Anti-Movements
in America

THE
RISING STORM

H[iram] W. Evans

ARNO PRESS

A New York Times Company

New York / 1977

Editorial Supervision: JOSEPH CELLINI

———◆———

Reprint Edition 1977 by Arno Press Inc.

Reprinted from a copy in the State
  Historical Society of Wisconsin Library

ANTI-MOVEMENTS IN AMERICA
ISBN for complete set: 0-405-09937-1
See last pages of this volume for titles.

Manufactured in the United States of America

———◆———

Library of Congress Cataloging in Publication Data

Evans, Hiram Wesley.
   The rising storm.

   (Anti-movements in America)
   Reprint of the 1930 ed. published by Buckhead Pub.
Co., Atlanta.
   Bibliography: p.
   1. Catholic Church in the United States. 2. Church
and state in the United States. I. Title. II. Series
BX1770.E8 1977   261.7   76-46075
ISBN 0-405-09948-7

The Rising Storm

THE
RISING STORM

AN ANASYSIS OF THE GROWING CONFLICT
OVER THE POLITICAL DILEMMA OF
ROMAN CATHOLICS IN AMERICA

By DR. H. W. EVANS

ATLANTA
BUCKHEAD PUBLISHING CO.

Printed in the United States of America
Buckhead Publishing Co.
Atlanta, Georgia

POLITICAL CATHOLICISM

"*As an outward and visible church and a State founded on law and on force, Roman Catholicism has nothing to do with the Gospel, nay, it is in fundamental contradiction with it. That this State has borrowed a Divine lustre from the Gospel, and finds this lustre extraordinarily advantageous, cannot avail to upset the verdict. To mix the Divine with the secular, and what is innermost in man with a political element, is to work the greatest of mischiefs, because the conscience is thereby enslaved and religion robbed of its solemn character. It is inevitable that this character should be lost when every possible measure which serves to maintain the EARTHLY empire of the church—for example, the sovereignty of the Pope—is proclaimed as the Divine Will.* * * **

"*No one who looks at the present political situation can have any ground for asserting that the power of the Roman Church is on the wane. What a growth it has experienced in the Nineteenth Century!* * * * *As a State this church lives today, to a not inconsiderable extent, on its history, its old Roman and medeaval history;—and it lives as the Roman Empire of the Romans. But empires do not live forever.*"

Dr. Adolf Harnack,
Rector, University of Berlin.

From "What is Christianity?," Pages 283-5.

AUTHOR'S FOREWORD

Ever since American complacency was shattered by our discovery of the national disunity which had crept upon us during the last generation, this country has been engaged in a self-analysis which is probably without parallel in history. An incalculable amount of time and thought has been spent on the effort to diagnose and prescribe—or to prescribe without diagnosis.

Yet there is one phase that has barely been touched, and most inadequately. Traces of its presence are to be found in almost every discussion, and a realization of it is widespread, yet only one American has undertaken even to state fully this cause of discord, much less to analyze it and determine its weight, influence and menace. It is time that this be done, for it is inevitable that before the discussion is ended, and the diagnosis completed, all hypocrisies will be thrown aside and the question brought down to fundamentals. This is one of those fundamentals. It is the attitude of the twenty-three million American Catholics toward a civilization purely Protestant in its origins, philosophy and institutions, and their effect upon it. This is the subject of this book.

It has been with no anticipatory pleasure that I have undertaken this work; only a firm belief that in the Catholic Question we are for the first time approaching a real diagnosis of our national disunity, and a conviction that the question must be fully and honestly faced before we can begin to restore national unity, could have brought me to attempt it. But my conviction has grown with my study, and I now am absolutely sure that unless the question is met and settled, it will produce a crop of evils of the utmost menace.

Not the least of the considerations which tended to deter me is that my chief reward will be abuse. Even Charles C. Marshall, whose work has been as diplomatic and conciliatory as it is valuable, has been met with denunciation, but no answers. How much more I may expect, since I have thought it necessary to make a social and political appraisal of the conditions found!

It is with no hope of avoiding this that I state my position, which I believe to be that of all fair-minded Americans. We wish most heartily that Catholicism were a religion only, and that it had no political implications. We wish that it contained no principles and supported no campaign which we could not ignore under the principle of religious toleration. We have no desire to interfere with any man's faith; no wish to bring a religious conflict into American politics. But we find the conflict there already, growing, and threatening to grow to monstrous proportions. It is in no spirit of intolerance, but one of a desire for truth and for the peace of the country, that we insist on having the issue made clear.

This much having been said, let me add that I cannot claim this book to be impartial in the sense of being a purely judicial verdict upon the issues involved. I can claim only accuracy, truth, careful study and the desire for fairness. In the main, there is no attempt to solve the issues; merely to clarify them. I have not tried to prove that American principles are superior or even that they are right. I believe in them; my purpose has been to show that they are threatened, at what points, by what means, and how greatly.

H. W. EVANS.

CONTENTS

PART I. THE CONFLICT IN IDEALS

CONTENTS

CONTENTS

CONTENTS

CONTENTS

CONTENTS

CONTENTS

CONTENTS

PRINCIPAL PUBLICATIONS CITED

AMERICA, A Catholic Review of the Week; published under the auspices of the Jesuits, New York.

AMERICA COMES OF AGE, A French Analysis, by Andre Siegfried. (Harcourt, Brace & Company, 1927.) References to the 15th printing, February, 1929.

AMERICAN HISTORICAL DOCUMENTS, compiled by Charles W. Eliot. (P. F. Collier & Son, 1910.)

CATHOLIC ENCYCLOPEDIA, An International Work of Reference on the Constitution, Doctrine, Discipline, and History of the Catholic Church. Impramatur of John Cardinal Farley, Archbishop of New York. (The Encyclopedia Press, Inc., New York, 1913.)

CATHOLIC YEARBOOK, An Annual published with the Approbation of the Hierarchy of the United States of America. Impramatur of Patrick Cardinal Hayes, Archbishop of New York. References are to the 1928 edition.

COMMENTARY ON CANON LAW, by the Reverend P. Charles Augustine, O. S. B., D. D., professor of Canon Law. Impramatur of John J. Glennon, Archbishop of St. Louis. (B. Hurder Book Co., 1921.)

COMMONWEAL, The, A Weekly published by the Calvert Publishing Corporation, New York, to interpret Catholicism to non-Catholics.

COMPENDUM OF DOGMATIC THEOLOGY, A, by H. Hurter, S. J., A Textbook for Use in Theological Seminaries. (B. Hurder Book Co., St. Louis, 1909.)

CONTRAST, The, by Hilaire Belloc (Robert M. McBride & Co., 1924.)

DOGMATIC CANONS AND DECREES, Impramatur of John Cardinal Farley, Archbishop of New York. (The Devin-Adair Co., 1912.)

ENCYCLOPEDIA BRITANNICA, The, References to the Eleventh Edition. (New York, 1910-11.)

PRINCIPAL PUBLICATIONS CITED

GOVERNOR SMITH'S AMERICAN CATHOLICISM, by Charles C. Marshall. (Dodd, Mead & Co., 1928.)

GREAT ENCYCLICAL LETTERS OF LEO XIII, The, Compilation of Translation from Approved Sources, with preface by the Reverend John J. Wynne, S. J. Impramatur of John M. Farley, Archbishop of New York. (Benziger Bros., 1903.)

KU KLUX KLAN, The, by John Moffatt Mecklin, Ph. D. Professor of Sociology, Dartmouth. (Harcourt, Brace & Co., 1924.)

L'AMERICANISME, by Albert Houtin. A study of the Americanism movement in the Catholic Church. (Paris, 1904.)

MANUAL OF THE HOLY CATHOLIC CHURCH, The, by the Reverend Dr. James A. Govern. Impramatur of James Edward Quigley, Archbishop of Chicago. (The Catholic Art & Publication Office, 1906.)

MANUAL OF CHRISTIAN DOCTRINE, The, by A Seminary Professor. Impramatur of D. J. Dougherty, Archbishop of Philadelphia. References are to the forty-fourth edition, 1925. (John Joseph McVey.)

OUTSPOKEN ESSAYS, Series II, by W. R. Inge, Dean of St. Paul's, London.

SERMONS ON ECCLESIASTICAL SUBJECTS, by Henry Edward Cardinal Manning, Archbishop of Westminister, American edition, New York, 1873.

STATE AND THE CHURCH, The, by the Reverend John A. Ryan. Impramatur of Patrick J. Hayes, Archbishop of New York, 1922.

SURVIVALS AND NEW ARRIVALS, by Hilaire Belloc. (The MacMillan Co., 1929.)

Part I

The Conflict in Ideals

CHAPTER I

THE CATHOLIC ISSUE

Re-appearance of the conflict—Questions that must be answered
—Danger of ignoring the issue—Its actual importance—Definition of the question—Charges of intolerance against all
who attempt any discussion of it—The effect and limits of
prejudice—The true issue not religious but political—What
is "Americanism?"—Catholic opposition—Anti-American
ideals of which Catholics are accused—The question of assimilation—Foreign origin of the issue—Factors to be considered—Permanent solution imperative.

THE re-appearance of the conflict over the political position of Roman Catholics in this country
caused deep distress to the majority of Americans.
It forced upon public attention a condition which
for centuries has caused untold evil, but which all
hoped and many believed had been made impossible
for us by the separation of Church and State and the
principle of religious toleration. It revealed a cleavage portending serious danger to our national unity,
and it cast doubt upon the practical value of some
of our most cherished ideals.

It is not surprising, therefore, that the issue was
faced with reluctance or not at all, and that it was
debated with hysteria. It is not surprising, either,
that in the heat of a political campaign it was
almost impossible to give to the question that calm
and careful consideration which it must have. As
a result, these important questions are left unsettled:

*Was the conflict sporadic or is it chronic, with oc-
casional acute developments?*

How fundamental are the issues?

Does the cleavage hold a serious menace for America?

Can our ideals and institutions, as they now exist, prevent the development of dangerous hostilities?

Is compromise possible?

Can an armistice, such as is implied in the principle of toleration, continue indefinitely and solve the problem?

Will either party change its attitude enough to end the conflict?

From the day the campaign closed there has been a strong tendency to ignore or belittle the part played by the Catholic issue in the election, partly because so many dislike to face its unpleasant realities.

This ostrich-like attitude is extremely harmful. The issue has been acute in the past; it certainly will be so again. It is when the fever has somewhat subsided that the question can and should be carefully and calmly considered. It is only during a lull in such a struggle that reasoned and just conclusions can be reached.

For those who wish to minimumize the conflict, let us recall a little genuine testimony as to the overwhelming importance placed upon this issue at the close of the campaign. At that time "America," a prominent Catholic weekly, said:

"It was admitted by all, as the campaign came to a close, that the religious issue had been the predominant one in most parts of the country."*

Similarly, the "Commonweal" which is probably the most fair-minded of all Catholic publications, said:

"It is then, plainly evident now that if Smith is beaten —nobody ever says 'if Hoover is elected' * * * *—it will be a

*America, Nov. 10, 1928.

demonstration that inherited fear is more potent with, for instance, the aggrieved farmer than his own material welfare. For, if Minnesota, the Dakotas and several other western states go against Smith, it will be in spite of the fact that a majority there believe their material welfare would be promoted by Smith's election. They do believe it; and in spite of that belief, it is possible that they will vote against him because he is a Catholic."*

The Cincinnati "Enquirer," in summing up the campaign, had this to say:

"The cost to the Democrats of taking chances on religious prejudice was frightful, though it is conceded that the Democrats received a substantial vote from those of the Catholic faith, due to the church affiliation of their leader on the national ticket."

This illuminating comment from a Catholic source appears in an article by Dr. John A. Ryan:

"It is my deliberate judgment that the foregoing facts, in conjunction with many others that cannot be presented here, demonstrate that without the religious factor Governor Smith would not have been defeated. At any rate, no intelligent person who rejects this judgment can deny that the religious factor was of widespread and profound importance."**

To this should be added the fact that Massachusetts and Rhode Island, both normally Republican states but with a large Roman Catholic vote, went Democratic for the first time in any presidential election.

This is a measure of the conflict now existing in America because of Catholicism in politics. It must be remembered, too, that we cannot hope for permanent disappearance of the issue, since this is the fourth time in our history that it has arisen. It is notable that the present conflict has been more

*The Commonweal, Oct. 24, 1928, page 622.
**Current History, December 1928, page 378.

far-reaching and deep-seated than any previous one. It is also notable that, with each re-appearance of the issue, there has been less attack upon the spiritual faith and religious practices of Roman Catholics and a more complete concentration upon the political purposes and activities of the Catholic hierarchy and of individual Catholics.

Thus it was that the issue was finally narrowed and accurately defined. This issue, as it now stands today in the minds of millions of Protestants, is:

Are Roman Catholics in the mass hostile to American principles, and does their church foment and inculcate this hostility, directing its action in American politics, with or without the knowledge of the mass of Catholics?

Many Protestants fear this question must be answered in the affirmative. It is undeniable that if the Roman Church does, in fact, control its members in politics through the use of religion, then that power in American politics which is represented by the votes of Catholics must revert, in fact, to the Roman hierarchy and not to any part of the American people. All who voice any fear of this danger, however, are accused of intolerance and prejudice and of forcing religion into politics in violation of the American principle of toleration.

Notwithstanding this charge, thoughtful non-Catholics cannot grant full political confidence to Catholics until they are convinced that these fears are groundless. They will be convinced only by evidence—not by abuse.

It is no answer to this question, for example, to say that those who ask it are intolerant. Surely it is not in any degree an exhibition of intolerance to demand convincing evidence on so important an issue! Nor is it intolerant to hold these fears in view of the history and the present pronouncements of the Roman Church. Indeed, intolerance is often not only justified but imperative; no one maintains that all evil should be tolerated, and the border-line of toleration is passed at that moment when a thing which asks for tolerance becomes a serious menace. The question is whether the political position of the Roman Catholic Church in America is in fact menacing. To raise the cry of intolerance is merely to beg this question.

It is no answer, either, to say that fear of the Roman Church in America is due to prejudice, although it must be admitted at once that prejudice enters deeply into the question. Two kinds of prejudice are involved:

The first is that which Webster defines as "an opinion formed without due examination." Certainly this form of prejudice has some part in the attitude of vast numbers of Protestants on the Catholic question but so it does with Catholics, and so it does with the majority of citizens on practically every issue. Political questions are complex and usually difficult to understand in detail; it would be absurd to hope that any considerable number of citizens would be able to give "due consideration" to many of them. It may fairly be argued that any popular government must be a government by prejudice! To charge this form of prejudice against Protestants on the Catholic issue is merely to state a truism of popular government.

However, most of these popular prejudices are inheritances based upon some experience of the ancestors of those holding them. They are, as it were, an inherited wisdom, even though the reasons underlying that wisdom have been forgotten. As such they still command the utmost respect. They are steadfastly maintained until reasons appear why they should be abandoned. The burden of proof rests upon those who wish to dissolve such a prejudice. I believe that this is right but, right or wrong, it is so. The prejudice against Catholicism, inherited by modern Protestants from the bitter experiences of their forefathers, will very certainly remain until there has been full proof that it has become groundless.

The second kind of prejudice involved is less justifiable. It is defined by Webster as "leaning toward one side of the question from other considerations than those belonging to it." The only question "belonging" in this issue is the patriotic fitness of Roman Catholics. Their religious convictions have no bearing whatever. Nevertheless, it must be admitted that there are great numbers of Protestants whose antipathy to Catholics is based upon religious grounds.

Yet after all these considerations have been eliminated, the main issue remains and it is not a religious one. The question which has already been stated is still unanswered. To put it in another way, even with all prejudice and intolerance set aside, there remains in the minds of the great majority of non-Catholics a serious doubt whether Catholics are truly Americans in the mental and idealistic and patriotic meanings of the word.

It is not worth while to enter into a discussion of what Americanism ought to be. Our national traditions and the mental and spiritual attitude held by practically all Americans of the older stock show what Americanism actually is. It is merely playing with words and fogging the situation to claim, as some do, that the Americans themselves do not know what Americanism is or to say, as Edward Bok did, that "The first need is to Americanize the Americans." Americanism is the mental attitude of the great mass of old stock Americans.

Whether this Americanism is right or wrong, the important fact is its conflict with Roman Catholicism and with the mental attitude of the great mass of Catholics. The object of this book is to analyze the conflict and its causes, and to consider what should be done about it.

The fact of this conflict hardly needs proof. The reality of its menace to the continuance of Americanism is not yet recognized by many, but is nevertheless indisputable. It was very concisely stated by Professor Andre Siegfried, whose book on America has been widely hailed as the most illuminating of our time. He said:

"Is it possible to contemplate a United States that is neither Protestant nor Anglo-Saxon? This is the aim of an opposition which, however, is not constructive and resists only by instinct. And yet they persist. If their policy were to become constructive and they obtained control, we might have a new America resembling in many ways the New York of today; but to the old Puritan element it would seem a shocking perversion. The final destiny of the country is still in suspense, and it is unable to foretell what tomorrow will be its very soul."*

This was written before the candidacy of Alfred E. Smith crystalized the issue in 1924. To a large extent he gave the opposition coherence and leadership, and organized the forces described by Dr. Siegfried.

His defeat did not remove the menace of "perver-

* America Comes of Age, Page 146.

sion." It may be that he will never again be important in public affairs, but the forces which he represented will surely find other leaders.

The conflict, in the view of most non-Catholics,
is definitely caused by supposed beliefs of the Roman
Catholic Church, each of which has a distinct political effect. Most non-Catholics would be glad to
learn that American Catholics do not believe these
things, but they feel that full proof is required, since
each of them seems definitely to challenge and oppose some part of essential American principles.
These things, which the non-Catholics fear Catholics believe, are the following:

*That the Pope "holds on this earth the place of God
Almighty" on all subjects.*

*That the Pope's utterances on religion and morals
are infallible and irreformable.*

*That even outside of religion and morals, the Pope's
instructions are binding on all good Catholics.*

*That the Roman Church denies any difference between
American Catholics and all others.*

*That all "Liberalism" is condemned by all good
Catholics.*

*That freedom of conscience and religion, of speech
and the press, are considered "Liberalism."*

*That popular government is the result of such "Lib-
eralism" and is responsible for great evils.*

*That the separation of Church and State is to be
condemned as the cause of great evil.*

*That the Church has co-ordinate jurisdiction with the
State, and is never subject to it on any matter.*

That the Roman Catholic Church is supreme over any

State on any subject which it (the Roman Catholic Church) declares to affect morals.

That it specifically has, by Divine Right, jurisdiction over all education and all marriages.

That the Pope has the duty to annul any laws which he believes conflict with morals or the "natural rights" of the people.

That certain classes of marriages, though valid in law, are "no marriage;" that is, of any Catholic, except by a priest; any marriage between a baptized and an unbaptized person; any marriage by a magistrate.

That the Popes instruct Catholics in general to be active in national politics.

That the Popes instruct Catholics in politics to follow the guidance of the Holy See and the bishops.

That the Popes instruct Catholics to oppose in politics all doctrines hostile to the supremacy of the Roman Catholic Church.

That the Popes instruct Catholics to make use of popular institutions to bring nations back to the Roman Catholic ideal.

It is evident that if Roman Catholics hold to these beliefs it is impossible for any devout Catholic, with the consent of his church, to be also a good and patriotic American. If this is found to be true one more question remains:

Can either side change its attitude enough to end the conflict?

I think no one believes that the Americans will change, and few will argue that they should do so. This country has been predominantly Protestant from the first and its whole political philosophy and structure are based upon the Protestant idea. To change them would be to abandon everything that America has stood for. Moreover, the Catholic is, in the great majority of instances, a guest; he was admitted to this country in the expectation that he would assimilate Americanism; not that we would change ourselves to suit him! The question should therefore be stated thus:

Can Catholics change their attitude enough to end the conflict? Or more concisely: Can Catholics be assimilated to Americanism?

One point stands out at the very start. This problem is a foreign one. It appeared in America only with the coming of enough Catholic Irish and South Europeans to affect local elections, and it became national only when there was danger that they would hold the balance of power in a presidential election. The Roman Church is the only sect which has any close connection with any foreign organization. American Catholics look for control on certain questions to a foreign power, and are the only ones who do so and seek to justify it. They form the only religious body in America held together and controlled by a foreign power.

All these things are vital factors in the problem. An understanding of all these foreign conditions is therefore required. It is entirely probable that I, or any other American, will fail to analyze these foreign conditions to the satisfaction of the Roman Catholics. But at least we can analyze them from the American point of view, and it seems axiomatic that this American view-point is the chief essential in the consideration of a purely American condition and problem, even though the Roman Catholics will not admit the point.

Much of our discussion must therefore be based upon European history and conditions. Also, before we can approach the fundamental question of the impact of Catholicism on American development, it is necessary that we should understand as well as we may the nature, position, history and aims of the Roman Church, and the mentality—including spiritual and social outlook—of the people who chiefly control and compose it.

All this is analysis—the basis for correct understanding of the present situation. It is of small value in itself, however interesting it may be, unless it results in action. The first and pressing need is that, through understanding, Protestant Americans be brought to face the conditions that exist and to meet them—without prejudice or panic, to be sure—but with full realization of their serious nature.

The greatest value of this analysis, however, will be in its contribution to this final solution. There *must* be such a solution. Lincoln declared that this country could not exist half slave and half free; it is equally clear that it cannot exist half despotic and half free. By some means this conflict must be adjusted along the lines of American principles, so that every citizen shall be assured not only of religious liberty, but also of *political liberty free from religious interference*. The basis for such a solution is already prepared; it will be found when the situation is squarely faced. The closing chapters are devoted to a discussion of the lines along which such a permanent solution can be reached.

CHAPTER II

CHURCH AND STATE

Proper relation of churches to a free State and its politics not
   yet well defined—The question complicated by survival of
   medieval ideals—Slow growth of religious freedom—Equality
   of churches necessary in a democracy—Their functions and
   duties as to civic morals.

MUCH of the controversy over the political position of Roman Catholics in America is due to the
fact that the proper position of churches and of
religions in a modern State and its politics have
never been thoroughly discussed and defined. The
principle of the separation of Church and State,
which is an axiom with Americans, is a new thing
in the history of the world. It has not, like most
questions concerning both the Church and the
State, received the cumulative analysis of many
generations of thinkers. Both the rights and the
duties of church organizations and their members
in a free State are still subject to constant dispute and are extremely vague in the popular mind.
Thus there is no ready-made standard which can be
applied to the political conduct of American Catholics.

Instead we have, projected into the modern free
State, many of the ideals, assumptions, and inherent
prejudices belonging to the older, autocratic form
of government. Since the whole question hinges
upon the moral, if not upon the legal, rights of
churches and religious people in a democracy, it
seems desirable to attempt to reach an understanding
about them before undertaking a discussion of the
peculiar position of Catholics.

Until little more than two hundred years ago all peoples had lived under some form of a union of Church and State. Catholic writers claim this as a Catholic idea but it is such only by adoption. In the oldest known civilization, that of Mesopotamia, the rulers of the cities of Sumeria were both priests and kings.

This condition has continued down to modern times. The Sultan of Turkey, the Czar of Russia and even yet the King of England, have been nominally heads of the Church as well as heads of the State. If Rome can claim any originality in regard to the union of Church and State, it is in the idea that all State heads should be allied with and subject to a Universal Church. This is in contradiction to the older idea that the religion of each State should be peculiar to and practically co-terminus with the State itself. Under either theory, however, the support of the Church becomes a first business of the State, just as Mussolini has recently proclaimed the effective union of Church and State in Italy.

The theory underlying both forms of union is that a Divine Commission has been given to some living man, which constitutes him a supernatural autocrat, with power to delegate certain parts of his authority. To state this in simpler terms, the Catholic theory is that the kings rule by a Divine Right granted them by the Pope, who in turn has been Divinely commissioned by God.

Under this theory both the popes and the Catholic kings rule with complete supernatural authority. Under it exist two co-ordinate jurisdictions, one temporal and the other spiritual, each supplementing the other. The Church by Divine Authority tells men what they must believe and inculcates submission to the king; the State by the same Divine Authority tells them what they must do and enforces all beliefs taught by the Church. The State becomes in fact, as the Roman Church has long called it, the "secular arm" of Divine Authority.

Under this system heresy and treason are so nearly alike that little distinction is possible. A man who defies the authority of the State is automatically rebellious against the power of the Church; one who doubts the authority of the Church becomes in that instant a rebel against the king. It was under this theory that the "secular arm" of the Spanish government executed those who had been found guilty of heresy by the Catholic courts of the Inquisition. It was under the same theory that Queen Elizabeth executed Sir Thomas Moore and other Roman Catholics on charges of treason.

If it be granted that the authority of the Almighty over any people has been divided between a Pope and a king, it is obvious that the union of the two is not only logical but advantageous. The fear of hell-fire, of all the superstititions of priest-craft and of the unknown are brought to support the process of government; the sword of the State is made to strengthen the moral and spiritual influence of the Church. Together the two are almost irresistable and—if the theory of a Divine and infallible authority is accepted—it is certainly desirable that it should be clothed with the utmost power over humanity. Thus under an autocratic theory of government, the union of Church and State is an harmonious part of the whole structure.

Mankind has broken away from this theory slowly and little by little. Long after the Protestant

Reformation started no one put forward the claim of any right to individual judgment or freedom of conscience on the part of the common people. The early struggles were to establish the right of the head of each State to decide what his subjects should believe. It was not until the establishment of the American Colonies, whose inhabitants had almost violently freed themselves not only from European control but from European tradition, that the necessity for the separation of Church and State in a free government was realized.

Although every European State with an established Protestant Church had come to grant a certain measure of toleration to dissenters—largely as a necessary means toward preserving the peace—it was only in this country and then only after the Constitution had been completed, that men came to realize the inconsistency of any Established Church in a democracy. Once this inconsistency has been stated it is obvious. The theory of the modern democracy is that government rests upon the free will of the citizens, freely expressed. To permit a State to bring religion to the support of an existing administration would at once make impossible this necessary expression of free wills. Since it is not possible, as it has not yet been, to prevent some churches from thwarting the processes of democratic government by dictation to their communicants, it is at least imperative that no Church shall be supported and maintained by the government.

This principle that there should be no State religion and no Established Church involves certain rules; there must be no special privileges to any church; there must be no interference with the doctrine and worship of any church; no church can be forbidden; and every church must, from the point of view of the law, be regarded as a purely voluntary society, subject to the regulations which the State imposes upon any other voluntary society. That is, all churches must be equal before the law, and each must conduct itself toward the government, toward its members and toward non-members, on a basis of equality with every other church.

This is the American doctrine of the separation of Church and State. Under this principle America has achieved a larger degree of religious liberty and more perfect toleration than has ever before been seen. This principle has been applied so successfully that until now America has never had to consider seriously what regulations are necessary to enforce it, nor how it shall be enforced against any church which refuses to abide by the obligations it imposes.

From this review of the history and purposes of the two theories of the relation of the Church and State it is clear that the question of what that relationship should be does not stand alone. It is fundamentally involved with and dependent upon the theory of human rights on which the State is founded. On the autocratic theory a State Church is justified and necessary; on the democratic theory a State Church or any church which attempts to exercise or even to assert any function belonging to the State, is intolerable.

Let us look for a moment at the functions of a State Church. Because of the close union between the two co-ordinate jurisdictions, the State safely leaves to the Church moral questions and those bearing upon education and marriage. It becomes not only the right but the duty of the Church to govern these matters and on them the citizen is free to do as he pleases so long as he obeys the laws of the Church. The State does not interfere.

The function of churches in a free State is totally different. Since there is no union, no church has authority to enforce its laws through discipline on morals, education or marriage. Thus social regulation and enforcement on all three must finally revert to the State. This is doubly true because in a free State there will not often be agreement among the many churches, and the State must act as arbiter over all. In a free State, too, the churches as voluntary associations must become subject to regulation by the State and they must not pursue the policy—which is entirely salutary under the autocratic theory—of attempting to coerce communicants in their political actions. This of course is the situation in America.

CHAPTER III

POLITICS AND RELIGION

Attempt to exclude churches from all political influence—The
difference between religion, church and morals—The need
of religious influence in politics—The right of churches to
political activity on moral questions—Their duty to conform
to the principles on which the State is founded—Rules which
should govern the political action of churches in America.

THE great desire among Americans to assure the utmost toleration, and their confusion of mind as to the exact relation of religion and politics, have caused an attempt in this country to extend the principle of the separation of Church and State to include a separation of politics and religion. Before attempting to pass upon the merits of this attempt it is necessary that three distinctions should be clearly drawn.

The first is the distinction between a church and a religion. To the Protestant this distinction is very clear. Religion is a faith based upon personal relationship with the Almighty; any church is an organization of men holding the same faith, formed for purposes of mutual help and mutual achievement. In an autocratic church, however, the distinction is often denied and is far less clear. Indeed, it requires a close discernment to distinguish between an organization which enforces all the details of faith, and that faith itself. Nevertheless the distinction must be maintained if any sound conclusion is to be reached in regard to the proper relation of religion and churches to American politics and government.

Let me emphasize this, since Roman Catholics are so reluctant to admit the distinction. To Protestants there is a clear and a simple difference between the Roman Catholic faith and the Roman Catholic hierarchy's active participation in social and political affairs. Protestants can give full tolerance to the religious side of Roman Catholicism and yet attack its politics, and we should be able to do this without being accused of prejudice, bigotry and intolerance. To us, in other words, church politics and church religion are very different things.

The second distinction which must be made is that between religion and morals. A religion, to be sure, is greatly concerned with morals as the means of applying its principles to life, but morals can and do exist independently of religion. Also, men of many religions or of no religion at all can often agree upon a moral question. Religion, too, is a matter of faith which cannot be enforced politically in the modern world, while morality is a matter of conduct which is enforced more or less successfully and which is the basis of every legal code.

The third distinction is that between autocratic and democratic churches as to their functions in politics. The autocratic church directs the opinions and consciences of its members on all matters which it itself believes involve morals as well as religion. It is not created by nor controlled by its members but controls them. It speaks for them only in the sense that it determines what they shall desire. The democratic church, on the other hand, is—like a free government—the creature of its members and subject to their control. As an organization its opinions and policies are those which the members have voluntarily approved. It can function politically only as their representative.

It is perfectly clear that under these definitions religion as a spiritual code must be kept out of politics in a free government. Religion in politics always attempts to impose its beliefs upon others— to say to other men "Thou shalt worship *my* God and none other"—and is not only futile but a certain cause of bitterness and a probable cause of bloodshed.

It is equally clear that questions of morals do belong in politics and particularly in the politics of a democracy, since, under the principle of separation of Church and State, the State must take over the function of the regulation of public morals.

This is a proposition upon which both Catholics and non-Catholics can agree. The Roman Catholic Church maintains dogmatically that politics and religion cannot be divorced, since politics is the application of morals to public affairs and morals are definitely in the realm of religion. The position of the Catholic Church has been clearly stated by Cardinal Manning, who said:

"Now I may be asked, Why should the Holy Father touch on any matter of politics at all? For this plain reason: because politics are a part of morals. What the moral law of the Ten Commandments is to the individual, politics are to society. Politics are nothing more than the morals of society—the collective morality of Christian men united together under social law * * * *—Politics are morals on the widest scale."*

This proposition is equally in harmony with the best American tradition, in spite of the recent clamor against "dragging religion into politics." There is no more authoritative document on American principles than Washington's Farewell Address. In a passage too little remembered he said:

*Sermons on Ecclesiastical Subjects, Vol. II, page 83.

"Of all the dispositions and habits, which lead to political prosperity, Religion, and Morality are indispensable supports. * * * And let us with caution indulge the supposition, that morality can be maintained without religion. * * * Reason and experience both forbid us to expect, that national morality can prevail in exclusion of religious principle. * * *"†

From this quotation it is perfectly clear that the founders of the nation did not desire to separate the State from Christian morality, based upon religion. They saw clearly that a free government must itself take over many of those moral functions which an autocratic government leaves in the hands of the State Church.

Since enforcement of morality is with us a function of government and finds its expression through legislation, which in turn is controlled by politics, private moral agencies have the right to political influence. More than this, the churches have not only every right but an imperative duty to be in politics in this country. Actually, they often are, though, to be sure, the Catholic Church has affected indifference to politics. But this has deceived few; in countries where public sentiment is strongly Catholic, the Roman Church is openly and often dominantly active in politics. Its apparent detachment here is a strategic pose for political purposes. Protestant Churches are also often compelled to be in politics; they must bear practical and concrete testimony to their moral convictions by an effort to have those convictions incorporated into the policies, institutions and laws of the State.

But—and here the third distinction comes in— in a free country the churches have a right to be heard and to take part in politics only on the same basis as all other democratic agencies. It follows

†American Historical Documents, page 260.

that only a democratic church can exert political influence which does not threaten the principle of separation of Church and State, and prevent the essential democratic function of the free expression of the will of the people. Protestant Churches make no claim to pre-eminence over each other or over the State, they truly represent the free will of their members, in no way threaten the principles of separation, and have no power to coerce their members by spiritual threats.

The Catholic Church, however, refuses to accept the distinctions between church and religion and between religion and morals, so that in working for what it considers moral policies it also automatically injects its temporal interests, policies and ambitions into politics. Moreover, it uses the religious faith of its members to prevent their political freedom. The Roman Catholic Church as an organization has vastly important policies and purposes which are entirely apart from its spiritual concerns, and we shall see that a Roman Catholic, to be fully approved by to his church, must accept and support not only its faith but its politics. No democratic church has any such policies nor any power to coerce its members.

Moreover, being autocratic, the Roman Catholic Church must maintain its claim to autocratic supremacy at all points, including political action. It must, therefore, in politics deny the supremacy of the State over itself at any point. It must deny the equality of other churches; it must deny toleration to other faiths; and it must particularly oppose the control by the State of morals, marriage and education. That is, it must in politics be hostile to the basic principle of the free State, teach this hostility to its members, and demand that they practice it. This is logical; we shall find that it is true.

Let me illustrate. The Roman Catholic Church, through control of the education of its members, instills into them a conscientious objection to all Liberalism, including the separation of the Church and State, freedom of conscience, freedom of speech and governmental control of education and morals. It is thus able practically to control their political actions and when it takes any position on political questions it is assured of their support.

The Protestant denomination which is most active in politics and which has been most vigorously accused of threatening the principle of the separation of Church and State, is the Methodist Church. This is more than a coincidence, since this church is historically an outgrowth of the Established Church of England and maintains more of the tradition of the autocratic church than does any other Protestant sect. It grants to its bishops powers far greater than those given to any other Protestant clergymen. Nevertheless, this church is fundamentally democratic, since its bishops are chosen and controlled by its members; it has no control over education; it has no authority over votes. It is in harmony with the institutions of free government, while the autocratic Roman Church is in conflict with them.

From this comparison the rules which should govern the political position of churches in a free State are clear. No church has any right at any time to inject into politics any question of religious faith or spiritual interest, but it has every right to exert its influence for the legal application of its moral convictions. This right is conditioned upon one thing: The church must conform to democratic principles and its political action must be directive and corrective but must not be subversive —nor coercive.

In the American State conformity to the principles on which the State is founded involves several points:

The church must be democratic in principle, so that it may represent the free opinion of its members but not control their opinion. In its attitude toward them it must refrain from control of their political action even indirectly, and even in respect to moral issues must confine itself to leadership and the teaching of what it considers to be the truth.

Second, no church may attempt any subversion of the principles of the State. Each church benefits by the toleration granted and it is morally bound to support the principle of separation of Church and State which makes that toleration possible.

Third, each church, since it occupies the status of a voluntary association, must hold itself subject to the State as are all other voluntary associations.

Fourth, each church must in itself fulfil the principle of democracy by placing itself on a basis of political equality with all other churches and by granting to all other churches that toleration which it receives for itself.

Fifth, every church must allow all its members to be wholly free politically, it must ask no favors for itself or its interests from any of its members who may reach public office, and it must not seek to influence any of its members in their official actions.

Finally, it must set up no conflict of sovereignty with

the State. It cannot claim for itself any right to over-rule the decisions of the State (that is, to resist the decision of the majority) nor to determine for itself what matters lie within its own jurisdiction. The Constitution of the United States clearly provides that the American State shall determine what matters lie within its own jurisdiction, and any church asking and receiving the protection of that Constitution must conform to this provision.

It is true that these obligations have never been laid down in American law. It may possibly be argued that they are not even moral obligations, since a man or a church holding opinions contrary to them has a right to maintain those opinions *in argument*. But this is the most that can be said, and there can be no question that any church benefited by American principles is bound *in practice* to observe those principles. Very certainly, any church which does not observe them is automatically in conflict with and a menace to American institutions.

Thus the claim of the Roman Catholic Church to a right to political influence is justified in principle and would be justified in practice if that church were to conform to American principles. The real question is as to the form and purpose of Papal politics in America and their effect upon the principles of the separation of Church and State and of human freedom.

CHAPTER IV

CATHOLICISM AND THE PAPAL THEORY

The various phases of Catholicism—Its religious and humanitarian work not under consideration—Its theory of Papal
Supremacy universally applied—This theory a survival from
the Dark Ages—How it is enforced under threat of eternal
damnation as well as present penalties—What the Papacy
claims — Supremacy of Ultramontanism in the Roman
Church—The recent doctrine of Infallibility—Its logical application in intolerance, control of education and marriage,
and supremacy over the State—Its effect on the patriotism
of American Catholics.

IN a country where freedom of conscience is a
principle, non-Catholics have no direct interest
in Catholicism except insofar as concerns its social
and political activities and purposes. To understand
these, however, it is necessary to take into consideration the several interlocking and interdepend-
ent phases of Romanism.

The Roman Catholic Church is first, of course,
an organized religion. This is no concern of non-
Catholics so far as it deals with theology and with
the relation between men and their Maker. Catholics' religious beliefs do not affect us unless they
attempt to extend religious authority and sanctions
into civil and political life; that is, unless the
Catholic Church insists upon including its temporal
and political activity, influence and purposes in the
category of religion.

The second characteristic of the Catholic Church
which must be considered, and the one which probably gives it its greatest hold upon its communicants,
is its humanitarian work. Romanism cares for the
physical ailments of its people, helps them in

trouble and ministers to their distresses. It has vast financial resources for this work, but even more important than these resources are the unpaid services of its great brotherhoods and sisterhoods. Through them it is able to extend a care which goes far toward establishing gratitude in all whom this service touches.

Similar to this is the spiritual peace which the Catholic Church gives. When it denies to its members any freedom of conscience or right of decision in moral matters, it also removes from them all need for searching of souls. They can consult their priest and follow his advice in the comfortable assurance that the moral responsibility for their actions rests upon him. If human weakness prevents their carrying out the full letter of his instruction, there is still a way open for the remission of sins through penance, and the good Catholic may die in the conviction that his salvation has been completely assured. This, to be sure, Protestants consider a form of moral anesthesia but it is—like a physical anesthetic—an antidote to mental pain which Protestantism does not offer.

It is these two great palliatives of human distress which have made the Roman Catholic Church so nearly impervious to outside attack and to the consequences of internal evils.

The Catholic humanitarian work is beyond praise. The spiritual ministrations—although to a Protestant they are a delusion and especially an evasion of personal responsibility—seem to Catholics an unmixed good. A Protestant could have no right to criticize either, were it not for the fact that the Catholic hierarchy uses both as a basis for forcing the acceptance of its autocratic theory in civil affairs.

In return for the comforts it gives to its communicants, the Roman Catholic Church requires of them only one article of faith which is essentially different from the creed accepted by all Christians. But this belief is one which has so direct and powerful a social effect that it becomes for the entire non-Catholic world the most important characteristic of the Catholic Church. This is their dogma that Christ gave a direct, universal and exclusive commission as His earthly agent to Peter and to all who succeed to Peter's throne.

Non-Catholics could easily ignore this doctrine if it were held merely as a theologic theory, or if the Catholic Church limited its effect to willing believers. But in fact it is not limited in any way; it is pushed to the utmost possible bounds in civil as well as spiritual affairs, is insisted upon in every detail and applied to Protestants and unbelievers as rigidly as the power of the Catholic hierarchy permits.

Our interest, therefore, as citizens of America, is not with a religion but with the vast international organization whose announced purpose is to enforce in practice every possible jurisdiction over men which can logically be based on this autocratic theory.

From a social and political aspect, the Roman Catholic Church is a politico-priesthood, self-perpetuating and exclusive, claiming sole and complete jurisdiction over all mankind on all moral questions with all their social implications. This, by reason of its claims first to a divine commission and, second, to supernatural and infallible guidance.

The Roman Church in this autocratic structure is a complete anachronism; a survival into modern times of the last and supreme embodiment of the ancient and almost savage idea of autocratic despotism through a self-perpetuating priesthood. There has never been any similar institution among civilized men. To find a parallel we must go to Lhasa, deep in the mountains of the Himalayas, where the Dalai-Lama, although selected by examination of the entrails of a bull calf instead of by the election of a college of cardinals, is believed by all Tibetan Buddhists to be an actual re-incarnation of the Guatama Buddha himself and as such to hold the same power over mankind as that claimed by the Pope.

It is of no importance to a non-Catholic whether this theory of Papal power is held in full sincerity by all Catholics or whether it is simulated because of worldly ambition, greed for money and power and the vast temporal interests of the Church. It is not important, either, whether Catholics call it "purely religious" or admit the fact of its political character. The important thing to non-Catholics is that the Papal Theory, held by some 330,000,000 souls in the civilized world, has had, has today, and will have for untold generations, a terrific impact upon the social and political life of all nations which include any considerable number of Catholics among their population.

Before beginning a study of the Papal Theory, let us consider briefly the punishment with which the Roman Catholic Church threatens all Catholics who question or resist it in anyway. This is the punishment of excommunication, which to a Catholic means an assurance of eternal damnation.

To a Protestant or any non-Catholic, such a threat is childish and silly. When a man tells one of us to "go to hell," we may resent it but are in no way spiritually disturbed. It is far different with a Catholic. He believes that Christ gave to Peter and Peter's successors the power to "loose and to bind" as set down in Matthew 16:19:

"And I will give to thee the keys of the kingdom of heaven. And whatsoever thou shalt bind upon earth, it shall be bound also in heaven; And whatsoever thou shalt loose on earth, it shall be loosed also in heaven."*

To any Catholic this means that Peter's successor, the Pope, has complete power to save his soul or to damn it eternally. Such a sentence from the Pope is to him more real and inescapable than the sentence of a human judge who says: "You shall be hanged by the neck until dead."

The Roman Catholic Church pronounces this sentence in its "bulls of excommunication," and these imply also such temporal evils as the church is still able to inflict. Excommunication cuts off a Catholic from all social intercourse except with his immediate family. He is an outcast from decent society; the social position of a condemned murderer is high and comfortable in comparison to that of an excommunicated Catholic.

In the days of the temporal power of the Popes such a man could be barred from obtaining the necessaries of life; no one could even give him a cup of water without risk of sharing his punishment. In those days too, he was removed from the protection of the temporal law, and if he failed to purge himself within a year, was handed over to the Inquisition, its tortures and hideous death.

However feeble the threat of excommunication seems to us who are non-Catholics, we must re-

*Murphy Edition of the Bible.

member that it is a punishment more terrible to a Catholic than any which could ever possibly be meeted out to a Protestant. It is by this supernatural threat that the Roman Catholic Church coerces its members.

The threat of excommunication is definitely laid down in regard to obedience to the Pope in civil life in canons of the Roman law, and for the enforcement of every dogma, law or even rule laid down by the Pope and his hierarchy. It applies to all such laws as have been quoted in this book, or may be quoted. Canon 2334 provides that:

"Those who issue laws, ordinances or decrees against the liberty and rights of the church incur excommunication."*

That is, if the Congress of the United States were to pass a law which the Pope believed to infringe upon the claims of the Roman Catholic Church, and the President approved it, both Congress and the President could be excommunicated, as could also any court which attempted to enforce such a law. It must be remembered that jurisdiction over all moral questions is considered by the Roman Catholic Church to be one of its rights.

The same Canon provides in the second place that:

"Those who, in order to impede the exercise of ecclesiastical jurisdiction in the internal as well as external forum, either directly or indirectly have recourse to any secular power, incur excommunication."*

That is, if at any point any person appeals to the laws of the United States as against any law or jurisdiction of any ecclesiastic of the Catholic Church, that person could be visited with the utmost penalty claimed by the Popes—*the penalty of eternal damnation.*

*Commentary on Canon Law, Vol. 8, page 335.
**Ibid, page 337.

It is interesting to note that the Roman Church has enforced this Canon as late as 1928 by excommunication of French Canadians in Rhode Island who had appealed to the American courts against a bishop accused of misappropriation of church funds.

Canon 2344 provides that:

"Any person who has either directly or indirectly injured or libelled the Roman Pontiff, the Cardinals, Papal Legates, Roman Congregations, Tribunals of the Roman Court and their higher officials, or one's own Ordinary (bishop),* or has excited criticism of their acts, documents, decrees, decisions or sentences, or animosity against them, shall be punished by whatever penalty his ecclesiastical superior thinks fitting."**

This last is a "blanket decree," putting complete power of enforcement in the hands of the Roman Church. Under this Canon the Roman Catholic Church is in a position to command full obedience for anything it chooses, and use its whole power for enforcement.

Thus the Papacy is prepared, under its own law, to enforce its decrees. If a non-Catholic offends, by excommunicating him the Pope notifies the faithful that the offender is worthy of no consideration, and may not receive even social civility. And for its own people the penalty is instant ostracism, denial of all the comforts of religion, and assurance of damnation unless there is complete surrender.

It should be noted, too, that the Roman Church still uses physical punishment when it has the power.

*Note: An Ordinary is an ecclesiastic having original jurisdiction, as an abbot for his monastery, a bishop for his See, and the Pope for the entire church.
**Commentary on Canon Law, Vol. 8, page 380.

The theory upon which the Papacy is founded and which controls every act of the Roman Catholic Church was briefly and completely defined by Pope Leo XIII, who was very largely responsible for its application in its modern form. In speaking of the power of the popes he said:

"We hold upon this earth the place of God Almighty."*
He also said:

"Everything, without exception, must be subject to Him, and must serve Him, so that whosoever holds the right to govern, holds it from one sole and single source, namely, God, the Sovereign Ruler of all. There is no power but from God."**

This, of course, means the Pope, since Catholics believe that God's power is transmitted through that person. If this were not sufficient, he dilates on the subject as follows:

"In defining the limits of the obedience owed to the pastors of souls, but most of all to the authority of the Roman Pontiff, it must not be supposed that it is only to be yielded in relation to dogmas of which the obstinate denial cannot be disjoined from the crime of heresy. Nay, further, it is not enough sincerely and firmly to assent to doctrines which, though not defined by any solemn pronouncement of the (Catholic) church, are by her proposed to belief, as divinely revealed, in her common and universal teaching, and which the Vatican Council declared are to be believed with Catholic and Divine faith.   But this likewise must be reckoned amongst the duties of Christians, that they allow themselves to be ruled and directed by the authority and leadership of bishops, and above all of the Apostolic See."***

The theory of exclusive Papal control of all Christian morals is fully set forth by Canons 218 and 219 the Roman law as revised in the Code of 1922 as follows:

*The Great Encyclical Letters of Leo XIII, Page 304.
**Ibid, Page 109.
***Ibid, page 194.

"As the successor to the primacy of St. Peter, the Roman Pontiff has not only the primacy of honor, but also supreme and full power of jurisdiction over the universal church, in matters of faith and morals as well as in those pertaining to the discipline and government of the church throughout the whole world. This power . . . is independent of all human authority."

"The Roman Pontiff legitimately elected obtains, from the moment he accepts the election, the full power of supreme jurisdiction by Divine Right."*

This Papal claim was reaffirmed by the present Pope in 1922:

"The Divine origin and nature of Our power, as well as the sacred right of the community of the faithful scattered throughout the entire world, require that this sacred power should be independent of all human authority, should not be subject to human laws."**

It was again laid down for American Catholics, following the restoration of temporal sovereignty to the Pope in the spring in 1929, by the National Catholic Welfare Conference in the following statement:

"No earthly recognition can add to the Divine Commission of the Papacy. The independent sovereignty which is rightfully hers and which has finally been restored to the church, will but evidence to the world the supernatural and supra-national mission with which the Visible Head of the church has been commissioned since Christ spoke to Peter."

It is not to be supposed that this doctrine has been accepted, even inside the Catholic Church, without opposition. There has been a party within the church—and sometimes a strong one—which has advocated a theory of power in the bishops— a theory that comes under the name of Episcopalism. The theory of Papal Supremacy is known in its

*Commentary on Canon Law, Vol. II, page 207.
**Translation in the Forum, Jan. 1928, page 53.

modern form as Ultramontanism. The fact with which we are immediately concerned is that this latter theory is now in complete control of the Catholic hierarchy and its policies (as will be shown in a later chapter) and that whatever opposition remains has been practically destroyed.

Ultramontanism has been defined more accurately than a Protestant could perhaps define it by two Catholic writers. Professor J. J. I. Von Dollinger wrote in 1865:

"The Ultramontane view can be summarized in a single, concise, and luminous proposition; but out of this proposition are evolved a doctrine and a view that embrace not merely religion and the church, but science and the State, politics, morals and the social order—in a word, the whole intellectual life of men and nations. The proposition runs; The Pope is the supreme, the infallible, and consequently the sole authority in all that concerns religion, the church, and morality; and each of his utterances on these topics demands unconditional submission—internal no less than external."*

Franz Xaver Kraus classes as supporters of Ultramontane doctrines the following:

"(1) Whoever places the idea of the church above that of religion; (2) whoever confounds the Pope with the church; (3) whoever believes that the kingdom of heaven is of this world, and maintains, with medieval Catholicism, that the power of the keys, conferred on Peter, includes secular jurisdiction over the princes and nations; (4) whoever holds that religious conviction can be imposed by material force, or may legitimately be crushed by it; (5) whoever is always ready to sacrifice a clear injunction of his own conscience to the claims of an alien authority." **

* The Encyclopedia Britannica, Vol, XXVII, Page 571.
**Ibid, Vol. XXVII, Page 570.

All these claims, and others which are characteristic of Ultramontanism, are flawlessly logical if we accept the first proposition that the popes "hold upon this earth the place of God Almighty" and that they have supreme jurisdiction on all moral questions—that is on any question which involves right and wrong.

If we accept the Papal Theory we must accept the dogma that the Pope is infallible. It would be absurd to suppose that Almighty God would allow His representative to make mistakes. It follows also that no Pope can ever have made any mistakes, that all dogmas and policies of the Papacy from its foundation till now have been correct and that no one of them can ever be corrected or reformed. There may be further revelations, but they must follow the line already laid down.

This doctrine was set forth in the Constitution *Pastor Aeternus*, promulgated by Pope Pius IX in 1870, as follows:

"We teach and define as a divinely revealed dogma, that the Roman Pontiff, when he speaks *ex cathedra—i. e.* when, in his character as Pastor and Doctor of all Christians, and in virtue of his supreme apostolic authority, he lays down that a certain doctrine concerning faith or morals is binding upon the universal church—possesses, by the Divine assistance which was promised to him in the person of the blessed Saint Peter, that same infallibility with which the Divine Redeemer thought fit to endow His Church, to define its doctrine with regard to faith and morals; and, consequently, that these definitions of the Roman Pontiff are irreformable in themselves, and not in consequence of the consent of the church."*

It also follows logically that the Pope and his followers can grant no tolerance to any other re-

* The Encyclopedia Britannica, Vol. XIV, Page 511.

ligion. Since the Pope speaks for God under the Papal Theory, he knows absolutely what is right and what is wrong. Tolerance in religion is based upon the theory of human error, but the Pope, under the Papal Theory, can make no human error and therefore ought not to grant any tolerance. Freedom of conscience is also forbidden to any believer in the Papal Theory, for under this theory if a man's conscience disagrees with the Pope's edict, then the conscience must be wrong and has no rights.

The Encyclopedia Britannica states the development of this principle of intolerance:

"Ultramontanism is the embodiment of intolerance towards other creeds. The general presupposition involved is that a man cannot be saved except within the Catholic Church. Since, however, on the one hand, in virtue of a theory advanced by Pius IX against the Emperor William I of Germany, in a letter which has since become famous— every Christian, whether he will or no, belongs to that church by baptism, and is consequently pledged to obey her, and, on the other hand, since the State lies under the obligation to place the 'secular arm' at her disposal whenever one of her members wishes to secede, the most far-reaching consequences result.

"In the past this principle led to the erection of the Inquisition, and, even at the present day, there exists in the Curia a special congregation charged with its application. On the Roman Catholic side the employment of compulsion against heretics has never been acknowledged as a blunder; and this method of silencing opposition has found champions in the bosom of the church down to the most recent years. But the development of modern culture has rendered these exploits of an unbridled fanaticism impossible, and no government would consent to enforce the once obligatory sentences of ecclesiastical courts. (**Remember that Italy has since agreed to do this!**)

"As a result of this situation, the Catholic condemnation of heresy—though as stringent as ever in principle—has assumed less dangerous forms for the heretic. Nevertheless, it proved capable, even in the 19th century, of imposing onerous restrictions on the heterodox, and practical exemplifications of this hostile attitude persist to the present day.

"The embittering influence of Ultramontanism may be further traced in its attitude towards the baptism of non-Catholics, for it seeks to establish the rule that baptism conferred by Protestants is invalid through defect of form or matter, or even of intention, and that, consequently, the rite must be readministered, at least conditionally, to proselytes joining the Roman Church.

"Finally, ample scope for the display of tolerance—or intolerance—is found in the mixed marriages between Protestants and Catholics, which, as a result of the modern facilities for intercommunication and the consequent greater mobility of population, have shown a large increase during the last few decades—in Germany, for instance. Here, again, Ultramontanism has done much to aggravate the pernicious feud between the two creeds."*

This principle of Papal Sovereignty is fully stated in the writings of Roman Catholic authorities. Pope Pius IX in Proposition 37 of his famous Syllabus (1864) said that to hold that "national churches, withdrawn from the authority of the Roman Pontiff and altogether separated, can be established," is pernicious error.

That great compendium of Roman Catholic teaching, the "Catholic Encyclopedia," declares that the Roman Catholic Church "regards dogmatic intolerance, not alone as her incontestable right, but as her sacred duty."**

Pope Leo XIII is explicit on this point:

* The Encyclopedia Britannica, Vol. XXVII, Page 572.
** Catholic Encyclopedia, Vol. XIV, Page 766.

"The (Roman Catholic) church, indeed, deems it unlawful to place the various forms of Divine worship on the same footing as the true religion, but does not, on that account, condemn those rulers who, for the sake of securing some great good or of hindering some great evil, allow patiently custom or usage to be *a kind of sanction* for each kind of religion having its place in the State."*

Another vital and logical deduction from the Papal Theory is that the Catholic Church must control all education, prevent any teachings which conflict with its opinions and policies and inculcate its own theories. This also is true if the Papal Theory is true, since that theory assumes that the Catholic Church knows the truth. To permit any teaching opposed to it is therefore to permit the teaching of wrong. To quote again from the Encyclopedia Britannica:

"Since Ultramontanism cannot hope to realize its political ambitions unless it succeeds in controlling the intellectual and religious life of Catholic Christendom, it attempts to extend its sphere of influence in all directions over culture, science, education, literature and the forms taken by devotion. This endeavor is the third great characteristic of Ultramontanism. Wherever its operations can be traced, they are dominated by the conviction that all stirrings of independence must be repressed, and any advance beyond the state of immaturity and nonage checked at the outset.

"Nor are its criticisms limited to theology alone: its care extends to philosophy, history and the natural sciences. Even medicine has not escaped its vigilance, as is proved by the prohibition of certain surgical operations. The development of these efforts may be easily traced from decisions of the Congregation of the Index and the Holy Office in Rome.

"Ultramontanism, too, labours systematically to bring the whole educational organization under ecclesiastical supervision and guidance; and it manifests the greatest repugnance to allowing the future priests to come into touch

* The Great Encyclical Letters of Leo XIII, Page 127.

with the modern spirit. Hence the attempts to train its growing manhood in clerically regulated boarding schools and to keep it shut out from the external world in clerical seminaries, even in places where there are universities. Again, it works zealously to bring the elementary schools under the sway of the church. Since it regards the training and instruction of childhood as inseparable, and holds that the former is essentially the work of the church, it contests the right of the State to compel parents to send their children to the State schools and only to the State schools. In logical sequence to these tenets it seeks to divorce the school from the State—a proceeding which it terms educational freedom, though the underlying motive is to subordinate the school to the church. In the domain of religion, Ultramontanism tends to foster popular superstitions and to emphasize outward forms as the essence of religious life, for it can only maintain its dominion so long as the common people remain at a low spiritual level."*

The final conclusion which can logically be drawn from the Papal Theory, and which controls the attitude of the Catholic Church, is the doctrine of the supremacy of the Pope over all Christian States. So far as we in America are concerned there is no need to recall the history of this doctrine; nor of the co-ordinate doctrine of temporal rulership. These can have no direct effect upon American life.

The modern political doctrine maintained by the Roman Catholic Church, however, does have a great effect in this country and may easily have one much more powerful, if it directly influences the loyalty of Catholic citizens. It is this doctrine which causes the gravest doubt in the minds of Americans as to the fitness for citizenship of Catholics in any free government and even a doubt as to their loyalty to America.

* The Encyclopedia Britannica, Vol. XXVII, Page 571.

CHAPTER V

THE CLAIM TO POLITICAL SUPREMACY

The doctrine of two co-ordinate jurisdictions—Its apparent fairness over-ruled by the more fundamental claim to Papal Supremacy—Leo XIII's demand for subservience of the State —His nullification of the State's laws—Temporal supremacy of the Pope defined by Romanist authorities—Patriotic loyalty of Catholic citizens subject to Papal control—This logically inevitable under the Papal Theory—The basic conflict with all principles of civil liberty.

THE modern doctrine of the supremacy of the Pope over the State is somewhat confused by the form in which it is laid down. This is by means of setting up and defining what the Roman Catholic calls "the two co-ordinate jurisdictions"—that of the Church in spiritual and moral matters and that of the State in secular matters. The form in which the doctrine is stated permits Catholic apologists to make the specious claim that this church does not attempt to interfere with the State. This claim has misled many Protestants and is the basis on which rests the defense of the political position of Catholics in America today.

Dr. John A. Ryan, one of the foremost American Catholic scholars, lays down the doctrine in these words:

"The Catholic doctrine concedes, nay, maintains, that the State is co-ordinate with the Church and equally independent and supreme in its own distinct sphere."

Leo XIII states the basis on which this theory rests:

"The Almighty, therefore, has appointed the charge of the human race between two powers, the ecclesiastical and the civil, the one being set over divine, and the other over human, things. Each in its kind is supreme, each has fixed limits within which it is contained, limits which are defined by the nature and special object of the province of each, so that there is, we may say, an orbit traced out within which the action of each is brought into play by its own native right."*

These statements sound fair enough, but they must be considered in connection with the more fundamental dogma that the Pope has jurisdiction over all moral questions and that politics are in fact the application of morality to civic affairs. The Roman Catholic Church makes no claim, in this doctrine, to jurisdiction over questions which *in its own opinion* are entirely secular and civil. But it does claim jurisdiction over any question which is moral, and the right to decide whether any question is a moral one. It definitely includes under morals education, marriage, international peace, and domestic peace. It is clear that under these definitions the Catholic Church may bring into its own jurisdiction, at its own option, the most important interests of all human beings and may in theory—so far as it is able—annihilate the rights of all who are not Roman Catholics. In fact, these claims and these purposes are definitely laid down by the highest Catholic authorities.

Thus Leo XIII proceeds with his definition of the relation of Church and State:

"From these pronouncements of the Popes it is evident that the origin of public power is to be sought for in God Himself (*speaking through the Pope, of course*), and not in the multitude, and that it is repugnant to reason to allow

* The Great Encyclical Letters of Leo XIII, Page 114.

free scope for sedition. Again, that it is not lawful for the State, any more than for the individual, either to disregard all religious duties or to hold in equal favor different kinds of religion; that the unrestrained freedom of thinking and of openly making known one's thoughts is not inherent in the rights of citizens, and is by no means to be reckoned worthy of favor and support. In like manner it is to be understood that the Church no less than the State itself is a society perfect in its own nature and its own right, and that those who exercise sovereignty ought not so to act as to compel the Church to become subservient or subject to them, or to hamper her liberty in the management of her own affairs, or to despoil her in any way of the other privileges conferred upon her by Jesus Christ. In matters, however, of mixed jurisdiction, it is in the highest degree consonant to nature, as also to the designs of God, that so far from one of the powers separating itself from the other, or still less coming into conflict with it, complete harmony, such as is suited to the end for which each power exists, should be preserved between them."*

It will be understood, of course, that the harmony to which Leo refers is to be attained by subservience of the State to the Catholic Church. In case the State does not, under his definition, draw its power from God through the Popes, he declares that its laws are void. He says:

"Lawful power is from God, and whosoever resisteth authority resisteth the ordinance of God; wherefore obedience is greatly ennobled when subjected to an authority which is the most just and supreme of all. But where the power to command is wanting, or where a law is enacted contrary to reason, or to the eternal law, or to some ordinance of God, obedience is unlawful, lest, while obeying man, we become disobedient to God."**

Since Leo in writing this, and all Roman Catholics in reading it, assumed that the Pope "stands

* The Great Encyclical Letters of Leo XIII, Page 126.
** Ibid, Page 144.

on this earth in the place of God Almighty,'' the actual meaning of this paragraph to them is as follows:

"Lawful power is from God (*whose vice-gerent and spokesman is the Pope*), and whosoever resisteth authority resisteth the ordinance of God (*through the Pope*); wherefore obedience is greatly ennobled when subjected to an authority (*of the Popes*) which is the most just and supreme of all. But where the power to command is wanting (*because of denial of the Pope's power*), or where a law is enacted contrary to (*the Pope's*) reason, or to the eternal law, or to some ordinance of God (*as laid down by the Pope*), obedience is unlawful, lest, while obeying man, we become disobedient to God (*through His agent, the Pope*)."

Even more outspoken is this statement:

"If the laws of the State are manifestly at variance with the divine law, containing enactments hurtful to the (*Roman Catholic*) Church, or conveying injunctions adverse to the duties imposed by (*the Roman Catholic*) religion, or if they violate in the person of the supreme Pontiff the authority of Jesus Christ, then truly, to resist becomes a positive duty, to obey a crime . . .''*

Thus the Popes definitely and at all points put themselves above the State and put their decrees above the laws of the State in the obligations they lay upon their followers. Leo, moreover, shows clearly that he considers this granting of co-ordinate jurisdiction to any State as a concession on his part and not as a right of the State. He says:

"We are convinced, in this, that the holy and venerable authority of the (Roman Catholic) Church, which in God's name rules mankind, upholding and defending all lawful authority, has been despised and set aside. The enemies of the public order, * * * make an unflagging attack

* The Great Encyclical Letters of Leo XIII, Page 185.

upon the Church of God * * * Such, too, is the purpose of the seizing of the temporal power, conferred many centuries ago by Divine Providence on the Bishop of Rome, that he might without let or hindrance use the authority conferred by Christ for the eternal welfare of the nations."*

Later in the same Encyclical he says:

"We shall never cease to strive that our authority may meet with due deference; * * * because it is an ascertained fact that, when the temporal sovereignty of the Apostolic See is in question, the cause of the public good and the well-being of all human society in general are also at stake."**

And finally, in a passage which might be taken as being purely spiritual if it were not a part of this same Encyclical which calls for the restoration of temporal power to the Popes, he says:

"Since God has made the nations of the earth for health, when He founded the Church for the welfare of the peoples, and promised that He will abide with her by His assitance to the end of the world, We firmly trust that, through your endeavors, the human race, taking warning from so many evils and visitations, will submit themselves at length to the (Roman Catholic) Church, and turn for health and prosperity to the infallible guidance of this Apostolic See."***

Dr. Wernz, one of the foremost modern Catholic commentators on the Catholic Canon Law, interprets this clearly:

"It is false to say that the theory of the indirect power (of the Roman Church) is incapable of being put to practical use at the present day, for if at the present day certain civil laws should be declared invalid by the Church, then these laws would actually be devoid of all binding force."

* The Great Encyclical Letters of Leo XIII, Page 10-11.
** Ibid, Page 15.
*** Ibid, Page 19.

Similarly, Huto Hurter in a textbook officially authorized for use in Catholic Theological Seminaries in America, quotes with approval the following statement by the Italian Jesuit Palmieri:

"On account of the positive, though indirect, subjection of the civil authority to the authority of the primate (Papacy), the Roman Pontiff can not only forbid the civil authorities any measure that would hurt the Church, but he can also prescribe to them (the civil authorities), anything that is necessary, or even very useful, for the (welfare of the) Church; for he has the power to loose and to bind in everything that is conductive towards the good government of the Church and towards the right administration of the Christian commonwealth."*

Thus also Dr. Macksey, one of the most learned Roman Catholic writers, says that:

"In case of direct contradiction, making it impossible for both jurisdictions to be exercised, the jurisdiction of the (Roman) Church prevails and that of the State is excluded."**

This doctrine is brought absolutely down to date by other Popes since Leo. Pope Pius X in 1906, in his Encyclical "Vehementer Nos" said:

"It is indeed an utterly false and pernicious doctrine that the interests of the State should be separated from the interests of the Church."

We have thus reached a full understanding of the Catholic doctrine of co-ordinate jurisdiction. The Papacy regards every State as its subject and as incompetent to perform any functions except those which the Pope permits. In regard to all civil government the attitude of the Pope, in spite of the fair-sounding statement of Leo, is still that "We

* Compendium of Dogmatic Theology, Vol I, Page 446.
** Catholic Encyclopedia, Vol. XIV, Page 251.

stand upon this earth in the place of God Almighty''
and that all power reverts ultimately to the Pope.

Bringing this doctrine down to its practical application for a Catholic citizen of any country, it
amounts to this; that the loyalty given by any
Roman Catholic citizen to his nation is given only
by permission of the Pope, that it is subject to the
Pope's control, that it is definitely limited by the
Pope and that it may be further limited, temporally
recalled or completely destroyed by the Pope's
decree. In other words the supreme loyalty of every
good Roman Catholic, in temporal and political as
well as in religious matters, must be given only to
the Pope.

This is the ultimate and practical working out
of the Papal Theory in modern civil life. It is
utterly logical; certainly no man who believes that
the Pope *does* stand in the place of Almighty God
can refuse him supreme loyalty. This position is
the only one possible for the Catholic Church—
and for any good Catholic.

Thus the whole structure built on the Papal
Theory is bound together in a flawless chain of
logical reasoning. *If* the Pope stands in the place
of God and is infallible, then intolerance becomes
a duty, then education must be controlled, then the
church headed by that Pope must be granted primacy
and then the supreme loyalty of all believers must
give to the State no supremacy over the church. It
is impossible to deny any one of these doctrines
without at the same time denying that the Pope is
God's vice-gerent.

But if this *is* denied, then the whole authority
of the Roman Catholic Church falls to the ground

in religious as well as political matters. This does not mean that the Roman Catholic Church can be destroyed by logic; its humanitarian work is too great and the spiritual comfort it offers its communicants is too satisfying to give way to anything so cold as reasoning. But it is true that the Catholic Church logically must hold to each of all these doctrines. Logically also, the Catholic Church must enforce them. So far as it can, it does.

Under Canon 2214, the Catholic Church claims the right, free from all human authority, "to punish subjects who transgress her laws with spiritual as well as temporal penalties."* The Canon goes on to proscribe the penalties to be used in inflicting these punishments and advises persuasion and admonition at first but adds that "gentleness should be combined with firmness, judgment with mercy, and leniency with severity."

As Leo said:

"To cast aside obedience * * * is therefore treason, not against man only, but against God."**

The means of punishment used, and the supernatural threat which the Roman Church holds over the heads of its subjects, have already been described.

The result of the Papal Theory in practical politics is a political policy or polity by the Roman Catholic Church that is in conflict with the rights of all who are not Catholics.

Hilaire Belloc, one of the most distinguished Catholic writers, declares, "the Roman Catholic

* Commentary on Canon Law, Vol. VIII, Page 59.
** The Great Encyclical Letters of Leo XIII, Page 110.

Church is in its root principle at issue with the Civic definition both of freedom and of authority."* This is stating it mildly; under the Papal Theory the Roman Catholic Church is the implacable enemy of modern liberty and must seek to pervert the principles of every modern free nation.

Moreover, in fact, it deliberately undertakes by political means to impose its subversive ideas upon such nations. Its position is thus defined by the Encyclopedia Britannica:

"Thus Ultramontanism is not to be conceived as a theological movement, but as the programme of a party whose principles are in fundamental opposition to modern culture, modern education, modern tolerance and the modern State—a party which seeks to carry out its campaign against the society of today, not by bridging the gulf betwixt creed and creed, but by widening it, by awakening religious fanaticism, and by closing the way to a peaceful co-operation of Catholics and non-Catholics in the highest tasks of culture and human civilization."**

This is a position and policy which is frankly acknowledged, in other words, by American Catholics. The "Commonweal" gives this definition of the purpose of the Papacy:

"The work of the Holy See is not so much with the individual soul, which receives its guidance from the pastor nearest at hand; it is rather with the forces having a bearing upon the moral and religious life of the world. And of these none has anything like the standing of governments. The State not only has the right to regulate the temporal welfare of its subjects, but in practice it carries out a program of social legislation which frequently envisages spiritual ministration."***

* The Contrast, Page 160.
** The Encyclopedia Britannica, Vol. XXVII, Page 573.
*** The Commonweal, February 20, 1929.

A notable consequence of these policies of the Papacy has been, even in recent years, the alienation of the educated class in Catholic countries. The reason for this, to quote once more from the Encyclopedia Britannica, is:

"The developments of the last decade of the 19th century had clearly shown that the educated *bourgeoisie,* the *tiers etat,* in whose hands the supreme power had since 1848 become vested throughout Europe, was either entirely lost to the church or, at all events, indifferent to what were called Ultramontane tendencies. The educated *bourgeoisie,* which controls the fields of politics, science, finance, administration, art and literature, does not trouble itself about the great spiritual universal monarchy which Rome, as heir of the Caesars, claimed for the Vatican, and to which the Curia of today still clings. This *bourgeoisie* and the modern state that it upholds stand and fall with the notion of a constitutional state, whose *magna carta* is municipal and spiritual liberty, institutions with which the ideas of the Curia are in direct conflict."*

This is the Papal Theory, which rules the Roman Catholic Church today, in its purpose and its practice and its results. It can be stated in a single sentence. The Pope is a Divinely chosen and guided autocrat who has the right (enforced so far as he has the power), to suppress all freedom, spiritually, mentally and politically, and all Christians owe him implicit obedience.

I have shown that the Papacy opposes freedom. It is not my purpose to discuss the question whether freedom for mankind is desirable. The whole Papal policy toward modern thought can be summed up in the phrase "They make a mental wilderness and call it peace."

* The Encyclopedia Britannica, Vol. XX, Page 719.

CHAPTER VI

THE GROWTH OF PAPAL DESPOTISM

Papal Theory not known to Early Church—Its origin about 850 A. D.—Two great forgeries which supported it—Catholic opponent of Dogma of Infallibility exposes falsifying of history —Also shows inconsistency of claim to "Pontifical Succession"—The evil record of the Papacy in the Middle Ages.

THE Roman Catholic Church maintains as a dogma that Papal Autocracy has been claimed by the bishops of Rome from the earliest days of the church and that the power of the Pope is derived by unbroken "Pontifical Succession" from St. Peter. This claim has been reiterated so constantly that most Protestants, as well as Catholics, have accepted it.

A notable recent instance of this was in Alfred E. Smith's reply to the letter of Charles C. Marshall in 1927. Mr. Marshall had cited statements of recent Popes as showing the position of the Roman Catholic Church. Mr. Smith replied that he had drawn charges based on these utterances "from the limbo of defunct controversies." Even more recently Professor David S. Muzzey of Columbia University, said:

"If we were to take the official views of the Papacy literally there would be cause for concern. It has condemned the separation of the Church and State and other ideals that we hold sacred in America, but there is little cause to fear that the official pronouncements of the Catholic Church in Rome will take effect here. The Pope has been reduced from his sovereignty, except as a matter of pretense. The medieval language in which he speaks is a gesture which is not enforced."

This opinion is possible only for those who ignore the facts of history, for recent history of the Papal Theory shows a continual expansion of claims to power. Autocracy was not asserted by the bishops of Rome for centuries, and was then only gradually developed. There have been periods when it was almost abandoned even by the Popes; however, the Papacy in the last half century has been recovering from one of its periods of great weakness and it has strengthened its claims by enlarging and applying to modern conditions all the despotic dogma of the Middle Ages—not of the Early Church.

The present form of the Papal Theory is thus of recent re-construction and is more fully developed than at any time in the history of the Papacy. It is a very human trait to strengthen instead of abandon a false position which has cost opposition and even defeat. It is this trait which has controlled the policy of the Roman Catholic Church for three generations.

In the early days of the Christian Church there were five great ecclesiastical Sees (or bishoprics) and Rome was little, if any, more important than the others. When St. Gregory was elected Bishop of Rome in 590 A. D. the accepted theory was that the church was governed under the combined authority of the patriarchs of Rome, Constantinople, Alexandria, Antioch and Jerusalem. The Roman Bishop opposed this system, but favored having the three Sees of Rome, Alexandria and Antioch joined in supremacy. Certainly no idea of any Divine Autocracy of the Bishop of Rome had entered any one's mind at this point.

About two hundred and fifty years later, however (the middle of the IX Century) appeared one of the two great Roman Catholic frauds, in the documents now known as the "False Decretals." These forgeries were of immense importance, yet very little is known as to their origin. Apparently they were prepared about 850 A. D., and quite likely at Le Mans, France. Their author is wholly unknown, but their purpose is clear enough.*

Some Catholic prelate found himself in conflict with the civil authorities, and wished to strengthen his position. His idea was to do this by increasing the power of the bishops, emphasizing the stability and cohesion of the church, and magnifying the authority of the Pope. He therefore took a perfectly authentic collection of canonical documents which was being used by the church in Spain, and added to them forged letters and decrees which he attributed to former Popes, besides revising and editing the authentic documents to make them prove the points he wished to make. Out of the entire collection, nearly one hundred and fifty letters are now known to be pure fabrications, and this includes all the earlier ones (before 385 A. D.) on which is based the assertion that the early Roman bishops claimed supreme authority.

Included in the "False Decretals" is an earlier forgery of great importance, the "Donation of Constantine." This was a supposed grant by the Emperor Constantine, in gratitude for his conversion by Pope Sylvester, to that bishop and his successors forever, not only of spiritual supremacy over all other bishops and over all matters of faith and worship, but also temporal dominion over Rome, Italy, and "the provinces, places and cities of the

* The Encyclopedia Britannica, Vol. VII, Page 915.

western regions"—that is, over all the Roman
Empire of the West. The history of this forgery
is also obscure, but it was probably concocted about
775 A. D. for use in a quarrel between the Pope
and Charlamagne.* Thus the claims to temporal
power began in a human—not divine—commission,
and a forgery at that!

These two great frauds produced no important
results for some time. The Donation was not seriously used by any Pope until about 1050 A. D., by
Leo IX. Even after that, when it was more frequently employed, the Popes still depended mainly
on the Gospels for their claim to Divine Authority,
as set forth in the Decretals.

These also came into circulation slowly and
had very little effect upon the claims of the Papacy
even after Nicholas I became Pope. It is in his
writings after 864 A. D. that we really trace the beginning of the Papal Theory, and he was the first
of the Popes to undertake any serious intervention in
temporal affairs. Later Popes enlarged their claims.**

Thus it is upon two forgeries—the "False
Decretals" and the "Donation of Constantine"—that
the Papal Theory originally rested and was originally developed. Both documents were accepted as
authentic until well into the XVIth Century. It
was during this time that the theologians, finding
it necessary to justify the Papal claims, went back
to the Gospels and from them built up their grandiose
interpretation of Christ's words to Peter.

It is quite certain that this theory was not held—
certainly it was not predominant—during the early

* The Encyclopedia Britannica, Vol. VIII, Page 408.
** Ibid, Vol. VII, Page 917.

days of the church. No more damning statement
of the case can be made than that delivered by
Bishop Strossmeyer in the Vatican Counsel in 1870,
when he opposed the decree which declared the
Pope infallible. Bishop Strossmeyer said:

"I say no more, my venerable brethren; and I come now
to speak of the great argument—which you mentioned before—to establish the primacy of the Bishop of Rome by
the rock (petra). If this were true, the dispute would be
at an end; but our forefathers—and they certainly knew
something—did not think of it as we do. St. Cyril in his
fourth book on the Trinity, says, 'I believe that by the
rock you must understand the unshaken faith of the apostles.' St. Hilary, Bishop of Poitiers, in his second book on
the Trinity, says, 'The rock (petra) is the blessed and only
rock of the faith confessed by the mouth of St. Peter;' and
in the sixth book on the Trinity, he says, 'It is on this rock
of the confession of faith that the Church is built.' 'God,'
says St. Jerome in the sixth book on St. Matthew, 'has
founded His Church on this rock, and it is from this rock
that the Apostle Peter has been named.' After him St.
Chrysostom says in his fifty-third homily on St. Matthew,
'On this rock I will build my Church—that is, on the faith
of the confession.'

"Now, what was the confession of the apostle? Here it
is—'Thou art the Christ, the Son of the living God.' Am-
brose, the holy Archbishop of Milan (on the second chapter
of the Ephesians), St. Basil of Seleucia, and the fathers of
the Council of Chalcedon, teach exactly the same thing.
Of all the doctors of Christian antiquity St. Augustine occupies one of the first places for knowledge and holiness.
Listen then to what he writes in his second treatise on the
first epistle of St. John: 'What do the words mean, I will
build my Church on this rock? On this faith, on that which
said, 'Thou art the Christ, the Son of the living God.' In
his treatise on St. John we find this most significant phrase—
'On this rock which thou hast confessed I will build my
Church, since Christ was the rock.' The great bishop believed so little that the Church was built on St. Peter that
he said to the people in his thirteenth sermon, 'Thou art
Peter, and on this rock (petra) which thou hast confessed,

on this rock which thou hast known, saying, Thou art Christ, the Son of the living God, I will build my Church—upon Myself, who am the Son of the living God: I will build it on Me, and not Me on thee.' That which St. Augustine thought upon this celebrated passage was the opinion of all Christendom in his time.

"Therefore, to resume, I establish: (1) That Jesus has given to His apostles the same power that He gave to St. Peter. (2) That the apostles never recognized in St. Peter the vicar of Jesus Christ and the infallible doctor of the church. (3) That St. Peter never thought of being Pope, and never acted as if he were Pope. (4) That the Councils of the first four centuries, while they recognized the high position which the Bishop of Rome occupied in the church on account of Rome, only accorded to him a pre-eminence of honor, never of power or of jurisdiction. (5) That the holy fathers in the famous passage, 'Thou art Peter, and on this rock I will build my Church,' never understood that the Church was built on Peter (super Petrum) but on the rock (super petram), that is, on the confession of the faith of the apostle. I conclude victoriously with history, with reason, with logic, with good sense, and with a Christian conscience, that Jesus Christ did not confer any supremacy on St. Peter and that the bishops of Rome did not become sovereigns of the Church, but only by confiscating one by one all the rights of the episcopate. (Voices—'Silence, impudent Protestant! Silence!,)

"No, I am not an impudent Protestant. History is neither Catholic, nor Anglician, nor Calvinistic, nor Lutheran, nor Arminian, nor schismatic Greek nor Ultramontane. She is what she is—that is, something stronger than all confessions of faith or the Canons of the Ecumenical Councils. Write against it, if you dare! but you cannot destroy it, any more than taking a brick out of the Coliseum would make it fall."

In spite of this record of history, the Popes did claim supremacy from about the year 1,000 A. D., but in practice they exercised very little. There was, for instance, no claim by the Pope that he could depose any bishop or fill his place—up to that time bishops had been elected by the clergy of the diocese, since the early days of the church, when the custom of general election by the whole church disappeared. The supreme authority of the Pope over the bishops came as a result of the desire of the bishops themselves for aid against deposition by their subordinates or by the temporal authority.

In practice, during this period, the Pope was considered a court of appeals upon disputed questions, but his intervention even in ecclesiastical affairs was limited and sporadic. The Pope was, indeed, the head of the church but he used his authority only intermittently and without having any strongly centralized government. Till this time, too, the Pope, like all bishops, was chosen at an election in which the clergy and laity took part, but only those of his own diocese. In practice, a new bishop of Rome was chosen by the principal members of the Roman clergy and nobility, and then set before the people, who gave their approval by acclamation.

It was the appearance of the great Hildebrand in the councils of the Papacy which removed the Roman See from control of the Roman nobles. This change was made in 1059 and from that time secular influence in the selection of the Pope largely disappeared, although Austria retained a veto power over the election of the Popes until recent years. When Hildebrand became Pope under the name of Gregory VII, together with many real reforms he attempted to enforce a claim that kings should be subject to the Pope and that he should be able to enthrone or depose them at his own will—practically, this was an effort to restore the Roman Empire, but with the Pope as Emperor. This claim caused a tremendous outburst of indignation and before his death Gregory himself practically abandoned his political pretentions, as is shown by the fact that the man whom he nominated as his successor was known to be far more moderate. These pretentions, however, had been transferred into legal and canonical principles by the church's casuists and although Gregory's successors made little attempt to enforce them, they were passed on to distant heirs and reappeared in future struggles. During the Dark Ages they did in fact give the Popes the power of the Ceasars, and they make Catholicism the political successor to Imperial Rome. They are the basis of the Papal Theory today.

Thus it was more than a thousand years after the death of Christ before the idea of the Papal Autocracy appeared in anything approaching the form in which it stands today.

Another claim of the hierarchy is that the divine blessing upon Peter and the divine commission of rulership to him have come down in unbroken "Pontifical Succession." To some extent this is a religious question, and one with which we are not concerned, but since it is essential to the idea of infallibility and is therefore a cornerstone of the Papal Theory, it deserves a brief mention. This idea is no more historic than the previous one. Let me quote again from Bishop Strossmeyer:

"But you will tell me these are fables, not history. Fables! Go, Monsignori, to the Vatican Library and read Platina, the historian of the Papacy, and the annals of Baronius (A. D. 897). These are facts which, for the honor of the Holy See, we should wish to ignore; but when it is to define a dogma which may provoke a great schism in our midst, the love which we bear to our venerable mother Church, Catholic, Apostolic, and Roman, ought it to impose silence on us?

"I will go on. The learned Cardinal Baronius, speaking of the Papal court, says (give attention, my venerable brethren to these words): 'What did the Roman Church appear in those days? How infamous! Only all-powerful courtesans governing in Rome! It was they who gave, exchanged, and took bishoprics; and horrible to relate, they got their lovers, the false Popes, put on the throne of St. Peter's (Baronius, A. D. 912). You will answer, These were false Popes, not true ones; let it be so; but in that case, if for fifty years the See of Rome was occupied by anti-Popes, how will you pick up again the thread of Pontificial Succession? Has the Church been able, at least for a century and a half, to go on without a head, and find itself acephalous?

"Look now: The greatest number of these anti-Popes appear in a genealogical tree of the Papacy. * * *

"I grieve, my venerable brethren, to stir up so much filth. I am silent on Alexander VI, father and lover of Lucretia; I turn away from John XXII (1319), who denied the immortality of the soul, and was deposed by the holy Ecumenical Council of Constance. Some will maintain that this Council was only a private one; let it be so; but if you refuse any authority to it, as a logical sequence you must hold the nomination of Martin V (1417) to be illegal. What, then, will become of the Papal Succession? Can you find the thread of it?

"I do not speak of the schisms which have dishonored the Church. In those unfortunate days the See of Rome was occupied by two competitors, and sometimes even by three. Which of these was the true Pope?"

So "Apostolic Succession" must be rejected along with the theory of any primitive claim to Papal Supremacy.

Chapter VII

THE RENEWED DESPOTISM

Claim to Papal Supremacy lapses after the Reformation—Revived and re-affirmed because of vindictiveness of Pius IX—His struggle to force acceptance of complete Ultramontanism—Vigorous opposition inside the Church suppressed—The doctrines defined and expanded by Leo XIII—New era of Papal aggression forces ancient controversy on the modern world.

ALL claims to Papal Autocracy fell silent during the centuries following the Reformation. Indeed, many Popes of thase days went far toward compromise with Liberal ideas—they even repudiated and dissolved the Order of the Jesuits. We may pass over this period and come down to the middle of the last century, when the Catholic sovereigns dominated Europe and Protestant hostility to Catholicism had declined because of the weakness of the Papacy. It was then that it set out to regain all the power it had held in the Mindle Ages.

The leader in this movement was Pius IX. He was somewhat moderate and Liberal during the early years of his pontificate, but was embittered after being driven from Rome by the republican agitation of 1848. From that time onward he was an extreme reactionary, ruling Italian territory by the strength of French bayonets until the Papal States were finally wrested from him, and attacking all intellectual and religious progress as pestilent error. The change in him at this time was so great that it may fairly be charged that the modern reactionary attitude and the aggressive anti-Liberalism of the Papacy is due to the personal vindictiveness of this one priest. Pius IX was injured by Liberalism; he set Catholicism to fighting all Liberals.

Although it has no bearing on this discussion, it is interesting to note that Pius IX was the man who first proclaimed the doctrine of the Immaculate Conception as a dogma of the church.

Pius was a voluminous writer against progress, and summed up all of his attacks in what is known as his Syllabus, published December 8, 1864, condemning human liberty in all the forms which had taken shape during the Liberal movements of the two previous centuries. This was not new doctrine but a reaffirmation of the logical applications of the theory of Papal Autocracy to modern thought. It will be discussed at length in the next chapter.

In spite of the intolerance of this Syllabus, Pius took full advantage of the tolerance allowed in the Liberal non-Catholic countries and succeeded in strengthening the position of the Catholics in all those countries. This was greatly aided by immigration both in England and in the United States. Along with this, however, went a weakening of the Roman Church in the Catholic countries, due very largely to resentment against his extremely reactionary principles and policies.

The most notable achievement of Pius was the Vatican Council of 1870, which legally established the dogma of Papal Infallibility. This dogma completed and cemented the Papal Theory, and brought about a centralization of autocratic authority at Rome which would have appalled Catholics at any previous time in the history of the church.

This achievement was not an easy one and was made possible largely by an alliance with the

Jesuits which amounted almost to subjection to them.* The Jesuits have, since the founding of the order by Loyola, been the leaders in behalf of Ultramontanism in the Catholic Church. Although the Pope joined with them, and although years were spent in preparing the way for acceptance of complete Ultramontanism by the Vatican Council, a strong opposition developed. Germany, Spain, and to a lesser extent America, openly fought the proposal.

The opposition was led inside the Council by Bishop Strossmeyer, some of whose remarks have already been quoted. His other arguments against infallibility that are important were:

"If I have said anything which history proves false, show it to me by history, and without a moment's hesitation I will make an honorable apology; but be patient, and you will see that I have not said all that I would or could; and even were the funeral pile waiting for me in the place of St. Peter's, I should not be silent, and I am obliged to go on. Monsignor Dupanloup, in his celebrated Observations on this Council of the Vatican, has said, and with reason, that if we declared Pius IX infallible, we must necessarily, and from natural logic, be obliged to hold that all his predecessors were also infallible.

"Well, venerable brethren, here history raises its voice to assure us that some Popes have erred. You may protest against it or deny it, as you please, but I will prove it. Pope Victor (192) first approved of Montanism, and then condemned it. Marcellinus (296-303) was an idolater. He entered into the temple of Vesta, and offered incense to the goddess. You will say that it was an act of weakness; but I answer, a vicar of Jesus Christ dies rather than become an apostate. Liberius (358) consented to the condemnation of Athanasius, and made a profession of Arianism, that he might be recalled from his exile and reinstated in

*The Encyclical Britannica, Vol. XXVII, Pages 947-951.

his See. Honorius (625) adhered to Monothelitism: Father
Gratry has proved it to demonstration. Gregory I (785-90)
calls any one anti-Christ who takes the name of Universal
Bishop, and contrariwise Boniface III (607-8), made the
parricide Emperor Phocas confer that title upon him.
Paschal II (1088-99) and Eugenius III (1145-53) authorized
duelling; Julius II (1509) and Pius IV (1560) forbade it.
Eugenius IV (1431-39) approved of the Council of Basle
and the restitution of the chalice to the church of Bohemia;
Pius II (1458) revoked the concession. Hadrian II (867-
872) declared civil marriages to be valid; Pius VII (1800-23)
condemned them. Sixtus V (1585-90) published an edition
of the Bible, and by a bull recommended it to be read;
Pius VII condemned the reading of it. Clement XIV (1700-
21) abolished the order of the Jesuits, permitted by
Paul III, and Pius VII re-established it.

"But why look for such remote proofs? Has not our
Holy Father here present, in his bull which gave the rules
for this Council, in the event of his dying while it was
sitting, revoked all that in past times may be contrary to
it, even when that proceeds from the decisions of his predecessors? And certainly, if Pius IX has spoken *ex cathedra,*
it is not when, from the depths of his sepulchre, he imposes
his will on the sovereigns of the Church.

"I should never finish, my venerable brethren, if I were
to put before your eyes the contradictions of the Popes in
their teachings. If then you proclaim the infallibility of
the actual Pope, you must either prove, that which is impossible—that the Popes never contradicted each other—
or else you must declare that the Holy Spirit has revealed
to you that the infallibility of the Papacy only dates from
1870. Are you bold enough to do this?

"Perhaps the people may be indifferent, and pass by
theological questions which they do not understand, and of
which they do not see the importance; but though they are
indifferent to principles, they are not so to facts. Do not
then deceive yourselves. If you decree the dogma of Papal
Infallibility, the Protestants, our adversaries, will mount
in the breach, the more bold that they have history on their
side, whilst we have only our own denial against them.
What can we say to them when they expose all the bishops

of Rome from the days of Luke to his holiness Pius IX?
Ah! if they had all been like Pius IX we should triumph on the
whole line; but alas! it is not so. (Cries of: 'Silence, silence;
enough, enough!')

"Do not cry out, Monsignori! To fear history is to own
yourselves conquered; and, moreover, if you made the
whole waters of the Tiber pass over it, you would not can-
cel a single page. Let me speak, and I will be as short as
it is possible on this most important subject. Pope Vigilus
(538) purchased the Papacy from Belisarius, lieutenant of
the Emperor Justinian. It is true that he broke his promise
and never paid for it. Is this a canonical mode of binding
on the tiara? The second Council of Chalcedon had form-
ally condemned it. In one of its canons you read that 'the
bishop who obtains his episcopate by money shall lose it
and be degraded.' Pope Eugenius III (IV in original)
(1145) imitated Vigilius. St. Bernard, the bright star of
his age, reproves the Pope, saying to him, 'Can you show
me in this great city of Rome any one who would receive
you as Pope if they had not received gold or silver for it?'

"My venerable brethren, will a Pope who establishes a
bank at the gates of the temple be inspired by the Holy
Spirit? Will he have any right to teach the Church infallibility? You know the history of Formosus too well for
me to add to it. Stephen XI caused his body to be exhumed,
dressed in his pontificial robes; he made the fingers which
he used for giving the benediction to be cut off, and then
had him thrown into the Tiber, declaring him to be a per-
jurer and illigitimate. He was then imprisoned by the
people, poisoned, and strangled. Look how matters were
re-adjusted; Romanus, successor of Stephen, and, after
him, John X, rehabilitated the memory of Formosus. * * *

"Resuming once more, again I say, if you decree the
infallibility of the present bishop of Rome, you must establish the infallibility of all the preceding ones, without
excluding any. But can you do that, when history is there
establishing with a clearness equal to that of the sun, that
the Popes have erred in their teaching? Could you do it
and maintain that avaricious, incestuous, murdering,
simoniacal Popes have been vicars of Jesus Christ? Oh,
venerable brethren! to maintain such an enormity would

be to betray Christ worse than Judas. It would be to throw dirt in His face. (Cries, 'Down from the pulpit, quick; shut the mouth of the heretic!')

"My venerable brethren, you cry out; but would it not be more dignified to weigh my reasons and my proofs in the balance of the sanctuary? Believe me, history cannot be made over again; it is there, and will remain to all eternity, to protest energetically against the dogma of Papal Infallibility. You may proclaim it unanimously; but one vote will be wanting, and that is mine!

"Monsignori, the true and faithful have their eyes on us, expecting from us a remedy for the innumerable evils which dishonor the Church; will you deceive them in their hopes? What will not our responsibility before God be, if we let this solemn occasion pass which God has given us to heal the true faith? Let us seize it, my brethren; let us arm ourselves with a holy courage; let us make a violent and generous effort; let us turn to the teaching of the apostles, since without that we have only errors, darkness, and false traditions. Let us avail ourselves of our reason and of our intelligence to take the apostles and prophets as our only infallible masters with reference to the question of questions, 'What must I do to be saved?'

"When we have decided that, we shall have laid the foundation of our dogmatic system firm and immovable on the rock, lasting and incorruptible, of the divinely inspired Holy Scriptures. Full of confidence, we will go before the world, and, like the Apostle Paul, in the presence of the free-thinkers, we will 'know none other than Jesus Christ, and Him crucified.' We will conquer through the preaching of 'the folly of the Cross,' as Paul conquered the learned men of Greece and Rome; and the Roman Church will have its glorious '89. (Clamorous cries, 'Get down! Out with the Protestant, the Calvinist, the traitor to the Church!') Your cries, Monsignori, do not frighten me. If my words are hot, my head is cool. I am neither of Luther, nor of Calvin, nor of Paul, nor of Apollos, but of Christ. (Renewed cries, 'Anathema, anathema to the apostate!')

"Anathema? Monsignori, anathema? You know well that you are not protesting against me, but against the

Holy Apostles under whose protection I should wish this Council to place the Church. Ah! If wrapped in their winding sheets they came out of their tombs, would they speak a language different from mine? What would you say to them when by their writings they tell you that the Papacy had deviated from the Gospel of the Son of God, which they have preached and confirmed in so generous a manner by their blood? Would you dare say of them, 'We prefer the teaching of our own Popes, our Bellarmine, our Ignatius Loyola (founder of the Jesuits) to yours'? No, no! a thousand times, no! unless you have shut your ears that you may not hear, closed your eyes that you may not see, blunted your mind that you may not understand.

"Ah! If He who reigns above wishes to punish us, making His hand fall heavy on us, as He did on Pharoah, He has no need to permit Garibaldi's soldiers to drive us away from the Eternal City. He has only to let us make Pius IX a god, as we have made a goddess of the blessed Virgin. Stop, stop, venerable brethren, on the odious and ridiculous incline on which you have placed yourselves! Save the Church from the shipwreck which threatens her, asking from the Holy Scriptures alone for the rule of faith which we ought to believe and to profess. I have spoken: may God help me!"

No Protestant need add anything to this arraignment of the Catholic theory of Papal Infallibility!

Outside the Council the opposition was led by Professor J. J. I. Von Dollinger, who was at that time the leading Catholic historian. In a series of letters translated into almost every modern language, he showed the tendency of the Syllabus toward Papal Despotism and its incompatibility with modern thought. He showed, too, that the doctrine of Papal Infallibility rested upon the "False Decretals." Dollinger had long been a champion of freedom for the Catholic Church, but the freedom he claimed was the right to manage her affairs without interference from the State, and he charged that the champions of Papal Autocracy, and notably the Jesuits, desired freedom to stop the dissemination of modern ideas.

When the first vote was taken on declaring the Pope infallible one hundred and fifty prelates of the six hundred and one present rejected it. It was recognized that the doctrine could hardly be accepted as dogmatic if it was repudiated, in spite of the Pope's influence, by a quarter of all those present, although nearly half were Italians under his direct control. This meant, of course, that in the Catholic Church at large half of the prelates rejected Papal Supremacy. The leaders of the opposition to the Pope at last petitioned him to modify the terms of the dogma, but he took a position even more extreme. A part of the bishops present finally reversed themselves because of a desire to avoid a schism in the church and through loyalty to the Pope. Sixty-six retired from the Council, and the dogma was finally adopted by five hundred and thirty-three prelates with only two dissenting votes. The doctrine which it laid down has already been quoted.* Two prelates refused to accept it and were excommunicated. All others made "the loyal sacrifice of conscience."

The acceptance of that dogma marked the opening of a new era of increased autocracy in the Papacy. The power it gave the Pope has been used by succeeding Popes to strengthen and centralize that authority until it is today, in theory and in practice so far as they can make it, far beyond anything the church has known heretofore.

That well known bull, *Pastor Aeternus*, which contains the doctrine of infallibility, did not represent all the desires of Pius IX or the demands

* See Page 38.

of the Jesuits, but had been modified considerably to meet the strong opposition. Leo XIII proceded very shortly to strengthen the policy laid down. In his first Encyclical he proclaimed the temporal power of the Popes, one of the declarations which Pius IX had been unable to win from the Vatican Council. At the time this was generally regarded as a formal gesture, but it soon became evident that it was to be the main-spring of Leo's own policy with relation to the European governments. He steadily interferred with their politics; he attempted to coerce the consciences of the French Royalists and force them to break away from their political principles for the sake of temporal political advantage for himself. The same purpose led to his building up and directing the operations of the clerical party in Germany. The Encyclopedia Britannica says of him:

"The second phase in Leo's policy could only be accomplished with the aid of the Jesuits, or rather, it required the submission of the ecclesiastical hierarchy to the mandates of the Society of Jesus. The further consequence was that all aspirations were subjected to the thraldom of the Church. The pontificate of Leo XIII is distinguished by the great number of persecutions, prosecutions and injuries inflicted upon Catholic *savants,* from the prosecution of Antonio Rosmini down to the proscription directed against the heads of the American Church. Episodes, such as the protection so long extended to the Leo Taxil affair, and to the revelations of Diana Vaughan (the object of which last was to bring Italian free-masonry and its ostensible work, the unity of Italy, into discredit) together with the attitude of the Ultramontane press in the Dreyfus affair, and later towards England, the invigoration of political agitation by the Lourdes celebration and by anti-Semitism, were all manifestations that could not raise the 'system' in the estimation of the cultured and civilized world. Perhaps even more dangerous was the employment of the whole ecclesiastical organization, and of Catholicism generally, for political purposes. * * *

"* * * the ecclesiastical regime had not only taken under its wing the solution of social questions, but also claimed that political action was within the proper scope of the Church, and, moreover, arrogated to itself the right of interfering by means of 'Directives' with the political life of nations. This was nothing new, for as early as 1215 the English barons protested against it. But the weakening of the Papacy had allowed this claim to lapse for centuries. To have revived it, and to have carried it out as far as is possible, was the work of Leo XIII."*

The Britannica sums up as follows the results of Leo's policies:

"(1) An unmistakable decline of religious fervour in church life. (2) The intensifying and nurturing of all the passions and questionable practices which are so easily encouraged by practical politics, and are incompatible in almost all points with the priestly office. (3) An ever-increasing displacement of all refined, educated and nobler elements of society by such as are rude and uncultured, by what, in fact, may be styled the ecclesiastical 'Trottori.' (4) The naturally resulting paralysis of intelligence and scientific research, which the Church either proscribed or sullenly tolerated. (5) The increasing decay and waxing corruption of the Romance nations, and the fostering of that diseased state of things which displayed itself in France in so many instances, such as the Dreyfus case, the anti-Semitic movement, and the campaign for and against the Assumptionists and their newspaper, the *Croix*. (6) The increasing estrangement of German and Anglo-Saxon feeling."**

Leo XIII developed the doctrine of Papal Supremacy to its utmost limits on most points. Yet one extention of the centralization of all power in the Pope was made by the present Pope on August 17, 1929, when he laid down the fundamental laws for the Vatican City. Under them the administration of the city and all judicial power depends

*Encyclopedia Britannica, Vol. XX, Page 720.
**Ibid.

solely upon the Pontiff, who designated himself as the source of all law and power in the city. Even the College of Cardinals has no power over the city except during a vacancy in the Papacy. In the old Canon Law of 1607 A. D., the Pope had certain powers and the rest were delegated to other dignitaries. The present Pope reserves to himself all the power given to the Popes by this law, but makes the powers which it delegated to others depend upon his own pleasure!

It would seem that the Papal Theory has thus been brought to its fullest possible limits within wholly modern times, and that it can be extended no further. The Pope claims complete and unlimited domination over all men and all things, and his enforcement of that claim is circumscribed only by his actual power.

To carry his "infallible" will into effect, the Pope is equipped with an organization which is now admirably adapted to perpetuate forever the Papal Theory. It is a closed corporation, allowing admission to none except those who are approved because of their agreement with its purposes, who have been educated in accordance with these purposes and have shown ability in achieving them. It does not acknowledge any outside influence and does not admit the right of any other power whatever to control it in any way at any point. It is secret, self-sustaining, working under a discipline of more than military severity and above all held together by the most rigid vows as well as the actual consecration of many of its members.

It is absolutely at the command of the Pope.

The world has never seen an organization with such strength, solidarity and power of endurance.

All of this is concentrated by the Popes under the Papal Theory upon a revival in modern times of the Dark Ages and of the strong despotism which gave them their name. Leo XIII almost openly avowed this purpose when he said:

"There was once a time when States were governed by the principles of Gospel teaching. Then it was that the power and Divine Virtue of Christian wisdom had diffused itself throughout the laws, institutions, and morals of the people; permeating all ranks and relations of civil society. Then, too, the religion instituted by Jesus Christ, established firmly in befitting dignity, flourished everywhere by the favor of princes and the legitimate protection of magistrates; and Church and State were happily united in concord and friendly interchange of good offices."*

The Encyclopedia Britannica thus describes the modern policy of the Roman Church:

"The struggle for religious freedom has suffered no intermission since the beginning of the Reformation; and the result is that today its recognition is considered one of the most precious trophies won in the evolution of modern civilization; nor can these changes be reversed, for they stand in the closest connexion and reciprocity one with another, and represent the fruits of centuries of co-operation on the part of the European peoples. But Ultramontanism ignores this latest page of history and treats it as non-existent, aspiring to the erection of a new order of society, similar to that which Rome created—or, at least, endeavored to create—in the halcyon days of medievalism. For the justification of this enterprise, it is considered sufficient to point out that the several elements of its programme once enjoyed validity within the Church. But Cyprian of Carthage said long ago, *'Consuetudo sine veritate vetustas erroris est'* (custom without justice is merely vested wrong) and the bare fact of previous existence is no argument for the re-introduction of obsolete and antiquated institutions and theories.

* The Great Encyclical Letters of Leo XIII, Page 118.

"But, under the guise of a restoration on conservative lines, Ultramontanism—notwithstanding the totally different conditions which now obtain—girds itself to work for an ideal of religion and culture in vogue during the Middle Ages, and at the same time holds itself justified in adopting the extreme point of view with respect to all questions which we have mentioned.   Thus Ultramontanism is not to be conceived as a theological movement, but as the programme of a party."*

This is the Roman Church today.   This is the controversy which has been called "defunct," "obsolete" and "empty."

It ought to be defunct.   A policy such as that now held by the Roman Church should have no place in the modern world.   But the controversy is established by the Roman Church itself, it has been intensified by each succeeding Roman Pope, and it cannot die until the causes that give rise to it are removed.   Those causes lie in the claims and the practices of the Roman Church under the Papal Theory.

America has developed and tolerates a large variety of religious beliefs without question.   It has tolerated Catholicism.   Yet no church makes a more positive demand upon its followers than does the Papacy and in its attempt to enforce the Papal Theory upon American citizens it strikes directly at every principle of Americanism, and makes this conflict a vital one in American life.

* Encyclopedia Britannica, Vol. XXVII, Page 572.

CHAPTER VIII

THE WAR AGAINST LIBERALISM

What Liberalism is—Its relation to progress and freedom—Opposition from the Papacy logical and inevitable—Recent extention of opposition to include all phases of Liberalism—The conflict well understood except in Protestant countries—Enforcement of the Pope's teachings.

THE word "Liberalism" has been used in so many ways that its meaning is no longer definite. Lately, in particular, it has fallen into some disrepute because it has been employed as a cloak for so many anti-social and often immoral practices and ideas. However, it is a word which we must use in this discussion, for no other term covers the general principles involved in the historic meaning.

This historic meaning is clear enough. Under it "Liberalism" means a belief in human liberty and the freedom of the individual as against any imposed human authority. Its philosophy is based on recognition of human error in ourselves as well as in others. They are liable to error: therefore they have no right to enforce their opinions on us. Likewise, because of our own similar liability, we may not coerce them. This is Liberalism.

For more than three hundred years this principle has been the one controlling the progressive nations. Under it they have fought tyranny, ended many despotisms, destroyed slavery, established science, welcomed new ideas, cast off the bondage of unjust precedent, and achieved progress. Its growth has created modern civilization. Particularly under it they have maintained freedom of conscience and of thought ever since the day of Luther's revolt against Papal Supremacy. They have learned to distrust autocratic power in both Church and State and to resist it in both alike. Thus Liberalism has been the father of freedom, of Protestantism, of democracy, of science, of equal justice and of progress.

The Papal Theory is opposed to Liberalism in its every essence—it must be. Since the Pope is held to be beyond the possibility of error, it follows that he ought to enforce his beliefs on others, and that they have no right to set up their opinions against his. Liberty to disagree with him is merely liberty to fight against God—and this is unthinkable. It must (under the Papal Theory) be opposed by force as well as by teaching, and for the good of the rebel himself. This was the theory of the Inquisition, it is absolutely logical, and it has never been in the least degree abandoned or modified by the Roman Hierarchy. It is true that there have been some "regrets" over the vast tortures and slaughters of the Inquisition, but they have been on the ground that it was a mistake in policy and not that it was in any way wrong in principle.

It is inevitable, then, that the Papacy should fight Liberalism, and it has done so—with varying vigor—from the first. Certain Popes in the XVIIIth and XIXth Centuries, to be sure, showed Liberal tendencies and appeared on the way toward compromises with modern thought, but this ended with the Syllabus of Pius IX and the Dogma of Infallibility. Since then it will be found that, as with the whole Papal Theory, the Roman Church has intensified and strengthened its position because of the opposition it has met.

The Papal war on Liberalism has now been made

to include every phase of human liberty. The Vatican has come to present a great force—and the only great force—hostile to and obstructive of the characteristic tendencies of modern thought and life. The fact that this is so little understood in the Protestant countries like England, Prussia and the United States, and that opposition to the Papacy has to some extent relaxed in those countries, is only because in them Rome has not been strong enough to exercise the reactionary influence which she wields in the Catholic countries.

The undying Catholic opposition to Liberalism in all its forms is fully set forth in the utterances of the Popes. It is true that under the Dogma of Infallibility Catholics have a technical right to reject these utterances unless they are *ex cathedra*, but in practice the Roman Church does not encourage—to say the least—any exercise of this technical right. Pius IX in his Syllabus, declares (Proposition 22) that it is a deadly error to believe that:

"The obligation by which Catholic teachers and authors are strictly bound is confined to those things only which are proposed to universal belief as dogmas of faith by the infallible judgment of the Church."*

In other words, he holds them bound also to all teachings of the church, and of the Pope as its head. It must be remembered that the Popes are in a position to enforce this principle upon all Catholic teachers, and almost all Catholic authors. Pope Leo XIII goes even further when he says:

"If in the difficult times in which our lot is cast, Catholics will give ear to Us, as it behooves them to do, they will readily see what are the duties of each one in matters of opinion as well as action. As regards opinion, whatever

* Dogmatic Canons and Decrees, Page 193.

the Roman Pontiffs have hitherto taught, or shall here-after teach, must be held with a firm grasp of mind, and, so often as occasion requires, must be openly professed. Especially with reference to the so-called 'Liberties' which are so greatly coveted in these days, all must stand by the judgment of the Apostolic See.''*

In support of this demand for obedience outside the bounds of infallibility, Archbishop Ireland—the most liberal-minded of all American Catholic prelates—declared publicly in discussing "divisions among the Catholics of America, not in regard to truth in matters of faith and morals, but in tenden-cies and movements and in the adjustment to mod-ern circumstances and environment" that "separa-tion from Leo, opposition to his directions, is noth-ing less than rebellion." He added that "there should be for us but one tendency, one movement, one method of adjustment, those indicated by Leo.''**

In view of these pronouncements it will be seen how little practical value is to be found in the technical limitations on the Dogma of Infallibility. The quotations from the Popes which follow must be read with this clearly in mind. It is no reply to criticism, and no defense of Catholics, to say that "they are not articles of our faith." That is true, but they are laws imposed in the name of faith.

The Papal opposition to Liberalism was first laid down in the Syllabus of Pius IX, already re-ferred to. It was further defined by his great suc-cessor, Leo XIII, and has been brought down to date by Pius XI, the present Pope. It is enforced by the Canon Law.

* The Great Encyclical Letters of Leo XIII, Page 129.
** L'Americanisme, by Albert Houtin, Page 153. Trans-lation from the French by Prof. John Moffett Mecklin.

The general lines of opposition are stated in the following three "principle errors" in the Syllabus:

"5. Divine revelation is imperfect, and therefore subject to a continual and indefinite progress, corresponding with the advancement of human reason.*

"10. As the philosopher is one thing, and philosophy another, so it is the right and duty of the philosopher to subject himself to the authority which he shall have proved to be true; but philosophy (*that is, 'thought'*) neither can nor ought to submit to any such authority."**

This, it will be seen, declares that thought, truth and revelation are already perfect, and that this perfect thought should be forced upon mankind. Of course the Pope and his followers hold that it is only the Roman Church which knows what it is!

"11. The Church not only ought never to pass judgment on philosophy, but ought to tolerate the errors of philosophy, leaving it to correct itself."***

These propositions, which Pius declares to be pernicious errors, are the foundations of freedom of thought, of Liberalism and of progress.

Leo XIII defines the Roman attitude much more clearly. He thus limits all liberty:

"* * * the Church cannot approve of that liberty which begets a contempt for the most sacred laws of God and casts off the obedience due to lawful authority (*meaning that of the Pope*), for this is not liberty so much as license. * * * On the other hand, that liberty is truly genuine, and to be sought after, which in regard to the individual does

* Dogmatic Canons and Decrees, Page 189.
** Ibid, Page 190.
*** Ibid, Page 190.

not allow men to be slaves of error * * * and which, too, in public administration guides the citizens in wisdom * * *."†

This means, if it means anything, that both as individuals and as citizens, men must be restricted to such liberties as lie inside the bounds of truth as determined by the Pope. Later he says in regard to modern liberty and modern thought:

"Having a false and absurd notion as to what liberty is, either they pervert the very idea of freedom, or they extend it at their pleasure to many things in respect to which man cannot rightly be regarded as free.

"* * * We have shown that whatsoever is good in those liberties is as ancient as truth itself, and that the Church has always most willingly approved and practiced that good: but whatsoever has been added as new (*that is, modern liberal ideas*) is, to tell the plain truth, of a vitiated kind, the fruit of the disorders of the age, and on an insatiate longing after novelties. Seeing, however, that many cling so obstinately to their own opinion in this matter as to imagine these modern liberties, cankered as they are, to be the greatest glory of our age, and the very basis of civil life, without which no perfect government can be conceived, we feel it a pressing duty, for the sake of the common good, to treat separately of this subject. * * * ††

"Liberty, then, as We have said, belongs only to those who have the gift of reason or intelligence. * * * The end, or object, both of the rational will and of its liberty, is that good only which is in conformity with (*Catholic*) reason.

"* * * For, as the possibility of error, and actual error, are defects of the mind and attest its imperfection, so the pursuit of what has a false appearance of good, though a

† The Great Encyclical Letters of Leo XIII, Page 127.
†† Ibid, Page 135-6.   (Numbers in the following text refer to other pages in the same book.)

proof of our freedom, just as a disease is proof of our vitality, implies defect in human liberty. * * * Thus it is that the infinitely perfect God, although supremely free, because of the supremacy of His intellect and of His essential goodness, nevertheless cannot choose evil; neither can the angels and saints, who enjoy the beatific vision. St. Augustine and others urged most admirably against the Pelagians, that, if the possibility of deflection from good belonged to the essence or perfection of liberty, then God, Jesus Christ, and the angels and saints, who have not this power, would have no liberty at all * * * the possibility of sinning, is not freedom, but slavery. * * * (Page 138)

"Such then being the condition of human liberty, it necessarily stands in need of light and strength to direct its actions to good and restrain them from evil. (Page 139)

"For law is the guide of man's actions; it turns him towards good by its rewards, and deters him from evil by its punishments. * * * For, since the force of law consists in the imposing of obligations and the granting of rights, authority is the one and only foundation of all law—the power, that is, of fixing duties and defining rights, as also of assigning the necessary sanctions of reward and chastisement to each and all of its commands. But all this, clearly, cannot be found in man, if, as his own supreme legislator, he is to be the rule of his own actions. It follows, therefore, that the law of nature is the same thing as the eternal law, implanted in rational creatures, and inclining them to their right action and end and can be nothing else but the eternal reason of God." (Page 140)

It must not be forgotten that Leo claims to exercise in full the authority of God, so that all this means that liberty must be ruled by the Pope and subject to his limitations. He then makes a direct attack on Liberalism:

"Many there are who follow in the footsteps of Lucifer, and adopt as their own his rebellious cry; 'I will not serve;' and consequently substitute for true liberty what is sheer and most foolish nonsense. Such, for instance, are the men belonging to that widely spread and powerful organization who, usurping the name of liberty, style themselves Liberals. * * * (Page 145.)

"From all this may be understood the nature and character of that liberty which the followers of Liberalism so eagerly advocate and proclaim. On the one hand, they demand for themselves and for the State a license which opens the way to every perversity of opinion; and on the other, they hamper the (*Catholic*) Church in diverse ways, restricting her liberty within the narrowest limits, although from her teaching not only is there nothing to be feared, but in every respect very much to be gained." (Page 155)

These quotations might be extended greatly, but those given are enough to make the position of the Papacy clear. The present Pope re-iterated and even extended this position in a single phase on June 5, 1929, when he branded Mussolini's speech declaring for freedom of conscience, speech and religion as "heretical and worse than heretical." Certainly the Pope's opposition to Liberalism had not been abated on that date.

CHAPTER IX

DENIAL OF VITAL LIBERTIES

Our most important right is that of liberty of conscience and worship—This officially denied and condemned in recent utterances of the Popes—Freedom of speech also vigorously assailed—The right of liberal education, free from priestly control, and of State's authority over schools denied—How this
doctrine is enforced in America.

THE most vital of our liberties, and one without
the exercise of which any free government is impossible, is that of conscience and worship. Also,
this liberty has been proved necessary to the peace
of the world, as was shown once more by the
religious outbreaks in India and Palestine in 1929.
The Syllabus lists the following four propositions
as being wholly wrong:

"15. Every man is free to embrace and profess that
religion which, guided by the light of reason, he shall consider true.

"16. Man may, in the observance of any religion whatever, find the way of eternal salvation, and arrive at eternal
salvation.

"17. Good hope at least is to be entertained of the
eternal salvation of all those who are not at all in the true
(Roman) Church of Christ.

"18. Protestantism is nothing more than another form
of the same true Christian religion, in which form it is given to
please God equally as in the Catholic Church."*

If these are "errors," then freedom of conscience,
freedom of religion, hope of salvation except through
the Pope, and all hope for Protestants, are utterly
wrong. So, too, is tolerance and there can be no
basis for any Liberalism. Leo expands the idea:

* Dogmatic Canons and Decrees, Pages 190-191.

"Let us examine that liberty in individuals which is so opposed to the virtue of religion, namely, the liberty of worship, as it is called. This is based on the principle that every man is free to profess as he may choose any religion or none. * * * When a liberty such as We have described is offered to man, the power is given him to pervert or abandon with impunity the most sacred of duties, and to exchange an unchangeable good for evil; which as We have said, is no liberty, but its degradation and the abject submission of the soul to sin.*

"Wherefore civil society must acknowledge God as its Founder and Parent, and must obey and reverence His power and authority. Justice therefore forbids, and reason itself forbids, the State to be godless; or to adopt a line of action which would end in godlessness—namely, to treat the various religions (as they call them) alike, and to bestow upon them promiscuously equal rights and privileges. * * * (Page 150)

"Another liberty is widely advocated, namely, liberty of conscience. If by this is meant that every one may, as he chooses, worship God or not, it is sufficiently refuted by the arguments already adduced. But it may also be taken to mean that every man in the State may follow the will of God and, from a consciousness of duty and free from every obstacle, obey His commands (*meaning, of course, as laid down by the Popes*). This, indeed, is true liberty * * *. (Page 155)

"And as to tolerance, it is surprising how far removed from the equity and prudence of the Church are those who profess what is called Liberalism. * * * And because the Church, the pillar and ground of truth, and the un-erring teacher of morals, is forced utterly to reprobate and condemn tolerance of such an abandoned and criminal character, they calumniate her as being wanting in patience and gentleness, and thus fail to see that, in so doing, they impute to her as a fault what is really a matter for commendation." (Page 158)

The present Pope brings this doctrine down to date again in his letter of June 5, 1929. Mussolini

* The Great Encyclical Letters of Leo XIII, Pages 149-150 and following.

had said that other religions would be "permitted."
Pius insists that the word must be "tolerated."
The reason for this change is, strictly speaking,
that one "tolerates" evils which cannot be prevented, while to "permit" them means much more.
The use of the word "tolerate" in this case brands
Protestantism as an evil, just as in the case of those
evil houses which the French stignatize as *"maisons
de tolerance."* But even this is not enough for the
living Pope. He says other religions may be tolerated:

"* * * provided that it be and remains clearly and loyally understood that the Catholic religion, and it alone, is,
in accordance with the statute and treaties, the State Religion, with the logical and juridical consequences of such
a condition of constitutional right, especially with regard
to propaganda; provided it remain no less clearly and
loyally understood that the Catholic cult is not purely and
simply a permitted and admitted cult, but is that which
the letter and the spirit of the Treaty and the Concordat
will it to be."*

The reference to "propaganda" is particularly
interesting here. It will be some time before the
world will know just how far Pius intends to go
on this point—it is important that he has clearly
stated what he believes to be his rights. If Italy
accepts and enforces them, under this clause, it will
expell the Methodist, Baptist and Waldensian mis-
sions in Italy which have been such a thorn in the
Papal flesh. The whole machinery of the Inquisition was set up and functioned under this claim of
the Popes in regard to propaganda; the Popes prior
to being driven out of Rome in 1870 refused permission for an Anglican chapel in the city; the
Madiai family in Florence was imprisoned for dis-
tributing Bibles, and one of the last acts of temporal

*New York World, June 23, 1929.

rule of the Papacy was to seize a Jewish boy—who had been baptized by a servant without the consent of his parents—and bring him up as a Catholic. It seems clear that at least the Protestant churches were in the present Pope's mind when he said:

"All the greater, therefore, is our amazement at seeing advanced the idea that certain true and undeniable offenses against that sacred character can be tolerated (in Rome) in the name of liberty of conscience or of a wholly misplaced compassion."*

As to liberty of conscience Pius XI's letter of June 5, 1929, is explicit:

"It seems even less admissible to us to have meant the assurance of entire, intact, absolute liberty of conscience. It would be tantamount to saying that the creature is not subject to the Creator; tantamount to legitimization of every formation, or rather deformation, of conscience, even the most criminal and socially disastrous ones. Admitted that conscience escapes from the power of the State, recognized, as it is recognized, that in questions of conscience the Church, and she alone, by reason of Her divine mandate, is competent, it is by the same fact recognized that in a Catholic State liberty of conscience and discussion must be interpreted and practiced according to Catholic doctrine and law."*

It is worth pausing a moment to realize the full meaning of this statement of Papal policy in our own day. It means that Catholic law will be enforced upon non-Catholics in any State which accepts union with the Catholic Church; that their freedom of conscience and speech will be forcibly suppressed so far as the Pope pleases under the doctrine that intolerance is a duty; that whatever freedom is granted them will be by favor and not as a right. It means, too, that the present Pope maintains in full all the dogmas by which his predecessors justified the Inquisition, St. Bartholo-

* New York World, June 23, 1929.

mew's Massacre, and the religious wars of three centuries. It means, finally, that all devout subjects of the Pope must attempt to establish this condition in all nations.

Thus the opposition of the Papacy to the Liberal doctrine of freedom of conscience and religion is maintained in full force to the present time and applied so far as is possible. Against the corresponding doctrine of freedom of speech, Pius IX apparently did not think it necessary to speak in his Syllabus, since it is so obvious that when freedom of conscience and religion are denied, freedom of speech is impossible. Leo XIII, however, struck at it directly:

"We must now consider briefly liberty of speech, and liberty of the Press. It is hardly necessary to say that there is no such right as this, if it be not used in moderation, and if it pass beyond the bounds and end of all true liberty."[*]

The present Pope, too, in his letter of June 5th declares against liberty of discussion in Italy today. He says:

"It is inadmissible to have meant absolute liberty of discussion, including those kinds of discussion calculated easily to deceive the good faith of simple-minded hearers, discussion which may easily become dissimulated forms of propaganda not less dangerous for State Religion, and thereby for the State itself, especially in all it holds most sacred, to wit, the tradition of the Italian people and, most essential, its unity."[**]

If conscience, religion and speech are not to be allowed liberty, of course education cannot be free but must be under control of those who dictate to conscience. This is laid down in the Syllabus, which condemns the following ideas:

[*] The Great Encyclical Letters of Leo XIII, Page 151.
[**] New York World, June 23, 1920.

"45. The entire government of public schools in which the youth of a Christian State is educated, except (to a certain extent) in the case of episcopal seminaries, may and ought to appertain to the civil power, and belong to it so far that no other authority whatsoever shall be recognized as having any right to interfere in the discipline of the schools, the arrangement of the studies, the conferring of degrees, in the choice or approval of the teachers.

"46. Moreover, even in ecclesiastical seminaries, the method of studies to be adopted is subject to the civil authority.

"47. The best theory of civil society requires that popular schools open to children of every class of people, and, generally, all public institutes intended for instruction in letters and philosophical sciences and for carrying on the education of youth, should be freed from all ecclesiastical authority, control and interference, and should be fully subjected to the civil and political power at the pleasure of the rulers, and according to the standard of the prevalent opinions of the age."*

If these are errors, the truth is that Romanism should control all education for its own benefit!

Leo as usual expounds and expands this doctrine. He says:

"The more the enemies of religion exert themselves to offer the uninformed, especially the young, such instruction as darkens the mind and corrupts morals (*meaning, of course, instruction different from Papal doctrine*), the more actively should we endeavor that not only a suitable and solid method of education may flourish, but above all that this education be wholly in harmony with the Catholic faith in its literature and system of training, and chiefly in philosophy, upon which the foundation of other sciences in a great measure depends."**

And again:

"A like judgment must be passed upon what is called liberty of teaching. There can be no doubt that truth alone should imbue the minds of men; for in it are found the well-

* Dogmatic Canons and Decrees, Pages 198-199.
** Great Encyclical Letters of Leo XIII, Page 17.

being, the end, and the perfection of every intelligent nature; and therefore nothing but truth should be taught to the ignorant and to the educated, so as to bring knowledge to those who have it not, and to preserve it in those who possess it. For this reason it is plainly the duty of all who teach to banish error from the mind, and by sure safeguards to close the entry to all false convictions. From this it follows, as is evident, that the liberty of which We have been speaking, is greatly opposed to reason, and tends absolutely to pervert men's minds, in as much as it claims for itself the right of teaching whatever it pleases— a liberty which the State cannot grant without failing in its duty. * * *

"* * * * a perfect society was founded by Him—the Church namely, of which He is the head, and with which He has promised to abide till the end of the world. To this society He entrusted all the truths which He had taught, in order that it might keep and guard them and with lawful authority explain them; and at the same time He commanded all nations to hear the voice of the Church, as if it were His own, threatening those who would not hear it with everlasting perdition. * * * In faith and in the teaching of morality, God Himself made the Church a partaker of His divine authority, and through His heavenly gift she cannot be deceived. She is therefore the greatest and most reliable teacher of mankind, and in her dwells an inviolable right to teach them. * * * Therefore there is no reason why genuine liberty should grow indignant, or true science feel aggrieved, at having to bear the just and necessary restraint of laws by which, in the judgment of the Church and of Reason itself, human teaching has to be controlled. The Church, indeed—as facts have everywhere proved— looks chiefly above all to the defense of the Christian faith, (*Catholicism*) while careful at the same time to foster and promote every kind of human learning."*

The present Pope reasserted this in his letter of June 5, 1929:

"By logical necessity it must also be recognized that the full and perfect mandate for education belongs not to the State, but to the Church, and that the State can neither

*The Great Encyclical Letters of Leo XIII, Pages 152-155.

impede nor lessen the execution and fulfillment of this mandate, *nor even reduce it to the mere teaching of religious truths."*

This proposition is also enforced by Canon 1374 which states:

"Catholic children must not attend non-Catholic, neutral or mixed schools which are also open to non-Catholics. The local Ordinary (bishop) shall decide when attendance at such schools may be tolerated."**

It is in line with this policy that the Catholic Church has fought the public schools of America and elsewhere. It is not necessary to charge that the objection of freedom in education is caused wholly by fear of the truth; it doubtless is true that many Catholics believe a repressed education is the only means of preserving truth. Nevertheless it must be noted that Catholic education is the most effective means of inculcating the Papal Theory throughout the world and preserving the authority of the hierarchy. It has the further advantage of emphasizing the cleavage between Catholics and non-Catholics and thus contributes to the social and political solidarity of Catholicism. It goes without saying that these advantages to Catholicism are disadvantages to a free nation and to the freedom of individuals.

* The New York World, June 23, 1929.
** Commentary on Canon Law, Vol. VI, Page 414.

CHAPTER X

ROME'S MARRIAGE MONOPOLY

Catholic principles regarding marriage—Denial of all civil authority and of divorce—Leo's claim to exclusive jurisdiction over all Christians—His rejection of civil marriages—Opposition to mixed marriages—The Rota over-rides States and Protestant church—Roman exploitation of mixed marriages —Violation of freedom of unborn children—Blanket denial of all Liberal rights.

AS a part of its campaign against Liberalism, the Papacy claims control over the marriage of all Christians. It maintains that no deviation from its Sacraments can be tolerated, and it takes advantage of the romance of youth to force each succeeding generation into its system, and also to proselyte.

The Syllabus lays down the rules, branding the following ideas as errors:

"67. By the law of nature, the marriage tie is not indissoluble, and in many cases divorce properly so called may be decreed by the civil authority.

"71. The form of solemnizing marriage prescribed by the Council of Trent, under pain of nullity, does not bind in cases where the civil law lays down another form, and declares that when this new form is used the marriage shall be valid.

"73. In force of a merely civil contract there may exist between Christians a real marriage, and it is false to say either that the marriage contract between Christians is always a sacrament, or that there is no contract if the sacrament be excluded.

"74. Matrimonial causes and espousals belong by their nature to civil tribunals."*

* Dogmatic Canons and Decrees, Pages 204-5-6.

Leo in his first Encyclical took pains to deny the validity of civil marriage when he said that:

"Impious laws, setting at naught the sanctity of this great sacrament, put it on the same footing with mere civil contracts."*

A little later he denounced conditions under which:

"***things came to such a pitch that permission to marry, or the refusal of the permission, depended on the will of the heads of the State."**

He maintained the power of the church:

"Christ, therefore, having renewed marriage to such and so great excellence, commended and entrusted all the discipline bearing upon these matters to His Church. The Church, always and everywhere, has so used her power with reference to the marriage of Christians, that men have seen clearly how it belongs to her as of native right; not being made hers by any human grant, but given divinely to her by the will of her Founder." (Page 65)

In his attack upon civil marriage he said:

"Now since the family and human society at large spring from marriage, these men will on no account allow matrimony to be the subject of the jurisdiction of the Church. Nay, they endeavor to deprive it of all holiness, and so bring it within the contracted sphere of those rights which, having been instituted by man, are ruled and administered by the civil jurisprudence of the community. Wherefore it necessarily follows that they attribute all power over marriage to civil rulers, and allow none whatever to the Church; and when the Church exercises any such power, they think that she acts either by favor of the civil authority or to its injury. Now is the time, they say, for the heads of the State to vindicate their rights unflinchingly, and to do their best to settle all that relates to marriage according as to them seems good.

* The Encyclical Letters of Leo XIII, Page 18.
** Ibid, Page 61 and following.

"Hence are owing civil marriages, commonly so called; hence laws are framed which impose impediments to marriage; hence arise judicial sentences affecting the marriage contract, as to whether or not it have been rightly made. Lastly, all power of prescribing and passing judgment in this class of cases is, as we see, of set purpose denied to the Catholic Church, so that no regard is paid either to her divine power or to her prudent laws. * * * (Page 67)

"As, then, marriage is holy by its own power, in its own nature, and of itself, it ought not to be regulated and administered by the will of civil rulers, but by the Divine Authority of the Church, which alone in sacred matters professes the office of teaching. * * * (Page 68)

"Neither, therefore, by reasoning can it be shown, nor by any testimony of history be proved, that power over the marriages of Christians has ever lawfully been handed over to the rulers of the State." (Page 71)

A little later on he definitely states that the law of the church is superior to that of the State in regard to marriage:

"In like manner, all ought to understand clearly that, if there be any union of a man and a woman among the faithful of Christ which is not a sacrament, such a union has not the force and nature of a proper marriage; that *although contracted in accordance with the laws of the State, it cannot be more than a rite or custom* introduced by the civil law. Further, the civil law can deal with and decide those matters alone which in the civil order spring from marriage, and which cannot possibly exist, as is evident, unless there be a true and lawful cause for them, that is to say, the nuptial bond. It is of the greatest consequence to husband and wife that all these things should be known and well understood by them, in order that they may conform to the laws of the State, *if there be no objection on the part of the Church;* for the Church wishes the effects of marriage to be guarded in all possible ways, and that no harm may come to the children.

"In the great confusion of opinions, however, which day by day is spreading more and more widely, it should further be known that no power can dissolve the bond of Christian marriage whenever this has been ratified and consummated; and that, of a consequence, those husbands and wives are guilty of a manifest crime who plan, for whatever reason, to be united in a second marriage before the first one has been ended by death." (Page 80)

Finally he denounces marriages between Catholics and non-Catholics:

"Care also must be taken that they do not easily enter into marriage with those who are not Catholics: for when minds do not agree as to the observances of religion, it is scarcely possible to hope for agreement in other things. Other reasons also proving that persons should turn with dread from such marriages are chiefly these: that they give occasion to forbidden association and communion in religious matters; endanger the faith of the Catholic partner; are a hindrance to the proper education of the children; and often lead to a mixing up of truth and falsehood, and to the belief that all religions are equally good." (Page 81)

Once more the present Pope, in his letter of June 5, 1929, reasserted the Catholic position and promised excommunication to all who failed to obey the rules. He says:

"In the matter of marriage the Concordat procures for the family, for the Italian people, for the country still more than for the Church, so great a benefit that for its sake alone We would willingly have sacrificed life itself. And it is well said 'that there is no doubt that morally and before his religious conscience the practicing Catholic should celebrate canonical marriage.' But not so happily was it added that 'juridicially nobody can force him to it.' The Church, a perfect society in her own order, can and should do it, with the means at her disposal; and will do it; and does it up to the present moment, by placing outside the communion those of her members who have neglected or passed it by, preferring merely the civil marriage."*

Thus the Roman Catholic Church denies to the State all rights concerning the marriage of its citizens. It rejects and defies whatever laws the State

*New York World, June 23, 1929.

may make without its approval and teaches its people that these laws are of no effect whatever. It denies the morality of those citizens who comply with and depend upon the State laws, if those laws in any way conflict with its own regulations. As Charles C. Marshall has so vigorously pointed out:

"A direct conflict between the Roman Catholic Church and the State arises on the institution of marriage, through the claim of that Church in theory in the case of all baptized persons, quite irrespective of specific consent, Protestants and Roman Catholics alike, jurisdiction touching marriage is wrested from the State and appropriated to the Roman Catholic Church, its exercise reposing ultimately in the Pope. * * * The Church proceeds in disregard of the law and sovereignty of the State, and claims, at its discretion, the right to annul and destroy the bonds of the civil contract. * * * in the proceeding before that court (the Rota in the Marlborough case) the sovereignties of New York State and of England, and all that they had done, were ignored. * * * It would be difficult to find a more utter disregard of the sovereignty of States than this by the sovereignty of Rome, touching the comity which, in good morals and public decency, is supposed to exist between sovereign powers."*

To use the Marlborough case as an example, the Roman Catholic Church's decision on that case did the following things:

It declared that a marriage consummated under the laws of the sovereign state of New York, and valid under the laws of that State, was not a marriage at all.

It declared that a marriage consummated by another church, and valid according to the spiritual ordinances of that church, was no marriage.

It declared that a marriage whose validity had been affirmed by the action of British law was not a marriage.

It declared that a marriage which had stood for

*Governor Smith's American Catholicism, pages 57-61.

twenty-nine years and to which two children had been born, had never existed.

It implied that two Protestant children, born in wedlock valid under the law and made holy by the sanction of religion, were illegitimate and unblessed and then graciously conferred legitimacy upon them, in spite of its decision that their parents were never married.

It declared that a man who was not and never had been a Roman communicant had lived for many years in unholy union with a woman who was not his wife,— though his own belief, the laws of two nations, and the sanctions of a great Protestant church said that she was.

By this means it permitted one of the couple to contract a marriage with a Catholic which the Roman Church could hold "valid." Practically, it accomplished divorce by evasion.

Carrying out this policy, the Roman Catholic Church undertakes to say for all people—Catholics, Protestants and members of no Christian church— what are and what are not valid marriages. The following pronouncements are official:

"9. Marriage of all Catholics (both parties Catholics) before a minister or civil magistrate is no marriage at all.

"10. Marriage of all fallen-away Catholics (who have become Protestants or infidels) before a minister or civil magistrate is no marriage.

"11. Marriage of a Catholic to a non-baptized person is never a real marriage unless the Church grants a dispensation. Such a marriage before a minister or a justice of the peace is no marriage.

"12. Marriage of a Catholic to a Protestant (one never baptized in the Catholic Church) before a minister or civil magistrate is no marriage.

"13. Marriage of a Protestant to a Protestant (provided they were never baptized in the Catholic Church) is valid.

"14. Marriage of a Protestant (baptized) to a non-baptized party is no marriage.

"15. Marriage of a non-baptized man to a non-baptized woman is valid as a life-long contract. These parties do not receive, however, the Sacrament of Matrimony.

"16. There will be no marriage at all unless there be two witnesses—one witness with the priest will not suffice."*

Further than this, the Roman Catholic Church requires that all children of a Catholic marriage shall be brought up in the Catholic Church. Its laws are so amazing that they are worth setting forth in full. The following statement of them is also from the "Manual of the Holy Catholic Church," a book intended for a use among Roman Catholics corresponding to that of the family Bible, bearing the *imprimatur* of Archbishop Quigley, and with testimonials and endorsements from many important prelates in America. It says the requirements are:

"*First, That all the children that may be born of the marriage shall be baptized and brought up in the Catholic faith.*

"*Second, That the Catholic party shall have full liberty for the practice of the Catholic religion.*

"*Third, That no religious marriage ceremony shall take place elsewhere than in the Catholic Church.*

"*The following are the Promises to be signed before marriage:*

"*To Be Signed by the Catholic Party.*

" '*I the undersigned do hereby promise and engage that all the children of both sexes who may be born of my marriage shall be baptized in the Catholic Church, and shall be carefully brought up in the knowledge and practice of the Catholic religion, and I also promise that (according to the instructions of the Holy See) my marriage in the Catholic Church shall not be preceeded nor followed by any other religious marriage ceremony.'*   (*Signature*)

*Manual of the Holy Catholic Church, Section II, Page 187.

"To Be Signed by the non-Catholic Party.

" '*I the undersigned do hereby solemnly promise and engage that I will not interfere with the religious belief of_____, my future (wife or husband), nor with (her or his) full and perfect liberty to fulfil all (her or his) duties as a Catholic; that I will allow all the children of both sexes, who may be born of our marriage, to be baptized in the Catholic Church, and to be carefully brought up in the knowledge and practice of the Catholic religion.' (Signature)''*

Thus the Roman Church, by its insistence that it alone can make a marriage holy, uses this belief on the part of its people to increase its grip upon all with whom it comes into contact and so furthers its campaign for national and world domination. Its importance to the Roman campaign is shown by the fact that, although in many things Romanism has made some concessions to the American principles of self-government and self-control, in this it reverts to a complete denial of those principles and adds to its denial a deliberate insult to all people of other creeds.

Since the attitude of the hierarchy on the marriage sacrament directly or indirectly effects all non-Catholics, this has no claim on our religious tolerance. There is an indirect injury in the declaration that marriages under the laws of our States are in a large measure null and void and their children illegitimate. More serious and more immediate in its effect upon society is the requirement of Catholic education for all children of mixed marriages. This attempt, by precontract, to mortgage the religion and insure a reactionary outlook in a large part of the coming generation has been highly successful. Its evils are many.

This system, as is intended, gives to the Roman hierarchy a distinct advantage over other churches.

*Manual of the Holy Catholic Church, Section II, Pages 165-6.

All other churches must depend for their strength entirely upon the truths they teach. The Roman system substitutes dogmatism for truth.

This practice adds greatly in perpetuating the power of Romanism, and that not only among Catholics. It draws into the Catholic schools large numbers of children, at least half of whom should be trained in either free or Protestant schools. Thus it constitutes a far-reaching method of proselyting.

A worse evil of this system is that it violates the rights of unborn children. It is, of course, usual for every child to be brought up in the religion of its parents, but the Romanist system goes far beyond this—as is entirely logical under a theory which denies all right of private judgment. Rome does not admit that either the parents or the children have any right to freedom of education or religion; therefore it forbids the parents to exercise any discretion and prevents the child from learning anything about other religions so that he might judge truth for himself.   *202511*

Thus in its use of marriage the Catholic Church carries to its extreme limit its war against Liberalism, and insures continued recruits for that war.

In his usual clear and forceful language Leo XIII sums up the entire attitude of the Roman Church against Liberalism. Let it be remembered that in these paragraphs the expression "the authority of God" means to Leo and to all Catholics the authority of the Pope. Leo says:

"And now to reduce for clearness' sake to its principal heads all that has been set forth with its immediate con-

clusions, the summing up is this briefly: that man, by a
necessity of this nature, is wholly subject to the most faithful and ever-enduring power of God; and that as a consequence any liberty, except that which consists in submission to God and in subjection to His will, is unintelligible.
To deny the existence of this authority in God, or to refuse
to submit to it, means to act, not as a free man, but as one
who treasonably abuses his liberty; and in such a disposition of mind the chief and deadly vice of Liberalism essentially consists. The form, however, of the sin is mani-
fold; for in more ways and degrees than one can the will
depart from the obedience which is due to God or to those
who share the divine power.

"For, to reject the supreme authority of God, and to
cast off all obedience to Him in public matters, or even in
private and domestic affairs, is the greatest perversion of
liberty and the worst kind of Liberalism: and what We
have said must be understood to apply to this alone in its
fullest sense."*

He thus summarizes all those things which are
forbidden to good Catholics and definitely states
that they have the right of rebellion against any
government which interferes with Papal Supremacy:

"From what has been said, it follows that it is
quite unlawful to demand, to defend, or to grant
unconditional freedom of thought, of speech, or
writing, or of worship, as if these were so many rights
given by nature to man. For if nature had really
granted them, it would be lawful to refuse obedience
of God, and there would be no restraint on human
liberty. It likewise follows that freedom in these
things may be tolerated wherever there is just cause;
but only with such moderation as will prevent its
degenerating into license and excess. And where such
liberties are in use, men should employ them in doing
good, and should estimate them as the Church does;
for liberty is to be regarded as legitimate in so far only
as it affords greater facility for doing good, but no
farther.

* The Great Encyclical Letters of Leo XIII, Page 159.

"Whenever there exists, or there is a reason to fear, an unjust oppression of the people on the one hand, or a deprivation of the liberty of the Church on the other, it is lawful to seek for such a change of government as will bring about due liberty of action."*

The definition of what Leo means by "a deprivation of the liberty of the Church" involves the whole question of the relationship of Church and State under the Papal Theory. This requires a chapter to itself, because of its tremendous importance to modern nations.

It will be seen that the attitude of the Catholic Church toward every one of the principles of Liberalism and toward each form of human liberty is governed by the same line of reasoning. It is this:

For all practical purposes, so far as human beings are concerned, the Pope is God. He knows what is right and what is wrong and tells humanity what it must and must not do. To disagree with him is to rebel against God. This would be an injury both to the rebel himself and to the purposes of God and can not be permitted. Therefore there can be no freedom which would allow any individual to disagree with the Pope; no freedom except by his permission, no liberty in the sense in which the modern world understands it and no belief in any such liberty.

This is the attitude toward Liberalism and all human freedom which is required of all who accept the supremacy of the Pope; that is, of all good Catholics.

* The Great Encyclical Letters of Leo XIII, Page 161.

CHAPTER XI

THE POPE AND THE NATIONS—THEORY

The Papal Theory defined for practical use—Catholic control of
conscience as to law-obedience—Logical basis for Papal position—Statement of claim to political supremacy—Application of this claim to union of Church and State—Denial of
validity of laws not approved by the Popes—Claim of Pope's
right to decide on validity of American law made by American Catholics—Refusal of Roman Church to submit to the
State.

THERE might be little actual harm to the world
from the Papal Theory if it were held merely as a
speculative philosophy for discussion in the re-
fectories of monasteries, or for debate inside the
frescoed walls of the Vatican. The Papal claim to
a divine and supernatural supremacy, the violent
Ultramontanism and opposition to all Liberal principles, the whole reactionary autocratic theory and
polity of Romanism, would cause only a mild interest if they were not put into practice. It is with
the actual impact of these pretentions on modern governments and society that we are chiefly concerned,
and it is by the study of the direct attitude of the
Papacy toward sovereign nations that we must
form a true estimate of the fitness of Roman Catholics as citizens.

Fortunately the position of the Papacy has been
made perfectly clear. With its usual remorseless
logic it has applied its autocratic theory to every
relation of Church and State, and it has defined
exactly what are the duties of Roman Catholics as
citizens. Certainly, so far as politics and government are concerned, Catholicism presents no clois-

tered philosophy but a practical, definite, detailed and rigid code to govern Roman Catholics in all their relations with the modern State.

There are certain admirable phases of this code. It inculcates general obedience to law and faithful discharge of civic duties. Many passages from Papal Encyclicals are wholly fine, if they were allowed to stand alone. It is when we come to the rules for the discharge of civic duties and to the limits placed on Catholic obedience to law, that the gravest questions arise.

Two things must be borne in mind. First is that the attempt of any outside power to define the duties of citizens is an encroachment upon the rights of the State. Certainly the State itself has the sole right and duty of laying down the responsibilities of citizenship. It is every man's right, of course, to submit the action of his government to his own conscience, but a violation of individual conscience by some law cannot be accepted by any government as justification for disobedience of law. Any self-respecting State must punish disobedience to its laws; resistance (even because of conscience or Papal commands) is rebellion and, unless it overthrows the government, will be treated as treason. Such rebellion for conscience sake (but not disobedience) is, of course, justified under the principles of the Declaration of Independence. It will be seen that the Roman law takes a very different position in that it submits the acts of the State, not to the individual conscience of free citizens, but to the *"ipsi dixit"* of the Pope. Certainly, the moral authority of the State cannot justly be questioned by a conscience influenced by loyalty to an alien authority.

In the second place the question of the actual application of the Papal Theory is always present. The most extreme defenders of Romanism do not attempt to deny the violence of the conflict between the Papal Theory and modern ideas. What they do claim is that this theory is not intended for general application to modern nations, but applies only to "some ideal State" or a wholly Catholic nation. Archbishop Dowling, in referring to any conceivable union of the Church and State said, for example; "So many conditions for its accomplishment are lacking in every government of the world that the thesis may well be relegated to the limbo of defunct controversies."*

Yet in the year of our Lord 1929 we have seen the union of Church and State accomplished in Italy. It will be important to determine just how far it is intended to apply Catholic political claims to other countries in our own day.

With the development of Ultramontanism through the whole Papal Theory, the position taken in regard to the Church and State is logical, if the preliminary proposition that the Pope stands in the place of Almighty God be accepted. If that be true, the Roman Catholic Church can not encourage nationalism; the utmost it can logically do is to support local governments as agencies for the regulation of local society. If the Pope is God's vice-gerent, he can not be expected to permit any emphasis on national differences which would tend to establish differences inside his church. He must be cosmopolitan in policy in order to attain his international ends; he must combat national power in

* Quoted by Alfred E. Smith in his reply to Charles C. Marshall, Atlantic Monthly, April, 1927.

order to magnify his own, and he must prevent patriotism from interferring with the secular ambitions of his church. It is inevitable, then, that he will seek to maintain the supremacy of the Roman Catholic Church and to limit the jurisdiction of national governments, in so far as it is possible.

Once more we go back to the Syllabus of Pius IX for the basic principles of Ultramontanism as applied to the nations. The pernicious "errors" which he lists on this subject are the following:

"19. The Church is not a true and perfect society, entirely free; nor is she endowed with proper and perpetual rights of her own, conferred upon her by her Divine Founder; but it appertains to the civil power to define what are the rights of the Church, and the limits within which she may exercise those rights.

"20. The ecclesiastical power ought not to exercise its authority without the permission and assent of the civil government.

"21. The Church has not the power of defining dogmatically that the religion of the Catholic Church is the only true religion.

"22. The obligation by which Catholic teachers and authors are strictly bound is confined to those things only which are proposed to universal belief as dogmas of faith by the infallible judgment of the Church.

"23. Roman pontiffs and ecumenical councils have wandered outside the limits of their powers, have usurped the rights of princes, and have even erred in defining matters of faith and morals.

"24. The Church has not the power of using force, nor has she any temporal power, direct or indirect.

"25. Besides the power inherent in the episcopate, other temporal power has been attributed to it by the civil authority, granted either explicitly or tacitly, which on that account is revocable by the civil authority whenever it thinks fit.

"26. The Church has no innate and legitimate right of acquiring and possessing property.

"27. The sacred ministers of the Church and the Roman Pontiff are to be absolutely excluded from every charge and dominion over temporal affairs.

"28. It is not lawful for bishops to publish even letters Apostolic without the permission of Government.

"29. Favours granted by the Roman Pontiff ought to be considered null, unless they have been sought for through the civil government.

"30. The immunity of the Church and of ecclesiastical persons derived its origin from civil law.

"31. The ecclesiastical forum or tribunal for temporal causes, whether civil or criminal, of clerics, ought by all means to be abolished, even without consulting and against the protest of the Holy See.

"32. The personal immunity by which clerics are exonerated from military conscription and service in the army may be abolished without violation either of natural right or equity. Its abolition is called for by civil progress, especially in a society framed on the model of a liberal government.

"33. It does not appertain exclusively to the power of ecclesiastical jurisdiction by right, proper and innate, to direct the teaching of theological questions.

"34. The teaching of those who compare the Sovereign Pontiff to a prince, free and acting in the universal Church, is a doctrine which prevailed in the Middle Ages.

"35. There is nothing to prevent the decree of a general council, or the act of all peoples, from transferring the supreme pontificate from the bishop and city of Rome to another bishop and another city.

"36. The definition of a national council does not admit of any subsequent discussion, and the civil authority can assume this principle as the basis of its acts.

"42. In the case of conflicting laws enacted by the two powers, the civil law prevails.

"43. The secular power has authority to rescind, declare and render null, solemn conventions, commonly called Concordats, entered into with the Apostolic See, regarding the use of rights appertaining to ecclesiastical immunity, without the consent of the Apostolic See, and even in spite of its protest.

"54. Kings and princes are not only exempt from the jurisdiction of the Church, but are superior to the Church in deciding questions of jurisdiction.

"55. The Church ought to be separated from the State, and the State from the Church."*

Once more, also, we find that Leo XIII has expounded these principles in the most thorough way. He lays down this general rule:

"From this it is manifest that the eternal law of God is the sole standard and rule of human liberty, not only in each individual man, but also in the community and civil society which men constitute when united."**

This must be interpreted from his point of view, which is that the Pope is divinely commissioned to lay down "the eternal law of God." The same interpretation must be put on this passage:

"But as no society can hold together unless some one be over all, directing all to strive earnestly for the common good; every civilized community must have a ruling authority, and this authority, no less than society itself, has its source in nature, and has, consequently, God for its author. Hence it follows that all public power must proceed from God." (Page 108)

The requirement that the Church and State shall be united under the supremacy of the church is fully laid down in the following:

* Dogmatic Canons and Decrees, Pages 192 to 202.
** The Great Encyclical Letters of Leo XIII, Page 142. Numbers in the following text refer to other pages in the same book.

"We shall not hold to the same language on another point, concerning the principle of the separation of the State and Church, which is equivalent to the separation of human legislation from Christian and divine legislation. We do not care to interrupt Ourselves here in order to demonstrate the absurdity of such a separation; each one will understand for himself. As soon as the State refuses to give to God what belongs to God, by a necessary consequence it refuses to give to citizens that to which, as men, they have a right; as, whether agreeable or not to accept, it cannot be denied that man's rights spring from his duty toward God. * * * (Page 261)

"In fact, to wish that the State would separate itself from the Church would be to wish, by a logical sequence, that the Church be reduced to the liberty of living according to the law common to all citizens." (Page 262)

In his great Encyclical on "The Christian Constitution of States" he develops this point fully:

"So, too, is it a sin in the State not to have care for religion, as a something beyond its scope, or as of no practical benefit; or out of many forms of religion to adopt that one which chimes in with the fancy; for we are bound absolutely to worship God in that way which He has shown to be His will. (Page 111)

"From all these it is evident that the only true religion is the one established by Jesus Christ Himself, and which He committed to His Church to protect and to propagate.

"Over this mighty multitude God has Himself set rulers with power to govern; and He has willed that one should be the head of all, and the chief and unerring teacher of truth. * * *

"And just as the end at which the Church aims is by far the noblest of ends, so is its authority the most exalted of all authority, nor can it be looked upon as inferior to the civil power, or in any manner dependent upon it. (Page 112)

"In very truth Jesus Christ gave to His apostles unrestrained authority in regard to things sacred, together with the genuine and most true power of making laws, as also with the two-fold right of judging and punishing, which flow from that power.

"It is to the Church that God has assigned the charge of seeing to, and legislating for, all that concerns religion; of teaching all nations; of spreading the Christian faith as widely as possible; in short, of administering freely and without hindrance, in accordance with her own judgment, all matters that fall within its competence.

"Now this authority, perfect in itself, and plainly meant to be unfettered, so long assailed by a philosophy that truckles to the State, the Church has never ceased to claim for herself and openly to exercise. The apostles themselves were the first to uphold it, when, being forbidden by the rulers of the Synagogue to preach the Gospel, they courageously answered, *We must obey God rather than men.* This same authority the holy Fathers of the Church were always careful to maintain by weighty arguments, according as occasion arose, and the Roman Pontiffs have never shrunk from defending it with unbending constancy. Nay, more, princes and all invested with power to rule have themselves approved it, in theory alike and in practice. (Page 113)

"And assuredly all ought to hold that it was not without a singular disposition of God's providence that this power of the Church was provided with a civil sovereignty as the surest safeguard of her independence." (Page 114)

It will be seen that in these passages Leo takes a position absolutely opposed to the basic principles of any free government; he goes further and maintains that unless his rules are followed the laws of a free nation are without authority. In his Encyclical on "Human Liberty" he says:

"If, then, by any one in authority, something be sanctioned out of conformity with the principles of right reason, and consequently hurtful to the commonwealth, such an enactment can have no binding force of law, as being no rule of justice, but certain to lead men away from that good which is the very end of civil society.

"Therefore, the nature of human liberty, however it be considered, whether in individuals or in society, whether in those who command or in those who obey, supposes the necessity of obedience to some supreme and eternal law, which is no other than the authority of God (*i. e., the Pope*), commanding good and forbidding evil.*

"Moreover, the highest duty is to respect authority, and obediently to submit to just law; and by this the members of a community are effectually protected from the wrong-doing of evil men. Lawful power is from God, and who-soever resisteth authority resisteth the ordinances of God; wherefore obedience is greatly ennobled when subjected to an authority which is the most just and supreme of all. But where the power to command is wanting, or where a law is enacted contrary to reason, or to the eternal law, or to some ordinance of God (*that is, without the Pope's approval*), obedience is unlawful, lest, while obeying man, we become disobedient to God. Thus, an effectual barrier being opposed to tyranny, the authority in the State will not have all its own way, but the interests and rights of all will be safe-guarded—the rights of individuals, of do-mestic society, and of all the members of the common-wealth; all being free to live according to law and right reason; and in this, as We have shown, true liberty really consists." (Page 144)

In his Encyclical on "The Chief Duties of Christians as Citizens" he goes even further:

"Hence they who blame, and call by the name of sedi-tion, this steadfastness of attitude in the choice of duty, have not rightly apprehended the force and nature of true law. We are speaking of matters widely known, and which We have before now more than once fully explained. Law is of its very essence a mandate of right reason, proclaimed by a properly constituted authority, for the common good. But true and legitimate authority is void of sanction, unless it proceed from God the Supreme Ruler and Lord of all. The Almighty alone can commit power to a man over his fellow-men."**

* Great Encyclical Letters of Leo XIII, Pages 142 and following.
** Ibid, Page 184.

If this last statement is true in the sense which Leo means, that is, that the Pope is God's vice-gerent, it follows that no elected magistrate has any true power, unless from the Pope. To turn away from Leo for a minute, we have an interpretation of the law of the Roman Church for us in America set forth by the Reverend Doctor John A. Ryan. He states "that whether a particular act of the State is in obedience to the moral law can not be decided by the State itself but must be determined by some other tribunal."* He adds that "the Church, since it is the only authoritative interpreter of the moral law, has the right to pronounce upon the morality of political actions just as it has upon those of private individuals."** Thus it is clear that Dr. Ryan—an American and modern interpreter—limits the obligation of citizenship at the point where the Pope has fixed the supremacy of the Roman Catholic Church over the State, and that he considers the Roman Catholic Church a tribunal whose judgment of the morality of the laws is binding upon all its communicants above that of the State.

Along with the claim for the supremacy of the church, Leo denounces any attempts of the State to hold Catholicism as subordinate or as merely equal to other religions. Speaking of Liberal principles he says:

"Now when the State rests on foundations like those just named—and for the time being they are greatly in favor—it readily appears into what and how unrightful a position the Church is driven. For when the management of public business is in harmony with doctrines of such a kind, the Catholic religion is allowed a standing in civil

* The State and the Church, Page 43.
** Ibid, Page 46.

society equal only, or inferior, to societies alien from it; no regard is paid to the laws of the Church, and she who, by the order and commission of Jesus Christ, has the duty of teaching all nations, finds herself forbidden to take any part in the instruction of the people. With reference to matters that are of twofold jurisdiction, they who administer the civil power lay down the law at their own will, and in matters that appertain to religion defiantly put aside the most sacred decrees of the Church. They claim jurisdiction over the marriages of Catholics, even over the bond as well as the unity and the indissolubility of matrimony. They lay hands on the goods of the clergy, contending that the Church cannot possess property. Lastly, they treat the Church with such arrogance that, rejecting entirely her title to the nature and rights of a perfect society, they hold that she differs in no respect from other societies in the State, and for this reason possesses no right nor any legal power of action, save that which she holds by the concession and favor of the government.*

"To wish the Church to be subject to the civil power in the exercise of her duty is a great folly and a sheer injustice. Whenever this is the case, order is disturbed, for things natural are put above things supernatural; the many benefits which the Church, if free to act, would confer on society are either prevented or at least lessened in number; and a way is prepared for enmities and contentions between the two powers, with how evil results to both the issue of events has taught us only too frequently. (Page 124)

"Others oppose not the existence of the Church, nor indeed could they; yet they despoil her of the nature and rights of a perfect society, and maintain that it does not belong to her to legislate, to judge, or to punish, but only to exhort, to advise, and to rule her subjects in accordance with their own consent and will. By such opinion they pervert the nature of this divine society, and attenuate and narrow its authority, its office of teacher, and its whole efficiency; and at the same time they aggrandize the power of the civil government to such extent as to subject the Church of God to the empire and sway of the State, like any voluntary association of citizens." (Page 160)

 * The Great Encyclical Letters of Leo XIII, Pages 121 and following.

This is a clear definition and application of the principle that the church, and especially the Pope, must remain free from any human authority and that Catholics refuse to accept equality with other forms of religion. The same position was taken by the present Pope in his letter of June 5, 1929 when he said:

"It is always the Supreme Pontiff who intervenes and negotiates in the fullness of the sovereignty of the Catholic Church, and which he, exactly speaking, does not such so represent as impersonate, and which he rules by direct Divine mandate. Therefore, it would not be the Catholic organization in Italy which would be under the sovereignty of the State (Mussolini in a speech shortly before had asserted the sovereignty of the State) even though under favorable conditions, but it would be the Supreme Pontiff, the highest and sovereign authority of the Church. It is he who decides as he can and judges as he should for the great glory of God and the great well-being of souls."*

Thus the doctrine of Papal Supremacy over the State has been brought down to date, and is applied to America by American Catholic leaders. This doctrine logically gives to Catholic prelates the right to direct the actions of their followers in their relations to the State—that is, in politics and obedience to law. We shall see that they claim this right; this subject is so important as to deserve a separate chapter.

* New York World, June 23, 1929.

CHAPTER XII

DENIAL OF POLITICAL LIBERTY

Pope's claim to control of political actions of Catholics—His
insistence upon full obedience—The political effects of the
Catholic training of conscience—Conflicts of jurisdiction
with the State—The misleading offer of "arbitration"—
Papal toleration not as of right but for expediency—Papal
instructions as to political action of Catholics—Rebellion
authorized against any State which interferes with "liberty"
of Romanism.

THE Encyclicals of the Popes are full of assertions
of the right of the Roman Church, because of its
alleged supremacy over the State, to control the
political consciences and actions of its members.
Under these pronouncements no Catholic can exercise anything approaching political freedom with
the consent of his church. Some of these pronouncements have already been cited but are worth
repeating; others expand and enforce the doctrine.

The following from Leo XIII's "Christian Constitution of States" is worth quoting again because
of its bearing on this point:

"If in the difficult times in which our lot is cast, Catholics will give ear to Us, as it behooves them to do, they
will readily see what are the duties of each one in matters
of opinion as well as action. As regards opinion, whatever
the Roman Pontiffs have hitherto taught, or shall hereafter
teach, must be held with a firm grasp of mind, and, so
often as occasion requires, must be openly professed.

"Especially with reference to the so-called 'Liberties'
which are so greatly coveted in these days, all must stand
by the judgment of the Apostolic See, and have the same

mind. Let no man be deceived by the outward appearance of these liberties, but let each one reflect whence these have had their origin, and by what efforts they are everywhere upheld and promoted."*

He expands this idea at great length in his Encyclical on "The Chief Duties of Christians as Citizens." In it he says:

"It happens far otherwise with Christians: they receive their rule of faith from the Church, by whose authority and under whose guidance they are conscious that they have beyond question attained to truth.**

"The supreme teacher in the Church is the Roman Pontiff. Union of minds, therefore, requires, together with a perfect accord in the one faith, complete submission and obedience of will to the Church and to the Roman Pontiff, as to God Himself. This obedience should, however, be perfect, because it is enjoined by faith itself, and has this in common with faith, that it cannot be given in shreds;— nay, were it not absolute and perfect in every particular, it might wear the name of obedience, but its essence would disappear. Christian usage attaches such values to this perfection of obedience that it has been, and will ever be, accounted the distinguishing mark by which we are able to recognize Catholics. (Page 193)

"In defining the limits of the obedience owed to the pastors of souls, but most of all to the authority of the Roman Pontiff, it must not be supposed that it is only to be yielded in relation to dogmas of which the obstinate denial cannot be disjoined from the crime of heresy. Nay, further, it is not enough sincerely and firmly to assent to doctrines which, though not defined by any solemn pronouncement of the Church, are by her proposed to belief, as divinely revealed, in her common and universal teaching, and which the Vatical Council declared are to be believed with Catholic and divine faith. *But this likewise must*

* The Great Encyclical Letters of Leo XIII, Page 129.
** Ibid, Pages 192 and following.

be reckoned amongst the duties of Christians, that they allow themselves to be ruled and directed by the authority and leadership of bishops, and above all of the Apostolic See. And how fitting it is that this should be so any one can easily perceive. For the things contained in the divine oracles have reference to God in part, and in part to man, and to whatever is necessary for the attainment of his eternal salvation. Now, both these, that is to say, what we are bound to believe, and what we are obliged to do, are laid down, as we have stated, by the Church using her Divine Right, and in the Church by the Supreme Pontiff. (Page 194)

"Men of this high character maintain without wavering the love of obedience, nor are they wont to undertake any-thing upon their own authority. * * * There is, however, a difference between the political prudence that relates to the general good and that which concerns the good of in-dividuals. This latter is shown forth in the case of private persons who obey the prompting of right reason in the direction of their own conduct; while the former is the characteristic of those who are set over others, and chiefly of rulers of the State, whose duty it is to exercise the power of command, so that *the political prudence of private individuals would seem to consist wholly in carrying out faithfully the orders issued by lawful authori-ty.*" (Page 201)

"The like disposition and the same order should prevail in every Christian State by so much the more that the political prudence of the Pontiff embraces diverse and multiform things; for it is his charge not only to rule the Church, but generally so *to regulate the actions of Chris-tian citizens* that these may be in apt conformity to their hope of gaining eternal salvation. * * * Consequently, just as in the exercise of their episcopal authority the bishops ought to be united with the Apostolic See, so should the members of the clergy and the laity live in close union with their bishops. Among the prelates, indeed, one or other there may be affording scope to criticism either in regard to personal conduct or in reference to opinions by him entertained about points of doctrine; but no private person may arrogate to himself the office of judge which Christ our Lord has bestowed on that one alone whom He placed in charge of His lambs and of His sheep." (Page 202)

There can be no question of the meaning of this last quotation. Taken by itself it might have to deal only with spiritual judgment, but it is in a particular discussion of the duties of Catholic citizens, and as such clearly lays down the rule that they must take political orders from their bishops. This shows the difference between the Catholic and the Liberal interpretation of the rule that every man's conscience must determine his relation toward laws and government; the Catholic's conscience is not his own, but is entirely in the hands of his bishops and of the Pope.

This difference is vital: Protestants have no conscientious scruples about obeying the laws, nor any need to ask their consciences whether or not they will obey. Their law is that laid down by their government; they may try to change the law or government but in the meanwhile they obey. Approval of a law is left to the conscience under American principles, but obedience is not. Still less have our principles permitted any official to bring any law to judgment before his own private conscience in order to decide whether or not he shall obey or enforce it.

Under the rule laid down by Leo, any Catholic's supreme law is that laid down by the Pope. The Pope may instruct his conscience, and every Catholic's conscience, to hold scruples against obedience to any American law which the Pope does not approve. He may also instruct the consciences of all Catholic officials to refuse enforcement of the law.

The Pope maintains his right to do this in case of any conflict between the Church and the State. There are many such conflicts possible and some are already becoming actively important. American principles give to the State control of education, of marriage, of religious toleration, and of international relations. The Roman Church claims control of all these matters and certainly at any moment any one of them may break out into an active contest between American law and the orders of the Pope. A single instance is the right of the Catholic Church to teach a divided loyalty, if not an actual disloyalty, under the doctrine of the supremacy of the Pope over the American State. Certainly such teaching is dangerous to the peace and welfare of the State within the meaning of the Constitution; certainly it will sometime be forbidden; certainly it will produce active conflict.

Other conflicts are sure if bills now pending in several American States should be enacted. One would forbid any priest to require of couples coming before him for marriage a pledge abjuring the liberty of their unborn children. Another would forbid any one to teach that certain great categories of American marriages, involving millions of American citizens and in full compliance with American law, are "legalized concubinage." Another would restore the teaching of the Bible in the public schools. Any such measure, if made law by any State, would force upon Romanists the choice of obedience to the State or obedience to the Pope.

Leo laid down the rules which must govern a Catholic in any such conflict. He says:

"Now, if the natural law enjoins us to love devotedly and to defend the country in which we had birth, and in which we were brought up, so that every good citizen hesitates not to face death for his native land, very much more is it the urgent duty of Christians to be ever quickened by like feelings toward the Church. * * * We are bound, then, to love dearly the country whence we have received the means of enjoyment this mortal life affords, but we have a much more urgent obligation to love, with ardent love, the Church to which we owe the life of the soul, a life that will endure forever.

"For instances occur where the State seems to require from men as subjects one thing, and religion, from men as Christians, quite another; and this in reality without any other ground, than that the rulers of the State either hold the sacred power of the Church of no account, or endeavor to subject it to their own will. Hence arises a conflict, and an occasion, through such conflict, of virtue being put to the proof. The two powers are confronted and urge their behests in a contrary sense; to obey both is wholly impossible. No man can serve two masters, for to please the one amounts to contemning the other. As to which should be preferred no one ought to balance for an instant. It is a high crime indeed to withdraw allegiance from God in order to please men; an act of consummate wickedness to break the laws of Jesus Christ, in order to yield obedience to earthly rulers, or, under pretext of keeping the civil law, to ignore the rights of the Church; we ought to obey God rather than man. This answer, which of old Peter and the other apostles were used to give the civil authorities who enjoined unrighteous things, we must, in like circumstances, give always and without hesitation. No better citizen is there, whether in time of peace or war, than the Christian who is mindful of his duty; but such a one should be ready to suffer all things, even death itself, rather than abandon the cause of God or of the Church."*

The Catholic Encyclopedia lays down this doctrine very clearly for American Catholics when it says:

"In case of direct contradiction, making it impossible for both jurisdictions to be exercised, the jurisdiction of the Church prevails and that of the State is excluded."**

---

* Great Encyclical Letters of Leo XIII, Pages 183-184.
** Catholic Encyclopedia, Vol. XIV, Page 251.

Leo is not yet through with the subject, but declares his right to exclude the civil authority altogether. He says:

"But if the laws of the State are manifestly at variance with the divine law, containing enactments hurtful to the Church, or conveying injunctions adverse to the duties imposed by religion, or if they violate in the person of the supreme Pontiff the authority of Jesus Christ, then truly, to resist becomes a positive duty, to obey, a crime; a crime moreover, combined with misdemeanor against the State itself, inasmuch as every offense levelled against religion is also a sin against the State. Here anew it becomes evident how unjust is the reproach of sedition; for the obedience due to rulers and legislators is not refused; but there is a deviation from their will in those precepts only which they have no power to enjoin. Commands that are issued adversely to the honor due to God, and hence are beyond the scope of justice, must be looked upon as anything rather than laws.*

"No one can, however, without risk to faith, foster any doubt as to the Church alone having been invested with such power of governing souls as to exclude altogether the civil authority. In truth it was not to Caesar but to Peter that Jesus Christ entrusted the keys of the Kingdom of Heaven. From this doctrine touching the relations of politics and religion originate important consequences which We cannot pass over in silence.

"A notable difference exists between every kind of civil rule and that of the kingdom of Christ."**

We find one modification of this autocratic doctrine, which was stated in "America," a Jesuit weekly, during the 1928 campaign. "America" assures us that the Pope is willing to "arbitrate" any conflict between the Roman Church and the American government. It says:

"In any particular difference of opinion that may arise,

* The Great Encyclical Letters of Leo XIII, Page 185.
** The Great Encyclical Letters of Leo XIII, Page 196.

Leo says officially, the Church is always ready to arbitrate the conflict, and to do so with the greatest possible kindliness and indulgence."

To any one who does not accept the Papal Theory it may seem rather presumptious for a foreign Pope to offer arbitration with our government as to whether or not American Catholics shall obey American laws. Nevertheless the idea is logical to those who accept the doctrine of two co-ordinate jurisdictions, for abritration is the way of settling disputes between equal and sovereign powers. Of course no Protestant church would dare suggest arbitration with our government and of course no non-Catholic would concede—and our government cannot concede—that the Papacy is a power which has any right to offer arbitration in regard to the conduct of American citizens. The promise of "kindliness and indulgence" does not make this form of the claim of the supremacy of the Pope over our government any more pleasing.

In fact, however, this offer to arbitrate does not mean what non-Catholics would expect. Arbitration to us means the setting up of an impartial tribunal which shall hear and decide the case. Leo makes the Pope his own tribunal. He says:

"There are, nevertheless, occasions when another method of concord is available for the sake of peace and liberty: We mean when rulers of the State and the Roman Pontiff come to an understanding touching some special matter. At such times the Church gives signal proof of her motherly love by showing the greatest possible kindliness and indulgence."*

This means clearly that the Pope is ready—not to arbitrate—but to negotiate with our government

*The Great Encyclical Letters of Leo XIII, Page 115.

in regard to whether his subjects in America shall respect American law. It amounts to no more than an offer to listen to what we have to say in defense of our law. In view of all the other statements of Leo, it is perfectly clear that he reserves in the end, and no matter what our government may say, the right to tell his subjects whether or not they shall obey the law.

Before leaving the subject of the relation of the Church and State it is important to notice two concessions made by Leo, which, Catholics claim, permit the Catholic Church in America to conform to American principles. Leo says regarding separation:

"It is true that in certain countries this state of affairs exists. It is a condition which, if it have numerous and serious inconveniences, also offers some advantages—above all when, by a fortunate inconsistency, the legislator is inspired by Christian principles—and, though these advantages cannot justify the false principle of separation nor authorize its defense, they nevertheless render worthy of toleration a situation which, practically, might be worse."*

Dr. John A. Ryan in his book on the "State and the Church" tries to strengthen that by saying:

"The Pope did not intend to declare that separation is always inadvisable, for he had more than once expressed his satisfaction with the arrangement attaining in the United States."

It will be seen that this is far from an endorsement of the separation of Church and State, even in America. Even in making this concession, the Pope insists that the principle is false and it is clear that he intends to remedy this false principle whenever he has the power.

* The Great Encyclical Letters of Leo XIII, Page 262.

The second concession has to do with tolerance of other religions. He says:

"Again, that it is not lawful for the State, any more than for the individual, either to disregard all religious duties or to hold in equal favor different kinds of religion; that the unrestrained freedom of thinking and of openly making known one's thoughts is not inherent in the rights of citizens, and is by no means to be reckoned worthy of favor and support."*

"The Church, indeed, deems it unlawful to place the various forms of divine worship on the same footing as the true religion, but does not, on that account, condemn those rulers who for the sake of securing some great good of or hindering some great evil, allow patiently custom or usage to be a kind of sanction for each kind of religion having its place in the State. And in fact the Church is wont to take earnest heed that no one shall be forced to embrace the Catholic faith against his will, for, as St. Augustine wisely reminds us, 'Man cannot believe otherwise than of his own free will.' (Page 127)

"Yet, with the discernment of a true mother, the Church weighs the great burden of human weakness, and well knows the course down which the minds and actions of men are in this our age being borne. For this reason, while not conceding any right to anything save what is true and honest, she does not forbid public authority to tolerate what is at variance with truth and justice, for the sake of avoiding some greater evil, or of obtaining or preserving some greater good." (Page 157)

Certainly this is anything but true tolerance. It grants religious liberty, not as a right of man, but as a matter of expediency. It is a kind of contemptious truce under which the Popes, in effect, declare that the suppression of tolerance is not worth the trouble it involves.

* The Great Encyclical Letters of Leo XIII, Page 126 and following.

Particularly interesting is the statement that the Catholic Church takes pains that no one should be forced to embrace the Catholic faith against his will. The Roman Church has always maintained this doctrine, to be sure, but with the same curious interpretations that justified the tortures and holocausts of the Inquisition. The attitude of the church is that it cannot force anyone into the church, but that it can coerce by force any one who is a member of the church. It maintains that all heretics come within its jurisdiction as "disobedient children"—and it includes within that jurisdiction all baptized persons, including Protestants and all who have at any time or in any way performed any of the Catholic religious observances. A Jew, for instance, could not be submitted to the Inquisition, but a Hebrew who had been baptized even against his will could be burned at the stake. The distinction is a rather fine one for Protestants, but is important if we are to understand what Leo means by this granting of tolerance.

Leo takes great pains to show that all Papal statements about politics are not merely opinions to be held by Catholics, but that they are to be put into effect so far as is possible by political action. He says:

"All, moreover, are bound to love the Church as their common mother, to obey her laws, promote her honor, defend her rights, and to endeavor to make her respected and loved by those over whom they have authority. It is also of great moment to the public welfare to take a prudent part in the business of municipal administration, and to endeavor above all to introduce effectual measures, so that, as becomes a Christian people, public provision may be made for the instruction of youth in religion and true morality. Upon these things the well-being of every State greatly depends. Furthermore, it is in general fitting and salutary that Catholics should extend their efforts beyond this restricted sphere, and give their attention to national politics.

"And this all the more because Catholics are admonished, by the very doctrines which they profess, to be upright and faithful in the discharge of duty, while if they hold aloof, men whose principles offer but small guarantee for the welfare of the State will the more readily seize the reins of government. *This would tend also to the injury of the Christian religion, forasmuch as those would come into power who are badly disposed toward the Church, and those who are willing to befriend her would be deprived of all influence.*

"It follows therefore clearly that Catholics have just reasons for taking part in the conduct of public affairs.

"For in so doing they assume not the responsibility of approving what is blameworthy in the actual methods of government, but seek to turn these very methods, so far as is possible, to the genuine and true public good, and to use their best endeavors at the same time to infuse, as it were, into all the veins of the State the healthy sap and blood of Christian wisdom and virtue."*

In other words, Catholics are instructed to use every means in their power to enforce all the Papal doctrines upon the State by means of political action. He says this even more clearly in the following passages:

"First and foremost it is the duty of all Catholics worthy of the name and wishful to be known as most loving children of the Church, to reject without swerving whatever is inconsistent with so fair a title; to make use of popular institutions, so far as can honestly be done, for the advancement of truth and righteousness (that is, of Catholic principles and policies); to strive that liberty of action shall not transgress the bounds marked out by nature and the law

* The Great Encyclical Letters of Leo XIII, Page 130.

of God; *to endeavor to bring back all civil society to
the pattern and form of Christianity which We have
described. * * * Nevertheless, above all things, unity
of aim must be preserved,* and similarity must be sought
after in all plans of action. Both these objects will be
carried into effect without fail if all will follow the guidance
of the Apostolic See as their rule of life and obey the bishops
whom the Holy Ghost has placed to rule the Church of God.
The defense of Catholicism, indeed, necessarily demands
that in the profession of doctrines taught by the Church
all shall be of one mind and all steadfast in believing.*

*"It is always urgent, and indeed the main pre-
occupation, to take thought how best to consult the
interests of Catholicism. Wherever these appear by
reason of the efforts of adversaries to be in danger,
all differences of opinion among Catholics should
forthwith cease, so that, like thoughts and counsels
prevailing, they may hasten to the aid of religion, the
general and supreme good, to which all else should
be referred."***

In a letter written to French Catholics at a time
of political crisis in that Republic, Leo made these
instructions specific:

"Therefore, on this ground, they can afford neither in-
dolence of action nor party divisions; the one would be-
speak cowardice unworthy of a Christian, the other would
bring about disastrous weakness.***

"Here We intend alluding principally to the political
differences among the French in regard to the actual republic. Page 255)

"Poor France! God alone can measure the abyss of evil
into which she will sink if this legislation, instead of im-
proving, will stubbornly continue on a course which must
end in plucking from the minds and hearts of Frenchmen
the religion which has made them so great.

* The Great Encyclical Letters of Leo XIII, Page 132.
** Ibid, Page 197.
*** Ibid, Pages 252 and following.

"And here is precisely the ground on which, political dissensions aside, upright men should unite as one to combat, by all lawful and honest means, these progressive abuses of legislation. The respect due to constituted power cannot prohibit this: unlimited respect and obedience cannot be yielded to all legislative measures, of no matter what kind, enacted by this same power." (Page 259)

In other words, in this specific case Leo definitely instructs French Catholics to abandon all political principles and forget all party differences, to defy the law and the government and to unite to carry out the Papal political program. Certainly the political activity of the Popes cannot go much further.

It does, however, go a little further. He authorizes rebellion and treason. He says:

"From God has the duty been assigned to the Church not only to interpose resistance, if at any time the State rule should run counter to religion, but, further, to make a strong endeavor that the power of the Gospel may pervade the law and institutions of the nations. And inasmuch as the destiny of the State depends mainly on the disposition of those who are at the head of affairs, it follows that the Church cannot give countenance or favor to those whom she knows to be imbued with a spirit of hostility to her; who refuse openly to respect her rights; who make it their aim and purpose to tear asunder the alliance that should, by the nature of things, connect the interests of religion with those of the State.*

*"Whenever there exists, or there is reason to fear, an unjust oppression of the people on the one hand, or a deprivation of the liberty of the Church on the other, it is lawful to seek for such a change of government as will bring about due liberty of action.***

* The Great Encyclical Letters of Leo XIII, Page 198.
** The Great Encyclical Letters of Leo XIII, Page 161.

Those are the rules which the Pope has laid down for Catholic citizens. It will be seen that he has not in any way limited them to any ideal State or to a "purely Catholic State." They are declared to be universal, and exceptions to them are to be tolerated only by his permission and for reasons of expediency.

No freedom whatever is allowed to Catholic citizens; their consciences must be submitted completely to the Pope's orders. They are not permitted to believe in Liberal principles, though they may practice them slightly if he allows. They are to place his orders above the law of the State and are to submit to the authority of government only so far as he permits. They are to be active in politics in order to carry out his program and to bring the State into harmony with the Papal Theory—which, if the State is a free government, means that they are to seek to pervert it utterly.

In brief, the Pope has ordered American Catholics to try to bring the American government under his control.

CHAPTER XIII

THE POPES AND DEMOCRACY

Attitude toward democratic government the first test for American Catholics—Conflicting definitions of "democracy"—Real meaning of the "neutrality" claimed by the Popes—Leo's antagonism to free government—His direct attack on Americanism—How the Papacy controls its subjects in a democracy—Requirements as to their obedience—Refusal to permit them to be politically free—Subversion of democracy through control of Catholic consciences—The primal conflict—Refusal of the Popes to make peace with progress and freedom.

DEMOCRACY is the embodiment in government of all those principles of liberty and human rights which have been the source and the glory of progress for the last four centuries. America, in spite of all imperfections, is the nation most definitely based on those principles; her destiny looks toward their complete fulfillment. The attitude of Roman Catholics toward a democracy, then, is the first test of their fitness for citizenship in our American democracy; it also governs their position in our politics and the position which non-Catholic Americans must take toward them. All the dicsussion hitherto has been to establish a basis for accurate judgment of the attitude of the Papacy and its followers on this one point. It is the chief one with which other American citizens are concerned.

We have seen repeatedly how the Popes and their apologists confuse thought and, whether intentionally or not, deceive non-Catholics as to their true position by the use of words which are familiar to us all, but to which they give meanings very different from our own understanding. The most notable instance of this is in the use of the word "liberty." To Americans this means one thing only: the right of every man to complete freedom of action, of conscience, and of judgment, so long as he actually obeys the law and remains loyal to our government. To the Catholic it means something very different: the right of every man to obey the Pope in full, and of the Papacy to carry on its policies and to enforce its own laws without hindrance or criticism. Lord Acton said: "When ecclesiastical authority is restricted, liberty is denied," which means that any interference with the vast spiritual, material or political purposes of the Popes, no matter how hostile they may be to the State or to all human liberty, is a denial of freedom. Certainly this has nothing in common with the American definition of freedom, yet this is what the Popes and their hierarchial followers mean when they speak of liberty!

We must not permit ourselves to be deceived by a similar difference in the definition of democracy. Here again the meaning is clear enough to Americans. Democracy is defined in scholarly terms as "a nation governed by the free synthesis of free minds." It was more simply defined by Lincoln as a "government of the people, by the people, for the people." The essential point is freedom of the people—their right to unhindered government of themselves. A true democracy is thus not merely a government under which men vote, or which has no king. Certainly Mexico, during the long rule of Diaz when half-enslaved peons were marched to the polls under the bayonets of the soldiery and obediently "re-elected" the dictator for term after term, was not—in our meaning—a democracy. Nor was England democratic so long as she maintained the "rotten borough" system by which six men in one village could out-vote a hundred thousand in a near-by city. Nor can any government be a pure democracy unless all men vote freely, and all votes have equal weight.

No one who has read the first part of this book can doubt the hostile attitude which must logically be taken toward such a government by the Papacy and it followers. Nevertheless the Popes have made several statements, quoted often by their apologists here, which might be taken as showing at least neutrality toward our democracy. American Catholics, from these statements, try to convince us that there is no inherent conflict between Catholicism and Americanism, and that the Popes permit them to support democratic principles. Three of these, all by Leo XIII, are most important:

"The right to rule is not necessarily, however, bound up with any special mode of government. It may take this or that form, provided only that it be of a nature to insure the general welfare."

"* * * the Church usually acquiesces in certain modern liberties * * *."

"* * * it is not of itself wrong to prefer a democratic form of government."*

These statements, taken by themselves, would seem to give full permission to all Catholics to be good Americans if they wish. By them the hand which the Papacy extends to a modern democracy is certainly clad in a velvet glove.

But the hand inside the velvet is still the iron fist of supernatural Papal supremacy over conscience

* The Great Encyclical Letters of Leo XIII, Pages 109, 158 and 162.

and action. Let us take the full text of each of these "reassurances" and include in them, in italics, those words which are necessary to show fully what they meant to Leo, and what they must mean to any person who accepts the Pope as the authorized representative of God Almighty. The first then reads as follows:

"The right to rule is not necessarily, however, bound up with any special mode of government. It may take this or that form, provided only that it be of a nature to insure the general welfare (*according to the principles the Popes have laid down*). But whatever be the nature of the government, rulers must ever bear in mind that God is the paramount ruler of the world (*speaking to mankind through the Popes*), and must set Him before themselves as their examplar and law (*as laid down by the Popes*) in the administration of the State."

This becomes very different from the first apparent meaning. It is merely a statement that the Pope will accept any kind of government so long as he can control it. The same is true of the second quotation:

"And although in the extraordinary condition of these times (*due to Liberalism which the Popes have condemned in general and in every detail*), the Church usually acquiesces in certain modern liberties, not because she prefers them in themselves, but because she judges it expedient to permit them (*since she is unable to do anything else*), she would in happier times exercise her own liberty (*and suppress all these liberties for reasons which I and other Popes have already made clear.*")

Most enlightening of all is the third "permission" of belief in democracy:

"Again, it is not of itself wrong to prefer a democratic form of government, if only the Catholic doctrine (*that the Pope is supreme over the State, and over all its acts, and over the consciences and political actions of its citizens*) be maintained as to the origin and exercise of power."

Certainly a democracy subordinate to the Pope, with citizens voting according to priests' orders, is hardly in accord with what Americans mean by that word. It is not a government by the people in any sense; it derives its powers from the Pope, not from the consent of the governed.

As to the Pope's attitude toward a true democracy Leo has left no doubt whatever. His statements from "The Christian Constitution of States," with the necessary clarifying interpolations in italics, are as follows:

"In political affairs (*in the kind of a State approved by the Popes*) and all matters civil, the laws aim at securing the common good (*according to Papal ideas*), and are not framed according to the delusive caprices and opinions of the mass of the people."*

"Sad it is to call to mind how the harmful and lamentable rage for innovation (*through Liberalism and the setting up of human rights as superior to kingly or Papal Authority*) which rose to a climax in the sixteenth century, threw first of all into confusion the Christian (*Catholic*) religion, and next, by natural sequence, invaded the precincts of philosophy (*including the theory of government*) whence it spread to all classes of society. From this source, as from a fountain-head, burst forth all those later tenets of unbridled license (*against Papal authority*) which, in the midst of the terrible upheavals of the last century (*caused by men's struggles for freedom*), were wildly conceived and boldly proclaimed as the principles and foundation of that new jurisprudence which was not merely previously unknown (*under Papal Supremacy*) but was at variance on many points with not only the Christian (*Catholic*) but even with the natural law (*as expounded by the Popes*).

* The Great Encyclical Letters of Leo XIII, Page **116**, and following.

"Amongst these principles the main one lays down that as all men are alike by race and nature, so in like manner all are equal in the control of their life; that each one is so far his own master as to be in no sense under the rule of any other individual; that each is free to think on every subject just as he may choose, and to do whatever he may like to do; that no man has any right to rule over other men. In a society grounded upon such maxims all government is nothing more nor less than the will of the people, and the people, being under the power of itself alone, is alone its own ruler. It does choose, nevertheless, some to whose charge it may commit itself, but in such wise that it makes over to them not the right so much as the business of governing, to be exercised, however, in its name." (Page 120)

This certainly is a clear and splendid definition of a democratic government, according to the principles embodied in the American Constitution. Leo goes on to express his opinion about it:

"The authority of God (*as exercised by the Popes*) is passed over in silence, just as if there were no God (*or He did not speak through the Popes*): or as if He cared nothing for human society; or as if men, whether in their individual capacity or bound together in social relations owed nothing to God (*and the Pope*); or as if there could be a government of which the whole origin and authority did not reside in God Himself (*and in the Pope as His vice-gerent*). Thus, as is evident, a State becomes nothing but a multitude, which is its own master and ruler. And since the populace is declared to contain within itself the spring-head of all rights and all power, it follows that the State does not consider itself bound by any kind of duty towards (*the Pope as the representative of*) God. (Page 120)

"The sovereignty of the people, however, and this without any reference to (*the Pope as the infallible spokesman of*) God, is held to reside in the multitude; which is doubtless a doctrine exceedingly well calculated to flatter and inflame many passions, but which lacks all reasonable proof and all power of insuring public safety and preserving order." (Page 123)

"Doctrines such as these, which cannot be approved by human reason (*so long as the Popes can dictate to reason*) and most seriously affect the whole civil order, Our predecessors the Roman Pontiffs (well aware of what their apostolic office required of them), have never allowed to pass uncondemned. (Page 125)

"From these pronouncements of the Popes it is evident that the origin of public power is to be sought for in (*the Popes as the only authorized agents of*) God Himself, and not in the multitude."   (Page 126)

These quotations might be extended indefinitely. One more is worth while:

"* * * the kind of civilization which conflicts with the doctrines and laws of holy Church is nothing but a worthless imitation and a meaningless name."*

These statements are all general.   But Leo took pains to strike directly at Liberalism in America. In his Encyclical on "True and False Americanism in Religion" he discussed as a matter of religion the question whether American Catholics should be allowed to believe in American Liberal principles. He said:

"* * * the project involves a greater danger, and is more hostile to Catholic doctrines and discipline, inasmuch as the followers of these novelties judge that a certain liberty ought to be introduced into the Church, so that, limiting the exercise and vigilance of its powers, each one of the faithful may act more freely in pursuance of his own natural bent and capacity. They affirm, namely, that this is called for in order to imitate that liberty which, though quite recently introduced, is now the law and the foundation of almost every civil community.   On that point We have * * * shown the difference between the Church, which is of Divine Right, and all other associations which subsist by the free will of men."**

* The Great Encyclical Letters of Leo XIII, Page 12.
** The Great Encyclical Letters of Leo XIII, Page 444.

From all these, and many more, it is quite clear the Popes oppose in root and branch the kind of democracy which we have in America, and which conforms to American Liberal principles. The kind of democracy they *do* like is only the kind which they control—as Leo said, one where "the Catholic doctrine be maintained as to the origin and exercise of power." And that most certainly is not American democracy.

No American Catholic (with one or two exceptions who have been promptly repudiated) has ever admitted that this is the idea of the Popes, or that there can be any conflict between their church and American principles. They have, however, declared that if there should be such a conflict the Roman Church could not control their actions, because, as Governor Smith said, "there is no ecclesiastical tribunal which could have the slightest claim on the obedience of Catholic communicant in the resolution of such a conflict."

In the first place this statement shows ignorance of the Catholic Church, unless those who make it intend to claim that a tribunal set up for just this purpose by the Pope is without authority in America—a claim which will hardly stand. Under Canon 255 the Congregation of Extraordinary Affairs is empowered to handle "especially matters that refer to the civil laws and to agreements of the Holy See with various nations."* It seems beyond question that such conflicts will come under "civil laws."

More important, by far, is the statement by Catholics that if such a conflict did arise they would

* Commentary on Canon Law, Vol. II, Page 263.

decide upon it according to the dictates of their consciences, "just as any Protestant would do." This is doubtless true, and in this answer lies the whole key to the conflict.

In the first place, there could be no conflict between any Protestant church and the government. No Protestant church has any political policies which might conflict with the principles, laws or policies of the government. No Protestant church claims any right to command its members to defy any law of the government. No Protestant church has any interest whatever in any function of the government beyond advocating laws for moral purposes; none has any interests which claim or need or could benefit by special action of the government. No Protestant as such will ever have any "conflict" with this government that needs to be referred to his conscience. The fact that the Catholics try to draw a parallel shows how completely they misunderstand the relation between the Protestant churches and the government.

In the second place, no Protestant could ever have any conscientious scruples about obeying a law, nor a Protestant official any scruples about enforcing it. He may approve or disapprove a law; that is his right. But he considers that in practice, because of the inherent nature of civil society, his conduct is subject to the collective moral sense of the community—that is, he should obey the laws even if he does not approve. To put it in another way: The Protestant considers that so far as conduct is concerned, we are subject to the moral supremacy of the State. Obedience to law does not need to be referred to our consciences. We will not allow our officials to refer any question of law enforcement to their consciences. The fact that Catholics believe such questions could possibly be referred to conscience shows again how different their attitude toward democratic government is from that of non-Catholics.

But setting aside both these considerations, the vital one is that if any question did arise non-Catholics would refer it to their *own* consciences, while Catholics must refer such questions to the Pope's conscience, or at best to a conscience which has been trained from babyhood to submission to the Pope "in opinion and conduct as well as in morals." Pope Leo makes this perfectly clear:

"* * * in controlling State affairs, means are often taken to keep those together by force who cannot agree in their way of thinking. It happens far otherwise with Christians (Catholics): they take their rule of faith (*as to State affairs*) from the Church, by whose authority and under whose guidance they are conscious that they have beyond question attained to truth."*

"* * * political prudence * * * is the characteristic of those who are set over others * * * whose duty it is to exercise the power of command, so that *the political prudence of private individuals would seem to consist wholly in carrying out faithfully the orders issued by lawful authority.*

"The like disposition and the same order should prevail in every Christian State, by so much the more that the political prudence of the Pontiff embraces diverse and multiform things; for it is his charge not only to rule the Church, but generally so *to regulate the actions* of Christian (Catholic) citizens, that these may be in apt conformity to their hope of gaining eternal salvation." (Pages 201-202)

This certainly means that the Pope claims the right to lay down orders for the political conduct of

* The Great Encyclical Letters of Leo XIII, Pages 192 and following.

Catholics; it seems also to mean that Leo holds the
threat of damnation over any who refuse to obey.

The following has already been quoted in another connection, but is so important that it is
worth reading again:

> "If in the difficult time in which our lot is cast, Catholics
> will give ear to Us, as it behooves them to do, they will
> readily see what are the duties of each one in matters of
> opinion as well as action. As regards opinion, whatever
> the Roman Pontiffs have heretofore taught, or shall here-
> after teach, must be held with a firm grasp, and, so often
> as conscience requires, must be openly professed. Espe-
> cially with reference to the so-called "Liberties" which are
> so greatly coveted in these days, all must stand by the
> judgment of the Apostolic See, and have the same mind."*

This is the conscience to which Catholics must
refer questions of conflict with the government—
"the judgment of the Apostolic See," and "especially with reference to the "so-called Liberties"
which are the fundamentals of American principles
and government. That is: the Pope sets up his
supremacy not only over the conscience of individual Catholics as to individual conduct, but as
to their relations with the State. He assures them
that by submitting to the Popes they shall beyond
question attain the truth. When the Pope has spoken
their position is like that of a Protestant when the
law has spoken—there is nothing to refer to conscience and nothing to do but obey. But with this
difference: that Protestants may disapprove while
they still obey the law, but Catholics are required
both to obey and to approve the Pope's rule, even
when it demands defiance of civil law.

* The Great Encyclical Letters of Leo XIII, Pages
129-130.

It does not require any "tribunal of the church" to make sure of conduct by all good Catholics pleasing to the Pope, when this condition is accepted. We had a recent instance of it in the case of the effort of the Knights of Columbus to force this country to intervene in Mexico—a direct attempt to apply the doctrine of the Pope's supremacy over the American government; to have us spend vast sums and sacrifice numberless American lives in order to enforce Papal Supremacy upon the free nation of Mexico; to injure this country for the benefit of the Papacy; to carry out the rule laid down in the Catholic school text-books* that "the principle duty of heads of States" is to defend and protect the Roman Catholic Church. It violated every American principle.

Instant and vigorous denials were made that the Roman Catholic Church had even suggested this action by the Knights of Columbus. If the denials were not true, then we have the spectacle of the Catholic Church directly bringing about the un-American and unpatriotic action by a large body of American citizens. But if the denials were true, we have proof that the Papacy indirectly, but no less effectively, can bring about such action through control of conscience. It had educated these Knights, it had taught them the doctrine of Papal Supremacy; it had laid down the rule that the interests of their own country must be sacrificed when the Roman Church could benefit. Therefore it had made sure that they would automatically carry out the Papal policy as against their own country; it had made them definitely un-American, and, if need arose, anti-American.

* Manual of Christian Doctrine, Page 132.

Another evidence of this was seen just before the 1928 election in an article published in "Unita Cattolica," a Catholic paper of Florence, Italy. This paper must know exactly what kind of pressure is brought to bear upon Catholics in Italian politics; it could not know of any agreement between Governor Smith and the Pope or the American hierarchy. Yet it flatly declared that Mr. Smith's election would be a distinct benefit to Catholicism. It is not important whether the paper put its trust in coercion or in conscience—it did expect that as an American official, Mr. Smith would serve his church.

So we see that in the politics of a democracy the consciences of Catholics are not their own; their church does not allow them to be politically free any more than it allows them to be spiritually free. It controls them in their political actions, as it does in their private lives, under threat of certain damnation. American Catholics vote under this threat with exactly as little choice and exactly as little fulfillment of the principle of democracy as the Mexican peons who voted under threat of Diaz's bayonets, if they devoutly obey their Pope.

They do not, they cannot, become an integral part of this or any other democracy. Their whole attitude toward the duties and rights of citizens of a democracy is hostile to that of non-Catholics and to the principles on which democracy is based. They do not become a part of the national conscience, or concensus of moral opinion, on which the free State depends, since the collective moral sense of the nation must be reached through the freedom of each individual conscience. Catholics are allowed no political conscience; they must vote according to the Pope's conscience. Thus they stand outside the national mind and conscience, and hostile to both. As the Encyclopedia Brittanica says "the modern State * * * stands or falls with the notion of a constitutional State, whose *magna charta* is municipal (political) and spiritual liberty, institutions with which the ideas of the Curia are in direct conflict."* It might have said the ideas *of the subjects* of the Curia, also.

Charles C. Marshall, the great lawyer whose studies have done so much to make the actual position of the Papacy clear, defines this situation more at length:

"There is in the sovereignty of the modern State a controlling power—the Civic Primacy of its People—from which the government is derived and by the consent of which it exists. In the sovereignty of the Roman Church there is a government, but its powers are not derived from its membership, nor do its powers exist by the consent thereof. The sovereignty of the Roman Church, is, in theory, derived from God alone and its powers are alone conferred by Him. It is in theory a sovereignty by Divine Right— *Jure Divino,* and therefore more than a church; it is a political community without a political superior at all vital points, and, therefore, it is a political sovereignty. Into whatever State it comes there are, in its theory, at once two sovereignties claiming jurisdiction over the moral life of men, and, whether the constitution of the State provides for their separation or their union, serious antagonisms inevitably result such as never arise in the case of other religious societies, which do not claim political sovereignty superior at any point to the sovereignty of the State.

"While both the State and the Church are thus in Roman Catholic doctrine two sovereignties, the sovereignty of the State is found in the people who create the government of the State. The sovereignty of the Church is not found in its members but in the Pope, on whom it is con-

* The Encyclopedia Brittanica, Vol. XX, Page 719.

ferred not by the Church or its members but by God Himself. The State derives its powers from the consent of the
governed. The Pope derives his powers irrespective of the
consent of the governed. The government of the State is
responsible to the people of the State; the government of
the Church is not responsible to the people of the Church.
The one is responsible power; the other is irresponsible
power, except on the *a priori* presumption that there is
a responsibility to God under supernatural theories accepted by the Roman Church and rejected by all the rest
of mankind."*

In the preface to the second edition of this book
Mr. Marshall sums up the situation thus:

"The conclusion is inevitable that Roman Catholic
citizens are radically differentiated from all others in their
relation to the social and political complex of life in the
American or modern State. The Roman Catholic solidarity
in the State (that is, the Catholics who are controlled by
their Church) cannot be a valid part of the collective conscience, or concensus of moral opinion, on which the civic
order of the State depends, for that collective conscience
or consensus, to be valid, must be arrived at under the
freedom of the individual conscience. Roman Catholics
are not free in conscience because of subordination, under
the penalty of damnation, in matters belonging to morals,
to the supremacy and infallibility of the Pope in his Divine
Right."**

There is a further conclusion to be drawn from
this. In any modern democracy the subjects of the
Pope influence the nation in exact proportion to
their numbers, and influence it toward the enforcement of the Papal Theory with all that it means
in reaction and Ultramontanism. That is, the
Pope's direct influence in a modern democracy is in
proportion to the number of his subjects; in our own

* The Roman Catholic Church in the Modern State,
Page 19.
** Ibid, Preface to the Second Edition, Page xiii.

country it grows as the number of Catholics grows and will grow yet stronger if they continue to increase. If they ever became a majority, or came to hold the balance of political power, then the Pope would control the nation and would be able to use our free institutions to make America the kind of a democracy he wants—a democracy in which the Catholic doctrine was maintained. Italy has shown us what happens in a modern State in which that doctrine is maintained.

The final conclusion is that our democratic institutions would cease to be a safeguard for liberty, but would instead become the instrument of tyranny, the moment Catholics attained political power; that the Pope would then exercise supremacy over our government as he has exercised it in Italy; and that he would destroy our liberties just as he has destroyed the liberties of that unhappy nation.

This concludes our study of the Roman Catholic Church today in its relation to modern nations and their politics. Let us review briefly what we have found.

The Roman Catholic Church is in its root principles opposed to all the Liberal principles on which the modern State and human liberty rest. As E. Boyd Barrett, an ex-Jesuit, has said: "patriotism in this country also operates against Roman doctrine and tends to undermine the orthodoxy of the American Catholic's position in regard to the Holy See. To reconcile pure, unadulterated Americanism with the Encyclicals of Pius IX and Leo XIII is impossible."* And as Hillaire Belloc, most distinguished of Catholic lay writers, said: "The Catholic

* The Forum, August, 1929.

Church is, in its root principle, at issue with the civic definition both of freedom and of authority."*

We have found that this Roman doctrine—although it is the outgrowth of proven frauds—so far from being outworn or merely a powerless tradition, has been strengthened in our own times—is being further strengthened even today. We have found that the doctrine of Papal Despotism has been made definite within the last sixty years, and has been more fully defined and more strongly enforced as lately as 1929. We have found that the long struggle for a compromise with Liberalism inside the Catholic Church ended in the complete triumph of Ultramontanism and reaction, and that this triumph has been cemented by two generations of Catholic education based wholly on that principle, so that all but a trace of Liberal thought has vanished from among Catholics.

We have seen that from this position the Papacy cannot now retreat, and that it cannot introduce the least compromise with the modern world, without destroying the logical basis not only of its polity but of its spiritual authority. The Papal position follows with inevitable logic from the primary Dogma of Divine Appointment, it has been made irreformable by the Dogma of Infallibility, and to depart from it in any degree and at any point would be to admit that the Papal Authority was *not* divine, and thus to undermine the whole structure of Catholic thought and faith.

We have seen that the Papacy has devised a method for using the liberty accorded the Catholic Church under a democracy for the purpose of destroying all the liberties of democracy, through the

* The Contrast, Page 160.

control of Catholic education and conscience. We have seen that it is using this method in political affairs, and that Catholics are in practice hostile to Liberalism, whether with or without the active leadership of the hierarchy.

Thus we find that the conflict between the Roman Church and all modern freedom is fundamental, is complete at every point, and is growing in intensity through the renewed aggression of Rome.

Pius IX "reprobated, proscribed and condemned" the proposition that: "The Roman Pontiff can, and ought to, reconcile himself and come to terms with progress, Liberalism and modern civilization."* His successors have more than lived up to his policy.

Since they will not come to terms, will not compromise, with "progress, Liberalism and modern civilization," then those who believe in progress, freedom and Liberalism cannot come to terms with them. It might be possible for the two religions to live together by mutual toleration and forbearance from aggression. But the Papacy is vigorously aggressive and intolerant.

Protestantism, Liberalism, freedom, must strike back or die. The storm is rising; the conflict is vital and inevitable.

The question remains: What will be the position of American Catholics in this conflict? Will they fight for American Liberalism or for the despotism of their Pope?

* Dogmatic Canons and Decrees, Page 209.

Part II

The Conflict in Politics

CHAPTER XIV

THE EUROPEAN MIND

The question of assimilation of European Catholics—Can they hold to their religion and reject the Pope's political leadership against Liberalism—Mental differences between races—The Catholic issue a recent importation from Europe—Acceptance of authority the basis for European mentality—Development of resistance due to Protestantism—Freedom in Europe still far from complete—The racial line of cleavage—Details of European state of mind—The contrast to American psychology most complete in Catholic countries.

SINCE the Roman Catholic Church is what we have found it to be, it is self-evident that the only hope for unity in America must be sought in the possibility that American Roman Catholics will refuse to follow the leadership of their church so far as American civil and political affairs are concerned. The Catholic Church, we have seen, is at every point hostile to the principles of human liberty and individual responsibility which control the great majority of Americans, which form the foundation of our civic structure and which until now have controlled our nation.

We may take it for granted that non-Catholic Americans will not abandon their principles. They have been developed through centuries of experience and consecrated with the blood of bitter struggle. They have justified themselves by making great all countries which have embraced them. They have produced in four centuries more progress and more opportunity for human happiness than all the ages had seen until they appeared. They cannot be sacrificed.

Moreover, we would not compromise them even for the sake of a truce with Catholicism. A recent writer defended Catholic resistance to American ideals on the ground that America had made no effort to meet Catholics' wishes. Why should we? America is our home, it is built upon convictions we cannot abandon nor change, and we believe we have every right to be masters in our own house. Whether immigration comes seeking sanctuary from persecution or for personal profit, it is morally bound to accept the conditions it finds here. Its willingness to do so is clearly implied when it seeks our hospitality for its own benefit. We share with it our freedom and our prosperity; we cannot fairly be asked for its sake to weaken the principles which underlie both. For, if it cannot accept these principles, it should not come; and if it finds some compromise necessary for the sake of its own peace, the compromise must in justice come from its side.

The question is, then, whether the Roman Catholics in America are able, or will be able, while holding the religious faith of the Catholic Church to reject its political ideas and refuse to serve it in its ceaseless warfare against American Liberalism. To put it in another way: the question is whether the great body of Catholics in America can and will become politically Americanized in spite of the hostility of the Papacy to Americanism. We have seen that the conflict is profound and unavoidable; what we must seek now is to find whether American Catholics will be found in this conflict on the side of their country or the side of their Pope. Will they insist on strife or permit peace?

Whether hope for religious peace is justified or not must be determined by a study of the Catholic people themselves. Are they the *kind* of people whose mental processes can be brought to understand and support American principles? Or are they the kind of people who naturally and instinctively prefer autocracy to individualism and outside control to self-reliance, not only in religious but in civic and political thought?

It is hardly necessary in these days to prove that there are fundamental differences between races and the different stocks within races. The idea that all men were of the same mental mold, and therefore that their acceptance of ideas depended purely upon the worth of the ideas themselves, has been abandoned by all thoughtful men. We know now that between two courses of action each individual will choose because of his own characteristics and psychological equipment. This is as it should be; a bold course is not a wise one for a timid man to take; diplomacy is impossible for a blunt one, and temporizing cannot successfully be attempted by a courageous and aggressive person. What is wise and fit for one man would be utterly unwise and unfit for another; each man must govern his life by the philosophy, code and policies which best express himself.

The world has come to know, too, that—for reasons which are not agreed upon—differences like those between men to a large extent divide different groups of men. The stolidity of the Russian, the thrift of the Scotchman, the tenacity of the Englishman, the gallantry of the Frenchman—all of these are proverbial and not without reason. Individual exceptions do not effect the general fact of these differences. No one can pretend that all people of a given race or nation are exactly alike or even that any handful of men could be found who are exactly alike. Nevertheless, we know that there are national and racial tendencies, characteristics and mental attitudes which dominate the action of any large number of the people of that race or nation; just as we know that there are characteristics which control the conduct of each breed of dogs or cattle in spite of the fact that each animal has its own individual traits.

These national and racial differences are written across the face of human history in letters so large that it is amazing that they should ever have been overlooked. Certainly it is no accident that the form of religion adopted by any man will be that which has appealed to the majority of his race. When we find that Hinduism is a religion of submission, that Confucianism is a philosophy of the most extreme conservatism, and that Mohammedanism and Shintoism are cults which idealize courage and aggression, and we see that each has been adopted by a distinct and very different type of human beings, we may know that there is a direct connection between the mental nature of the races and the psychology of the religion. It was not Mohammedanism that made the Arab and the Turk warlike; it was their war-like nature which made them embrace Mohammedanism. Certainly it was not Protestantism which has made the races of Northern Europe so aggressive and independent-minded; it was their courageous self-reliance which led them to develop and support Protestantism.

It is not important in this discussion to determine the reasons for these differences. How much they are due to race and inheritance, how much to training and environment, is not yet determined.

Nor is this necessary. The practical results are the same, since these differences exist and since they are persistent, in spite of changed environment, for generations.

Our problem now is to determine what differences exist between the bulk of Roman Catholics in the United States and those Americans who belong to the older stock, either by descent or by mental assimilation.

The fact that stands out in the beginning is that the great mass of Catholics in this country are either of recent immigration from Europe or have maintained a European attitude of mind. Certainly few of them are descendants of American pioneers. The Catholic year book for 1928, page 113, estimated that in 1807 there were only 150,000 Catholics in the new nation. Most of these, of course, were in the recently purchased territories of Florida and Louisiana whose settlers were almost all Catholics. As to Catholics in the original states, a letter sent in 1785 by the prefect apostolic to the Vatican, stated that there were 15,800 Catholics in Maryland, 700 in Pennsylvania, 200 in Virginia and 15,000 in New York.

Only the descendants of this handful of people can historically fairly claim the name of "American" Catholics. Certainly to estimate their living descendants at a million is to put the number too high; but even if we do this we find that twenty-two of the twenty-three million Catholics in America today are of more or less recent unassimilated immigration. That is, over ninety-five per cent of the Catholic problem is imported from Europe— this in addition to the direct and constant European control over American Catholics.

The answer to the question as to the possible assimilation of Catholics depends, then, upon Eurooean psychology and mental attitude.

Let us go to Europe and go back 500 years to the beginning of the modern era. At that time Europe (except Russia, which was still savage) was in the black night of the Dark Ages. It was bound in the iron system of feudalism, which had been only slightly relaxed even in England. Every man and every woman was held in immediate and galling subjection to a superior who was recognized by law and public opinion. The chain was complete from top to bottom. The man who tilled the soil could not leave the vicinity without permission; the so-called "free" man was held in personal, economic and military subjection to the lord of the manor; these lordlings held their property and their lives only by permission of the great lords who, in turn, were absolutely at the disposal of the kings. In all this system no man save the king truly owned anything; no property nor children, nor wife, nor life that could not be taken from him at the whim of every superior, and even emperors could be deposed, excommunicated and executed by the Popes.

No one could escape from this feudal bondage except by exchanging it for the different bondage of the Roman Church. In its monasteries men were free from the feudal authorities, but utterly subject to their own abbots and bishops. Over all these, as well as over the kings, stood the Popes.

The alliance between Church and State was almost complete. There were at times quarrels between the Popes and individual sovereigns, and Vatican impotence frequently tolerated a certain independence in the princes. But so far as any individual was concerned, Church and State were a unit, joined in the denial of liberty, in exploitation and in oppression. The whole system constituted a perfect despotism in the union of two autocracies claiming the same divine sanction and with the Pope as the supreme head of both. This is the structure from which modern Europe has grown; these are the conditions in which the mass psychology of Europe has its roots.

The keynote of this whole medieval system was *authority* both human and divine; authority that ruled every act of every individual; authority that controlled his thought, his conscience and his prayers; authority that was infallibly divine, that inseparably joined the priest's weapon of damnation with the ruler's weapons of steel, and that was inexorably enforced by both. From this authority no man had any appeal except to the good nature or self-interest of his superior.

During these ages this system of authority was accepted by all people. Some benefited and most suffered but no one challenged it. All government and all thought were based upon it.

There were, to be sure, for some people some things called "rights." Such were those of the Magna Carta in England which had been forced from King John by his barons, but which was so contrary to the prevailing thought that the Pope had declared it null and void. Such were the "rights" of the great nobles, but these were given them in each case by the express permission and kindness of the king. They depended upon his good faith. There were also certain customs to which usage had given the authority of law, such as those which granted immunity to heralds and troubadours. There was, particularly in England, that conservative force of habit which they called "custom of the country" and which few of the nobility dared defy because of the sullen resentment that it would arouse. None of these so-called rights, however, come within the meaning with which we use the word today. They were practically concessions to kindness and expediency made by limitless authority; they could be and often were revoked by the same authority. They did not spring from the people but descended to them. And at best there were no rights at all for nine-tenths of those who lived.

Under this system every man except the Pope was directly a subject of and responsible to some human authority. When that authority spoke there was required of the subject, whether it was king or peasant, nothing but obedience. His whole life was spent in seeking to please his superior. There was asked of him little private judgment, little self-reliance, little more self-control. Whatever a man had of these qualities was dedicated to the service of his superior and could be exercised only within the limits and for the purposes which that superior laid down. Any individualism, initiative or self-reliance which was against the interest and the wishes of the superior was instantly suppressed and terribly punished. Each man's life and thought and action depended on the will of the man next above him, until the ascending scale reached the throne of St. Peter.

Acceptance of authority was the dominant note in the psychology of Europe. It is from this habit of mind as a base that we must study European psychology today.

It must not be supposed that there was not constant seething below the surface of feudalism. Men often were in rebellion against the exercise of the authority, and sometimes against its principle. The story of those ages is bloody with the record of the revolts of peasants and burghers against intolerable tyranny; there were hordes of outlaws who could suffer nothing worse than to return under authority; the world ran red with the suppression of revolts.

Then came Martin Luther with an idea, the consequences of which he did not himself in the least foresee. He protested at first only against the sale of those "indulgences" for sin with which the Popes were financing the building of the great Basilica of St. Peter's. Luther had been a quiet university professor at Wittenberg and his mind, steeped in Biblical scholarship, rejected the idea that remission of sins could be bought for cash. So, in the ninety-five *theses* which he nailed to the door of the church, there was one which challenged the whole system of authority. This was his denial that the Pope had power to forgive sin.

So logical and so closely interwoven is the despotic theory of the Papacy that a denial of the Pope's authority at any point denies it at all points, for the Popes cannot be powerless on one subject and still hold complete power on others. It was not until long after he had announced his opposition to the indulgences that Luther himself realized this fact, but when he did he threw off the Pope's authority and began to preach his doctrine of the individual spiritual priesthood of all believers in Christ.

This doctrine spread like wildfire and where it spread the power of the Papacy was destroyed.

Moreover, since the temporal and spiritual authority had been so closely interwoven, men soon began to see that the temporal power which had been derived from the Popes was also without foundation. There sprang up the theory that the State was a divine ordinance, but that the ruling powers represented—not the Pope or the priesthood of the church—but this individual priesthood of the whole body of believers, and that the State drew authority from them.

This first position of Lutheranism and the whole Reformation was still far from democracy or from an understanding of individual human rights. Nevertheless, it supported the human revolt against authority with a holy and sacred principle, which has lived and grown into modern Liberalism and modern democracy. It is against this principle that the Papacy today, as in Luther's time, is fighting. It is for its suppression that the Papacy has once more assumed the aggressive after its centuries of weakness.

This principle has been accepted in varying degrees by the different races and nations. In the great wars which presently broke out to maintain the authority of the Pope through the Catholic princes, a sharp geographic and national cleavage appeared. Protestantism, in either the spiritual or the political sense, has had little development in Europe except north and west of a certain geographical line. This runs, in a general way, from the Polish frontier near the Bohemian border, west along that border and bending northward toward the mouths of the Rhine, and down through France to Bordeaux. Within this Protestant area are included those sections inhabited by Celts—Irish,

Scotch mountaineers and Bretons—who have remained Catholic, and the regions where the French Huguenots once lived, were persecuted and suppressed. But south of this line there are not, and practically never have been, many Protestants. Such Liberalism as has developed has been atheistic, and it has never won a secure foothold.

This line coincides, either by accident or because of racial character, almost exactly with the line which divides one of the three great European stocks from the other two. These three are the Nordic, the Mediterranean, and the Alpine. It was the Nordic race only in which Protestantism took hold. There are not today and there never have been more than a very few Protestants among the Mediterraneans and the Alpines. Scholars are not completely agreed as to the classification of the different stocks of men in these races but in general they are divided as follows: The Nordics include the North Germans, Scandinavians, Anglo-Saxons, and the descendants of the Norsemen who over-ran the northern provinces of France, except Brittany. The Mediterranean races are those predominating in South France, in Spain and in Italy, also Scotch highlanders, the Irish and the Bretons. The Alpines are the people of Southeastern France, chiefly in Alsace and Lorraine, the Bavarians and other peoples of Southern Germany, and the Slavs.

In Europe even the Nordic race has never entirely discarded the old medieval Catholic system. Certain vestiges of it survive in every country. In every one, for example, some form of union of Church and State remains, with an Established Church supported by the government and connected with it. Thus even in England, which is almost as democratic a country as this and which is completely tolerant, we have curious survivals. Certain prelates are members of the House of Lords by virtue of their position in the Established Church, and within a short time we have seen this political body in violent debate over the revision of the Prayer Book.

This universal connection between Church and State has prevented the natives of any European country from ever reaching the American attitude of mind toward the relation between Church and State. They are all accustomed to seeing one church above others and to seeing the government in some degree controlled on moral matters by this favored church. The degree in which this occurs varies tremendously; the State-Church has little actual political power in such countries as Germany and England, but the Catholic Church has overwhelming power in some Catholic countries.

There is thus in the European mind a distinct contrast to the American attitude, though in verying degrees.

Toleration, for example, does not to any European mean equality among churches or even social equality among members of all sects, since it is inevitable that a State-Church will have a preeminent social as well as political position.

There is never among Europeans the same sense of individual responsibility in regard to civic morals as among Americans, since under European customs civic morals are largely fixed by the State-Church. This implies an almost complete control of public morality by the State-Church. Legislative action by any European government on any purely moral matter is almost inconceivable to the European mind and would be vigorously resented and opposed.

We have seen the effect of this European mental attitude in this country in several recent instances. Governmental control of morals never meets with the approval of the new immigrants. Americans who still hold the European attitude of mind have resented and resisted even the government's attempt to suppress prostitution and gambling, instead of merely to regulate them after the European custom. They object vigorously to our governmental censorship of immoral plays, books, and pictures, although many of them accept without question the censorship on truth enforced through the Catholic *"Index expurgatorius."*

Especially, they have maintained that the prohibition law is an infringement of personal rights. From their point of view this is true though most of them without a moments hesitation would obey a similar prohibition if it came from the Roman Catholic Church, just as they refrain from meat on Friday. They are quite accustomed to seeing moral questions decided by a majority of prelates, but are unwilling to have them decided by a majority of votes. They refuse to accept the decision of the majority on moral questions as binding upon themselves.

The same mental tendency to submit to an imposed authority also marks the attitude of most Europeans in political matters. Under the influence of the Reformation their point of view, has, of course, been enormously modified from the completely submissive attitude of five hundred years ago, but submission is still normal.

Thus, both in religion and in politics, the philosophy of Europe is still very largely based upon the acceptance of imposed human authority. The great mass of Europeans still expect from individual men—priests or nobles—decisions on many matters which we in America insist on deciding either for ourselves or by the votes of the majority.

In other words, the average European exercises his individualism at points different from ours, and submits readily to being dominated at points where we demand freedom. He accepts domination from individuals, where we will accept it only from the State. This is true of the Continent as a whole—it is doubly or trebly true of the Catholic part of the Continent. In Catholic countries the stirrings of the Protestant spirit either in religion or politics have been comparatively faint, and the break from the Catholic mental tradition has been hardly noticeable. Whether this be due to training, to the actual power of authority to suppress Liberalism, or to the inherent nature of the different stocks and races of men who have submitted, is not important.

The great fact is that Europe as a whole, and particularly Catholic Europe, does not think, feel nor act as we do; that its mental background and attitude is in sharp contrast with ours. How great this contrast is we shall see when we come to the study of the American mind.

CHAPTER XV

THE AMERICAN MIND

Contrast between the New World and the Old—The difference in quality, proportion and purposes of ideals—Americanism the product of the Protestant revolt—Based on
rejection of self-constituted authority—Dominant note is
increasing freedom from Catholic tradition—Our institutions the practical embodiment of this philosophy—The
contrast in the ideal of freedom—Its limitations and duties
—The Puritan conscience—The ideal of equality—Of tolerance—Of the equality of churches.

ONE of the most penetrating writers of modern
times is Hilaire Belloc. He has highly developed
gifts of clear vision, sound analysis and forceful
statement. His great talents are devoted to the
support of the Roman Catholic Church; nevertheless many of his definitions of the conflict between
Romanism and Americanism cannot be improved.
They are proof that this conflict must be recognized
by honest thinkers on both sides.

Mr. Belloc in his book, "The Contrast," written
in 1923, attempted to define the difference between
this European psychology we have been studying
and that of America. In his opening pages he says:

"I discovered beneath all the superficial growth and
change the same profound, underlying spirit; the same
Personality—the soul of which is not ours."*

And again:

"The New World is wholly alien to the Old. Had time
proceeded further, were the language become admittedly
foreign, the architecture transformed to a new native type,
the institutions grown grotesquely diverse between America

* The Contrast, Page 15.

and Europe (as they will later be), the thesis would be of a different kind and differently approached, above all much easier to advance. The difficulty of presenting it today lies in the existing superficial similarities * * * which mask the essential truth."*

Mr. Belloc speaks also of the "intense *quality* of difference" and in this he has the key to the whole situation, for the difference between the European and the American attitude of mind is one of quality and of degree far more than of difference in kind. It is shown by the fact that Americans and Europeans use many of the same words but with utterly different meanings.

We have seen the difference which is given to the word "freedom" by an American and by a man who follows the teachings of Leo XIII; the same difference in less degree will be found between the understanding of any American and of any European. It is so with all words which we use in defining civic and social ideas. Statements of Europeans which include these words do not mean to them what they mean to us. In this chapter, however, we shall first try to define exactly what they mean to Americans.

The same general characteristics, both physical and mental, are present in all men and the differences between men lie in the differences in the proportion of these characteristics. All men, for instance, have the characteristic of height, but the difference of a tenth—seven inches—makes the difference between a tall man and a short one. Even less difference in mental activity distinguishes the leader from his subordinates. In the mental realm all men love freedom, but to some freedom is a consideration

* The Contrast, Page 15.

above all other things, while comfort or prosperity or peace come first to many. Also, different men direct their love of freedom toward different objects; they wish to be free in the pursuit of wealth, or pleasure, or power, or of conscience and of truth. The fact that these differences are in proportion and in direction, rather than in kind, does not reduce their importance, though it often obscures vital conflicts. This must be kept in mind in studying the contrast between American mentality and European.

We have seen that the dominant characteristic of the European mind in civil as well as in religious affairs lies in its acceptance of human authority. Americanism originated in the state of mind of Europeans who revolted—that is, *protested*—against this authority and came to a new continent to escape it. The predominant psychology of historical Americanism, then, is a state of active protest against the acceptance of self-imposed authority— against that state of mind which still dominates Europe.

It is necessary to recall historical facts only briefly. Political and economic protest, as well as spiritual Protestantism, were often involved. The Puritans, a dissenting and protesting sect against the half-free Protestantism of the English Church under the Stuarts, were also in economic revolt in many instances. The Scotch-Irish came in protest against both religious and civil oppression in the interest of the English Church and of the English merchants, more than because of the hostility of the Irish Catholics. The Cavaliers of the South came to secure religious and political freedom when the Puritans were attempting to destroy the Episcopal Church and the British aristocracy under Cromwell.

It was so in more recent times. The great German immigration in 1848 came because of the suppression of republicanism along the Rhine. Even the Irish Catholics, whose church was oppressed by the Episcopalian prelates and whose poverty was despoiled by English landlords, came in a very real spirit of protest.

Protestantism—religious, civil or economic, and often all three—protest against human authority over the souls, the bodies, the rights and the earnings of men—this was the spirit which animated, almost without exception, the men who made America. It is automatically antagonistic to the dominant European state of mind.

To this must be added certain other characteristics of the early immigrants. They had to give up a life which was settled and reasonably secure even if repressed; they had to face known hardships and unknown dangers, they had to abandon such advantages as civilization then gave for the crude and bitter conditions of pioneer life. Even the preliminary voyage across the ocean was fraught with danger and suffering such as would daunt any but the bravest. Finally, the immigrant often had to abandon practically all support from his fellows and trust himself almost wholly upon the resources of his own hands, brains and courage.

This meant that of all the protesters in Europe, only those came to America who were brave almost to recklessness, who were physically far above the average, who were comparatively insensitive to the need for comforts and refinements, and who demanded freedom as a necessity to be won at the cost of hardship or even of life itself. They were picked men, the "shock troops" of the Protestant idea. They cast off and despised Europeanism with an intensity that is probably incomprehensible even to those Protestants who elected to endure its restrictions rather than face the unknown ills of migration.

This characteristic of American psychology was marked from the first but was intensified by all the conditions of life during the first two and one-half centuries of American civilization. For example, the early Puritan preachers of Massachusetts tried to establish themselves as autocrats in the name of the "Bible Commonwealth," but were overthrown by the growing insistance of their followers upon individual spiritual priesthood and individual civil rights. The attempt to establish a State religion weakened and disappeared in one colony after another. The authority of the royal governors was more and more disputed until it became a mere shadow, and the right of participating in political affairs—that is of the ballot—was extended steadily to men of less and less education and property. The process was slow but inevitable, and it was the effect of this process, far more than the direct quarrel over taxation, that brought about the American Revolution. The fact is that, whether it was shown in taxation or other forms, European authority had become intolerable.

On the other hand, there was an intensification of all the mental characteristics of the early immigrants through the rigors of pioneer life. The constant warfare with the wilderness and the savages was as merciless a "selection of the fit for survival" as can be imagined. The price of life was not only health and vitality; survival required physical activity and skill, a courage that was not bullheaded but intelligent, enormous mental as well as physical endurance, complete self-reliance, instant presence of mind in emergencies and considerable powers of adaption and invention. Those who had not these qualities died. The American race that sprung from the survivors has inherited these qualities in a degree not known to any other people.

The American mental attitude, then, is based upon two characteristics, both of which differ sharply from even the most advanced and progressive mass-mind in any European country. These are in the fundamental insistence on individual rights, and in the extent to which American conditions have developed self-determination.

We have seen that the European mind is still in greater or less degree dominated by authority; that even in the most advanced countries there remain many habits of thought and custom which are the outgrowth of the old idea of the Divine Right of Popes and kings. We have seen also that the chief individual duty of man is obedience to authority and that initiative, self-reliance and self-determination are still largely repressed. We have seen that Europe has been working away from this condition for four centuries and that Protestant countries have done this far more successfully than Catholics, but that even those nations which have rejected the theory of Divine Right are not yet wholly free from the habits based upon that theory.

The New World only has been able to free itself from both the theory and the habit. America, and this is true also of all English colonies, has gone far beyond any part of Europe not only in free institutions but still more in mental habits. We have built our civilization, from the ground up, on an entirely different foundation from that of Europe.

We have been able to carry the Protestant idea into practical application which, if not complete, is still immeasurably farther advanced than with any European people. The complete break from European custom and influence which marked the colonial period, and the isolation which allowed the development of the fundamental idea of Liberalism, have produced in America more nearly full fruition than has been seen in any other time or nation. In addition, our mental attitude has been further changed from that of Europe by the simplicity and directness of thought and the habit of self-determination which were forced by pioneer conditions.

Thus the basis of our civilization and thought is predominantly not merely non-Catholic but anti-Catholic. Such ideas and mental habits as sprang from Catholic civilization are survivals that are fast weakening. Our mental habits, ideals, assumptions, even our instincts, follow logically from the proposition that there is no divinely appointed human authority, just as Europe's have been built upon the assumption that there is such an authority. America is the foremost development of the anti-Catholic idea. Whether or not Americans are religious, their mental habits and outlook all spring from this spiritual foundation, which is also the foundation of Protestantism.

This was recognized and clearly stated by Dr. Andre Siegfried, the brilliant French observer, in his recent book, "America Comes of Age," which has been widely hailed as the most enlightening study of American life written during our generation. He says:

"If we wish to understand the real sources of American inspiration we must go back to the English Puritanism of the Seventeenth Century, for the civilization of the United States is essentially Protestant. Those who prefer other systems, such as Catholicism, for example, are considered bad Americans and are sure to be frowned upon by the purists. Protestantism is the only national religion, and to ignore that fact is to view the country from a false angle."*

More than this, Protestantism, in the sense of revolt against politico-religious authority, is also the mental attitude of all non-Catholic Americans. Equally with Protestants and American Jews, all non-Catholics subscribe to and obey the philosophy and practical application of the Protestant idea. The contrast with Europe is not only sharp but complete; as to all but a few European countries it is fundamental and all-embracing.

This contrast shows itself in countless ways, but for the purpose of this book we may disregard all except those which have a direct bearing upon our social and governmental structure. Let us look at the American mental attitude in some detail, turning often to Mr. Belloc's book since it confirms our diagnosis to find such a large measure of agreement from a European Catholic.

First is the concept of freedom. All people claim and exercise some form or degree of freedom but the differences between them are so great that the word is meaningless until it is defined. To Americans the meaning of the word is based upon the denial of human authority and is this: that each man or woman shall have scope for all the exercise

* America Comes of Age, Page 33.

of his own conscience, his own intelligence, and his only individualism which does not affect the freedom of others or endanger society; that is, that all men have the right of self-determination free from individual human interference.

Because of the religious origin of the idea, however, freedom does not mean a right to license, even to an irreligious American. He does not believe that any person is entitled to a freedom which will permanently injure himself. To state it in another way: freedom to an American means the right of self-determination but not the right of self-debasement.

There is no need to discuss whether this is the best form of freedom; certainly it is not the only one; but just as certainly it is the American type. When people of other races speak of freedom they mean something other than this. Americans should realize, therefore, that a European interprets our principles of freedom as a promise to allow him the kind of freedom he understands.

To an American this European kind of freedom usually seems to be a freedom for self-indulgences. We observe many Europeans holding to habits which we consider vicious and forbid by law; habits which we believe weaken not only the individual but the social structure.

The whole history of America forbids our acceptance of such indulgences as justified under the right of freedom. Both the principles of Calvinist religion, which in one form or another was dominant in most of the early Americans, and the rigors of the pioneer's life which were common to the whole continent, punished such indulgences. The man who weakened himself by them was believed to incur eternal damnation; he was very likely to incur either starvation or Indian torture. American pioneer conditions visited a weakling with an almost certain and often painful death.

Moreover, the man who thus weakened himself weakened the community, and this was intolerable. When there were only a handful of settlers to meet the onslaughts of savages or subdue untamed wilderness, the failure of a single individual might mean death to all. His freedom to exercise his own self-reliance was complete, but every possible penalty of public opinion would be imposed upon him if he abused that freedom to the possible injury of his fellows.

Thus to the American, as to no other people, the right to freedom must be paid for constantly by the acceptance and discharge of all the communal responsibilities of that freedom. To us, to attempt another definition, freedom is a trust even more than a privilege.

The American idea of freedom, therefore, is strictly limited by the principle of the acceptance of the responsibilities of freedom. There is a double basis for this, one religious and the other social. From a social point of view, the American takes it for granted that freedom is not possible unless each individual observes all the rights of others and contributes his own strength toward maintaining conditions and political institutions which will safeguard freedom. More important, at least historically, is the Protestant idea of responsibility to conscience. Since the American accepts no priestly authority, he must depend for moral guidance upon his direct relation with the Almighty through the medium of his own conscience. When he is socially free, and even when he is not religious, he does not consider himself free from this control.

The Puritan conscience is recognized throughout the world as a thing peculiar to itself; admired, cursed and derided in turn. If we accept the word of the un-American writers of recent years it is responsible for infinite evil, is harsh, cruel and intolerant. But certainly it is much more than this. It imposes upon all who have it a strict sense, not only of individual, but of public, duty. The American commonwealth today stands as the embodiment in civil law of the Puritan conscience as it affects social life. Europeans welcome its insistence upon equal justice but reject its insistence upon such civic principles as are embodied in the prohibition law. No such discrimination is possible; to reject a part of the philosopy would destroy the whole—and Liberalism with it.

Thus, under the Protestant philosophy which controls American thought, conscience takes the place of priestly authority. As a means of maintaining high moral standards of personal conduct, three centuries have proved that it is far more vigorous and far more effective than any authority that can be exercised by a priesthood. It more than counteracts the danger that individual liberty will develop into license, as always occurs when freedom is granted to a people who have not this saving restraint.

The contrast between this attitude and that of Catholics is also recognized by Dr. Siegfried. He says of it:

"From this (the Protestant basis of American thought) arises the feeling of social obligation that is so typically Anglo-Saxon. The idea that his personality is being con-

stantly suppressed is almost painful to a Latin. He cannot
comprehend the Calvinist point of view that the group and
not the individual is the social unit and the foundation of
the religious structure.''*

The second great American mental concept growing out of the rejection of self-imposed authority
is that of human equality. The idea is so clear
that it is surprising how many attempts have been
made to misinterpret it and how successful they
have been in winning followers. To the American,
human equality is simply the statement in another
form of the principle that no man has a right to
authority over any other man. He has no right to
interfere with another man's conscience, his decisions, or his enjoyment of the fruits of his own
ability and his own energy. As Lincoln said in
regard to the negro:

"In the right to eat the bread, without leave of any,
body else, which his own hands earn, he is my equal * * *
and the equal of every living man.''**

This is the American idea of human equality—
this and nothing more. The American does not believe men are equal in ability or character or socially;
certainly he does not believe that they are all alike.
He recognizes personal, national, and racial differences, and pays due regard to them in his thought,
his actions, and his institutions. Recently there
has been an attempt to extend the principle of equality to cover the idea of equal political power.
Whatever value there may be in this ideal, it is not
historically American. There was not one of the
original thirteen states in which suffrage was not
sharply restricted, and such institutions as the

* America Comes of Age, Page 34.
** Abraham Lincoln, Vol. I, Page 289.

United States Senate and the electoral college show very clearly that the framers of the Constitution had no intent of allowing equal political power to all citizens.

Thus the American idea of equality is not at all that of the Socialist or the Communist; it is not at all the Roman Catholic idea of equal acceptance of a supreme authority; it is clearly and simply the Protestant idea of an equal right to self-determination under direct spiritual responsibility to the Almighty and civil responsibility to law.

The third American mental attitude springing from the Protestant theory is that of tolerance. Just as intolerance is logically necessary to all who believe that they are guided by Divine Authority, so tolerance is logically necessary to all who believe that every man has the right to seek divine guidance for himself.

As with the idea of equality, so with tolerance, there are definite limitations. Tolerance is required by American principles for every man's personal belief and for his relation with his Maker; it extends to every point of faith. But it has no application whatever to any man's social or civil conduct, no matter on what religious theory that conduct may be based. It does not allow opinions with which it is not in agreement to be applied socially.

These limitations are definite and are embodied in law. There is another limitation which has not yet been defined legally but which is today in the process of being defined. That is the question of the extent to which tolerance should be given to religious activities in politics. The results of the 1928 election show clearly that on this point, too, America intends to maintain a definite limitation on tolerance.

The fourth American mental attitude based on the Protestant idea, and one which was also involved in the 1929 campaign, is the equality of all churches. In one sense this is merely an extension of the principle of tolerance. It is based on the same reasons and is subject to the same limitations.

It has, however, another and different basis which springs from the rejection of the union of Church and State involved in the Papal Theory. Since individuals are believed to stand as equals before God, churches must likewise so stand. Therefore there must be no favoritism to one church over others; none may claim special privileges nor rights not common to all. A church is considered merely a voluntary association of its members instead of a Divine Society, and it must be willing to accept this position socially and politically. Any church which itself violates the principle of tolerance should thereby lose its own right to tolerance.

All these mental attitudes are based upon the rejection of human authority. There is another side to the American mind which is based upon the acceptance of an authority which differs in many ways from any that is known to the Roman Catholic system. This is the authority of the government. Of course every Catholic country has a temporal government and its citizens accept that authority, but both the powers of the government and the attitude of the citizens toward it are very different in America.

CHAPTER XVI

THE AMERICAN VIEW OF LAW

Authority of the American State on moral conduct—This necessary in a democracy—Automatically rejected by Catholics—
Application to education and marriage—The stability of
the American principle—Its effect on political conduct—
On law observance—On respect for the Constitution—On
attitude toward officials—On exploitation of governments—
Other contrasts with European ideas—The gulf between
American and Catholic minds—Failure of American institutions in Catholic countries.

ANY European government historically, and still
to some extent instinctively, is based upon the
idea of an imposed authority. Except in England
it does not spring from the people themselves in
any such way as with us. The Republic of France
may be taken for an example; there every man has
the ballot and yet the government itself is intrinsic-
ally autocratic and beaurocratic in its functioning;
nor does the Frenchman ever identify himself closely
with it. Except for the moment when he votes he
has no more share and interest in it than he did in
the days of Louis XIV.

To illustrate: to the European mind the position of a private citizen of a country has always
been like that of the private soldier in an army.
Orders and regulations came down from above and
he had nothing to do but obey. Under the old
autocratic system he had nothing to do, either,
with the selection of officers. The change that has
taken place in European governments has amounted
to about the same as if, in this army, the soldiers
were allowed to elect the officers. Regulations and
orders still come from above and the soldiers' chief
duty still is to obey.

The American idea is quite different. Americans recognize, of course, that authority is necessary in any social order and we have therefore created, accepted, and become a part of an authority which is just the opposite of the Divine Authority claimed by the Papacy; that is the Power of the People. However far popular government may have gone in Europe it is still a compromise, but with us it is a definite, concrete principle, accepted in all circumstances and applied under all conditions.

We have constituted in the Democratic State an authority which we accept far more than the European accepts the authority of his government. There was more than a half truth in the remark that "the voice of the people is the voice of God." To us "the voice of the people" certainly has replaced the Catholic "voice of God through the Pope" in all matters affecting social conduct. To be sure our American principle of human liberty implies that we shall give to the State as little right as possible to interfere with our conduct, but we do give to it many rights which Europeans do not consider belong to government, and which are exercised by the State-Church or not at all.

These chiefly concern moral matters. Where the European looks for moral mandates either to the Pope or an established church, the American accepts such mandates from the state or national governments. This is absolutely necessary if moral standards are to be maintained since—there being no church which has civil power—there can be no enforcement of morals except by the State.

Yet the European, and especially the Catholic, cannot accept this. He claims the right to submit laws of the State which affect morals to his Pope's conscience, and to obey its dictates. The conflict with American principles is complete so far as the Catholic is concerned, for to us it is intolerable that American laws should be submitted for judgment to a conscience trained by an alien authority, and loyal to it.

Two functions stand out which are logically claimed by the Roman Catholic Church under the autocratic theory, but which can not possibly be entrusted to any church under American principles. Those are the control of education and of marriage. To permit each separate church to set up unregulated schools and to divide the education of the nation's children among them, would be national suicide. To permit each separate church similarly to set up conflicting laws governing the marriage of its people would create a moral anarchy. American opinion recognizes these facts and unhesitatingly commits control of these matters to the State.

Less simple but equally powerful are the reasons which lead American opinion to commit to the State control over individual moral acts which have any social effect. Our custom in this matter has been challenged in the name of Liberalism by those people who have failed to recognize the limitations upon the principle of freedom. They maintain that freedom permits no limitations on individual moral conduct and that therefore the State has no right to attempt to impose such limitations. The fact is that, as has been stated, the American ideal of freedom does not extend to individual license and that it recognizes the necessity for social and moral control. Therefore this control must be placed in the hands of the only social authority, the State.

This governmental control of morals is directly opposed by Catholics. Hilaire Belloc states the reason:

"By the definition which is the very soul of Catholicism, religion must be for the Catholic *First,* a supreme authority superior to any claims of the State * * * *Fourthly,* a guarantee of individual freedom in all that is not of Faith. * * * the Catholic instinctively feels his right of personal choice in all that is not defined by creed."*

He goes on:

"Now it is clear that between this attitude and the attitude of a non-Catholic State which proposes 'tolerance' (that is, the definition of all religion as an individual concern), there is conflict. For 'tolerance' means indifference to those acts and doctrines which the State treats as private, *coupled with enforcement of certain acts and doctrines which the State insists upon treating as universal.*

"I am not here concerned with the evident falsehood of this word tolerance. I use it because it is the current word for this particular attitude which every State, not identified with Catholicism, must take up.

"I repeat, tolerance means today, in the mind of the modern statesman, and particularly in the mind of the American citizen, the enforcement of certain doctrines and practices, and, side by side with these, a complete freedom in such doctrines and practices as lie outside those limits.

"For instance, the American State enforces the doctrine of private property; the doctrine and practice of monogamy —not of monogamy in the sense of tolerating only one living wife, but in the sense of not tolerating two legal marriages with one person at the same time. It also forbids the purchase and transport of wine, but not those of Mrs. Stopes' books, etc.

"Up to the present day the position of the Catholic in the United States has insecurely fitted in with this modern conception of tolerance, through the fact that the dogmas

* The Contrast, Pages 160 and following.

taken for granted by the State, and enforced in practice, were mainly Catholic dogmas; and that the action of the State, where its dogmas differed from Catholic dogma, was mainly negative and permissive. But such a state of affairs cannot be permanent."

This Catholic attitude, unlike the attitude of the extreme Liberals, is logical. It is also an outstanding example of the conflict between the European and the American point of view, since in some degree this attitude is shared by all Europeans. They are used to seeing the government submit to the moral dictation of a church but cannot understand why, when it refuses such dictation, it should submit to the individual consciences of its citizens. Yet this is an inevitable development of the Protestant idea, even if European Protestants have not yet reached it. Since there must be moral control, where there is no accepted human authority on morals it is necessary and logical that this control should be vested in the only authority that can be recognized in a free State—the authority of the people through their legally elected representatives.

This situation has one great advantage for us which is recognized even by the Catholic Belloc, in that it preserves our moral and ethical standards against injury from any possible assertion of individualism, and from the weakening of the ecclesiastical authority, which in other countries has been depended upon to maintain morality. In Europe the spiritual authority of Catholicism is decaying, and with it morals also decay. Mr. Belloc thus analyzes the difference:

"Now in this situation England will, and must, behave as the rest of Europe behaves—that is, the loss of faith produces rapidly in England as in the rest of Europe a revolution in ethics; and the Pagan origins from which we sprang, noble and ignoble, reappear as the poor remaining fragments of Christian (Catholic) dogma are abandoned.

"But in the United States it is not so. The modern sceptical movement, the substitution of Opinion for Faith, leave the ethics of the nation, not unchanged indeed, but still in unbroken tradition, and that tradition is essentially Puritan."*

In other words, the Protestant basis of American thought gives us liberty without moral laxity and license, while to the European liberty does mean moral license. No wonder the Europeans complain of our moral laws!

The complete acceptance by America of the idea of popular government creates several mental attitudes which are almost unknown in Europe. One of these is the spirit of identification with the government. Each man feels himself a part of the government, our interest in politics is constant, our public affairs are openly conducted—even as to public scandals—and there is a frankness in all the actions of government such as is utterly unknown abroad. Also our political abuses are subject to a steady and gradual reformation, instead of being ignored until conditions become intolerable and an explosion occurs, as is more likely in Europe.

Again, because of our personal identification with the government, there is in this country much more of the spirit of common action. Although private interests have far too much influence with our government, they are nevertheless infinitely less powerful as against the national interest than are such private agencies abroad.

Most important of all, however, is that Americans, far more than Europeans, mentally accept

* The Contrast, Page 159.

public authority as binding. The laws and actions of the government come from our own volition and can be changed at will, but so long as they stand we believe that they must be accepted. The many violations of this principle do not affect the fact that it is an axiom of thought and conduct.

As a part of this, and also as a part of the acceptance of popular rule, comes the American habit of law observance. To be sure, there is no such observance of the letter of the law as marks the European mind. To the European a law is laid down by authority and must be observed just so far as that authority extends. But no further. To the American a law is an expression of the will of the people, since it can be changed by the people at any moment it is not sacred, but its authority extends far beyond any power of enforcement. It may almost be considered that to the American law observance is required by public welfare more than by authority, and as such is a demand upon his individual conscience rather than his obedience. Mr. Belloc speaks of this with surprise. After noting the obvious lacks of law observance in this country he goes on:

"* * * you may note the most surprising minuteness of respect paid to some regulations affecting a half-deserted countryside, a vast space in which the mere mechanical action of a police would be impossible, and where the carrying out of a law—apparently insignificant—clearly depends upon the respect paid to it by men too scattered to be coerced and even accustomed to private feud. Why is this?

"Both phenomena, the irregular and the regular action, spring from the same root; but the second is by far the more remarkable. The irregular action is the fruit of a looseness in social structure inseparable from an unprecedently large and rapid expansion over vast spaces and from a ceaseless foreign influx. The observance of law (and that in surprising detail), when it cannot be enforced, is the fruit of this same looseness of structure, in which the individual feels a menace to society and therefore to himself if law fails. It is the effect of a conclusion, more or less conscious, to which each man has come that in the absence of material force to uphold what was everywhere, and is still in a large part of the territory, a scattered society, only individual and voluntary co-operation can uphold it.

"I repeat, of the two American phenomena, lawlessness and adoration of law, the latter is far the more remarkable. A man of doubtful morals respecting a lonely letter box in a desert State, a lazy man mending his allotted piece of road on a mountain trail, impress me far more than a lynching or a shooting affray in the same country. These you may hear of in any place where distance and perpetual movement make order difficult to maintain. They are a natural concomitant of such conditions. But the spontaneous support of things necessary to the common life is a less explicable thing: and most admirable."*

A part of the American respect for law which distinguishes it utterly from anything to be found in Europe (except to some extent in England) is the respect for the Constitution. The Constitution to us is in all its provisions almost sacred. We add to it from time to time but many Americans regard any attempt to take from it even provisions which they disapprove as unwise, to say the least. The contrast in this attitude of ours between that of Europe is most brilliantly set forth by Mr. Belloc:

"It is the mark of long-established societies, shaped in tradition, that they extend the religious instinct to include their institutions. All the States of antiquity reposed upon such a practice and instinctively made of it their principle of continuity and of survival. Mediaeval and more recent Christian societies acted in the same fashion. The French before the Revolution had for the Papetian Monarchy just that religious awe which is felt for a national shrine or sacrificial rite. The whole of the West in the later Dark

* The Contrast, Page 133.

Ages and early Middle Ages had the same awe for the hierarchic bonds of society: the bond of feudal loyalty in temporal matters, the bond of official subordination leading up to the Papacy in spiritual matters.

"Modern Europe has, from a series of accidents, lost this cement. It has crumbled away. The various institutions familiar to men are each examined sceptically, each asked to give a reason for its existence, and therefore each undermined: and this is particularly true of the governmental institutions of the various countries into which our age-long occidental culture is now divided.

"It is remarkable that in the United States this ancient, profound and preservative instinct has revived to an intense life, and has attached itself to one central institution not yet a century and a half old: The Constitution.

"We have here the converse, the necessary supplement, to that permanent, unceasing watch and correction which corporate opinion and will in the United States sets over public servants. Deprived of such a check as this worship of the Constitution, the action of ceaseless criticism and correction would be disruptive. Provided with this check, a continual discussion of public affairs, a continual denunciation of dishonesty in public servants, does not breed instability.

"The Constitution of the United States has two main characters, one of method, the other of regulation. That of method is the provision of obstacles to change, that of regulation is the Supreme Court. * * *

"These two characters are peculiar to the society which they govern. There is nothing like them elsewhere on earth: but they could have no practical meaning save for the absolute quality of the respect they command. Commanding as they do that absolute respect, that religious awe, which forbids any question of their authority, they are wholly conservative of the Commonwealth."*

Another contrast based on the American idea of equality is our respect for an office without involving respect for the man holding it. The office represents

* The Contrast, Page 128 and following.

public power and public trust; the man is a temporary incumbent whose conduct has no claim on our
approval, who is subject to almost instant dismissal
and who carries out of office no more respect than
is due to his individual character. In the same way,
while we afford a very great respect and deference
to achievement and to the man who has won wealth,
we are inclined to contempt for his heirs.

The contrast with the European attitude is
complete, for almost without exception Europeans
respect a man because of his office, his wealth or
his inherited position and regardless of his own
character or achievements. A company of cockneys
will follow a "gentleman" officer to death no matter how worthless he may be, when they could not
be moved or controlled by the best of their own.
A German will step into the gutter to make room
for one of the "high-born" who is wholly despic-
able, when he would not accord any deference
whatever to the most brilliant citizen of low birth.
To put it briefly: America has almost completely
rid itself of the hampering effect of aristocracy,
while it still survives in Europe with an only
slightly diminished force.

A further feature of the American's attitude
toward the government, based on his share in it,
is his feeling of responsibility for its operation.
This feeling is still far too weak, but is distinctly
in advance of that which is common in Europe.
To the European, even though he may vote, the
government remains an outside authority in which
he has no personal interest and for which he has no
responsibility. The American believes that a good
citizen has a constant responsibility both to exert
personal influence and to stir up agitation against

any mis-government. Our failures are in practice but not in the universal acceptance of the principle.

A single example will make clear the contrast with European ideas: that is Tammany. It is not that Tammany has the habit of graft—there are too many political crimes by Americans to make this unique. But Tammany is open and shameless; it takes it for granted that exploitation of the government is a legitimate business; its leaders proclaim this creed. This attitude is impossible to American politicians; they steal, indeed, but do it shame-facedly and recognize their own degradation as Tammany does not. It is no accident that Tammany is made up so largely of Roman Catholics and is the most complete embodiment in this country of the European idea in politics.

A final characteristic of Americans is the habit of simplicity and directness of thought. Far more than with any other race the American will get to the heart of a problem, disregarding the various complications and modifications to it, although he knows very well that they exist. He will not bring them into consideration until he has answered the main question. This is in sharp contrast to the habit, which has been observed by anyone coming in contact with Europeans, of trying to get the whole of a vast and infinitely complex situation into view at one time.

There are two reasons for the American attitude. One is that when our forefathers revolted against Romanism they also turned against the elaborate legalism which is a part of it. The Roman Church had held them under a system set forth in obscurant and unintellible language, with an infinite variety of exceptions and "whereases." Our forefathers cast out this whole system of thought along with Papal Supremacy. They drew their rule from the Bible and submitted themselves to the simple command, "Thus saith the Lord."

The second reason for this lies in the conditions of pioneer life. They were simplified to the utmost; they required instant and direct decision. Thus the American man lost the habit of involved thought and has an instinct for simplified forthrightness. A practical effect of this is to be seen in our simplification of the process of manufacturing to create a mass production that has astounded the world, but it appears in less obvious forms in all American thinking.

Mr. Belloc, in discussing the European accusation that the American attitude of mind is "childish," has this to say:

"The American way of appreciating, approaching, judging the alien European thing, or, indeed, anything novel with which he is brought in contract, has nothing in common with imperfection, such as is connoted by the word 'child.' It has three qualities which struck the speaker of that very common, and most erroneous European judgment, but they struck him quite wrongly. It has the qualities of simplicity, directness and elimination: the combined result of these qualities grossly misleads the foreign observer. The American meeting with a problem will (as anyone who knows the Americans, however slightly, can testify) reduce that problem at once to its simplest terms, try to get to the core of it. He will then concentrate upon it, and for the purpose of concentration he will eliminate all its variables, although he knows very well that the variables are there. His process is that of the mathematician or of the student of physical science, and he pursues his own method more thoroughly than any other kind of man I know. That is why, I suppose, he solves his own problems, the only problems he is called upon to solve, with such astonishing rapidity and success. A child does none of these things. The difference between the American method and ours is not the difference between immaturity and maturity; it is the difference between one highly mature method and another; the difference between a mechanical and an organic method."*

It has been impossible to separate the various manifestations of the American psychology in any regular order, because they overlap and run together so constantly. The work should be attempted by a master psychologist. The utmost that has been attempted is to set down some of the cases in which the American mind operates very differently from the European mind. Certainly these prove˙that we have in America a mental attitude which is at vital points alien to European psychology based upon the Papal Theory and its survivals. As Mr. Belloc says:

"Europe and America are two systems, universes, creations, standing apart."**

Also he says again, speaking of the English, who are far more nearly American than any other Europeans:

"* * * an English group, remaining English, **could not** (I say) **live** in America; it would breathe an alien air and die."***

Thus there is between the American mind and the European a great gulf; a gulf which in the case of the Liberal Protestant nations is comparatively narrow and can still be bridged by mutual adjust-

* The Contrast, Page 22.
** Ibid, Page 37.
*** Ibid, Page 51.

ments but which, so far as the Catholic nations go, is of unplummed depth and infinite width and cannot possibly be crossed. The institutions of America have been built upon the Protestant philosophy; built to foster it and to secure it, and especially have been adapted to men who believe in it.

This state of affairs is vital in considering the attitude of American Catholics, with their European psychology. The fact that our institutions are well adapted to our own racial genius and mentality is beyond question. It is proved by their success, which has led to imitation throughout the world. But these imitations are feeble; the institutions which fit us are not fitted to peoples with a different racial genius. It makes it certain that when such people are brought under these institutions they will find themselves hampered and uncomfortable and will rebel more or less vigorously.

Particularly our institutions have failed in Catholic Europe. France is the only Catholic nation which much has more than a semblance of popular government. Spain, Italy, Poland, and Jugo-Slavia are under dictorships. France itself, although it has now maintained a republic for nearly sixty years, has passed through six revolutions since the Amercan Constitution was adopted and can even yet hardly be considered either stable or wholly democratic.

We may safely conclude that the failure of democracy in all these Catholic countries has been due to its conflict with the Roman Catholic ideals, instincts and mental habits which dominate their people, and which they have brought with them to America.

CHAPTER XVII

THE WORLD CONFLICT OF RELIGIONS

The question of Catholic action in practical politics—American confusion of thought—Catholic politics unconcealed in other countries—Catholics foresee growing political conflict in this country—The political character of Ultramontanism —Clericalism and its workings—Catholic revolts against it in France—The "heresy" of refusal to obey the Pope in politics—South American struggles against priests in politics.

SO far in this book we have considered almost entirely the mental side of the Roman Catholic issue; the conflict in ideas and ideals; the opposition in purposes and principles, the difference in the natural mental outlook and political aspirations of the peoples who are and are not Roman Catholics. We have found that the contrast between the two is infinitely deep and is all embracing; that the Catholics disagree with the non-Catholics on all points affecting human rights and liberties as well as on the principles underlying government and the relations of churches and their members to each other and to the State.

So far as non-Catholics are concerned, this mental attitude of Catholics is important only as it affects political conduct. If it were merely a belief which they held among themselves, even if it set them apart from other peoples as do the beliefs of many Jews, the social effect would not be serious. Our real concern is with the extent to which these Catholic principles produce political effect. The fundamental question, that must be answered to determine the fitness of Catholics for citizenship in a free nation, is whether they attempt in politics to carry out Catholic ideas and to enforce them upon non-Catholics and upon the government.

We come, then, to consideration of the practical side of the Catholic question and to an examination of how the conflict manifests itself in the world of events.

Three things stand out at the beginning. First, it is logically to be expected that such a complete conflict in ideas will instantly manifest itself in practical political conflicts. Second, Roman Catholic spokesmen, particularly in America, strenuously deny that there is such a conflict. Third, outside of America no one accepts this denial—not even Catholic laymen.

There is little need to enlarge on the first point. Once it is fully realized how great is the contrast between the Catholic and non-Catholic mind, no one can doubt that the conflict will appear in political form whenever the opportunity offers. No social structure and no governmental institution can be conceived which would be satisfactory to both types of mind. The disagreements are far more fundamental than any possible agreement on ordinary political or economic issues. Each side will inevitably, and rightly, seek to have the nation controlled by its own ideals and will attempt to impose them whenever there is any chance of success.

The denial of American Catholics that there is any conflict we may pass over for the moment. We shall find that the conflict does exist elsewhere and that foreign observers, including Catholics, see it already in operation in this country and expect it to increase. We will take up this denial later and seek to find how it is possible that it can be made by any honest and well-informed Catholic.

Let us look, then, at the third point—the fact that in all the rest of the Christian world neither Catholic nor non-Catholic denies the political conflict. We must have this situation thoroughly in mind before we can understand the present position of American Catholics.

The great fact is that this political conflict exists. We saw it in the 1928 campaign in America, though in that case the issue was not clearly drawn and was often denied. But throughout Europe and South America, in all countries where there is any considerable proportion of Catholics, this struggle is constant, open and vigorous. England and the Scandinavian countries are comparatively immune because of their small number of Catholics, but in Germany, where the Catholic minority is large, the conflict appears in full force.

This situation is vigorously stated by Hilaire Belloc, who says:

"Europe today is an exceedingly complex interlocking conflict, wherein one of two cultures, Protestant and Catholic (but each main side subject to innumerable variations and internal divisions) is slowly grappling with the other. From the smallest sub-unit to the largest group, intelligence in Europe today is consciously pitted against intelligence, tenacity against tenacity, will against will."*

It is only in the Protestant nations such as England and America that this situation has not been realized. Robert Dell, an English observer living in Rome, brings out this point. He says:

"I doubt whether the full significance of the agreement between the Pope and Mussolini has been generally rec-

* The Contrast, Page 21.

ognized in America, any more than in England. It is only
in Catholic countries that the Catholic Church is really
understood. In Protestant countries, where Catholics are
in a minority, they are necessarily to some extent liberal
because they need liberty for themselves and can get it
only if others have it too. If religious liberty were denied,
it would be denied to them, not to the Protestant majority. In Protestant countries, too, the Catholic ecclesiastical authorities rarely venture to dictate to their flocks
in political matters or to attempt to form a Catholic Party
in politics. * * *

"The consequence of all this is that in Protestant countries people get the idea that after all the Catholic Church
is in the same category as other religious bodies and the
fact that a public man is a Catholic is purely his own private
concern. It is held to be intolerant, as you recently held
it in America, to object to a candidate for high political
office on the ground that he is a Catholic. Anti-clericals
in European Catholic countries do not agree with you.
They say that the Catholic Church is above all an international political institution with a political policy of its
own and is always, potentially at any rate, as the London
'Nation and Athenaeum' said on February 16, 'the most
dangerous reactionary force in the modern world.' They
say that the Syllabus of Pius IX, whether technically
'infallible' or not, was an expression of the unchanging
teaching of the Catholic Church and that it is still true,
as Pius IX declared, that the Catholic Church cannot be
reconciled with modern civilization.''*

Although Mr. Belloc wrote in 1923, before the
first mutterings of the Catholic issue had appeared
in American national politics, he predicted that this
country could not long escape it and that we must
presently face the same situation as that which
confronts Europe. He said:

"In general, that conflict with which Europe is acquainted to the full, and which has filled the history of two
thousand years, from the time of Nero to our own, is inevitable.

* The Nation, March 27, 1929.

"Now we in Europe, being so familiar with this, taking it for granted, and knowing that the conflict is always potentially present, arrange for it in various ways; by certain compromises and anomalies in one time; by vigorous persecution in other times; by accepting corporate union between the faith and the civil power. In all these ways the strain is resolved or postponed, and an equilibrium, stable or unstable, preserved. But no one can know the United States without admitting that when the conflict shall there arise, an equilibrium will not be established or preserved, for the conflict will be novel and will seem monstrous. On the one side you have a plain affirmation that the law is the law and must be obeyed, and indignant surprise on the rejection of what seems so obvious and universal a rule. On the other, you will have, as you have had throughout history, resistance to and denial of that rule."*

Certainly this is anything but an agreement with the denial of a political conflict which is made by American Catholics. Mr. Belloc, however, was writing for cultured Englishmen whose knowledge of European affairs is so great that any book would be instantly discredited if its writer had the impudence to make such a denial. In fact, Catholic spokesmen do not attempt such denials in Europe except in technical language. But they apparently calculate upon American ignorance of European politics and permit themselves special latitude in statements intended for consumption in this country.

It is worth our while to spend some little time in looking at the Catholic conflict in Europe. The Roman Catholics are quite right in thinking we know little about it. Mr. Belloc is very likely to be right, since he knows so much about the Catholic Church, in saying that we Americans must soon face the same situation. And finally, it

* The Contrast, Page 164.

is in Europe that we may, so to speak, study Catholicism in its natural surroundings.

A brief glimpse of this European political conflict was seen in Chapter IV in the discussion of Ultramontanism.* The summary of the situation given by the Encyclopedia Britannica was so enlightening that it is worth repeating. It says:

"A second peculiarity of Ultramontanism is its confusion of religion with politics; it claims for the Roman Catholic Church the functions of a political power, * * * An instance of this interference with the duties of the individual citizens towards the State may be found in the fact that, till the year 1904, the Catholics of Italy were prohibited by the Pope from taking part in any parliamentary election."**

And again:

"Thus Ultramontanism is not to be conceived as a theological movement, but as the programme of a party whose principles are in fundamental opposition to modern culture, modern education, modern tolerance and the modern State."***

In regard to the present policy of the Papacy as established by Leo XIII, the Britannica says:

"* * * all these details * * * are overshadowed beyond all doubt by the one great fact that the ecclesiastical regime had not only taken under its wing the solution of social questions, but also claimed that political action was within the proper scope of the Church, and, moreover, arrogated to itself the right of interfering * * * with the political life of nations."****

This active attempt of the Roman Catholic Church to control political action gives rise to a

* See Page 37 and following.
** The Encyclopedia Britannica, Vol. XXVII, Page 571.
*** The Encyclopedia Britannica, Vol. XXVII, Page 573.
**** The Encyclopedia Britannica, Vol. XX, Page 720.

situation in European politics which is so strange to Americans that we hardly even know its name. In all Catholic countries it is known; it is called "clericalism." It is the control of the government, or—failing that—of a political party, in the interest of the Roman Catholic Church; a control that always subordinates all other interests to the interest of the Catholic Church. It produces an organization which uses religious faith as a political force and deliberately prevents, so far as it can, that free exercise of the popular will which is the basis of democracy. It may not be dominated by detailed orders from the Vatican, but it is always dominated by a state of mind which the vast Catholic hierarchial system has created for support of the Vatican policies. It is rather a modern development, and is the outgrowth of the renewed political aggression of the Papacy.

Clericalism is rampant in every country where there are enough Catholics to operate effectively as a separate force in politics. It is particularly vigorous, of course, in those countries which are religious battle grounds, such as Germany. Ever since the formation of the German Reichstag there has been in it a powerful party known as the "Centrists," which has always made the policies of the Vatican its first business. For this purpose it has been prepared to bargain with other parties, giving support to that one which would grant the largest part of its demands. Several times it has so embarrassed the government as to force the formation of new cabinets or even the actual dissolution of parliament. Clerical parties have appeared immediately in each of the new States which were set up by the Treaty of Versailles and in each of them today exercise enormous power.

Clerical political activities have usually been controlled by the Jesuits, with the result that almost every European country has banished them at one time or another. In spite of the fact that they have now practically captured the Roman hierarchy and Catholic education, laws against them are still on the statute books in such wholly Catholic countries as Spain, Portugal and France.*

The most notable of the struggles against clericalism in Europe has been that in France, where it has very largely been the dominant issue for two generations. The political aggressions of the French clergy were so great that they produced a revolt even among devout Catholics, and caused an agitation which in 1904 led to the separation of Church and State and the expulsion of many French monastic orders. Since that time French politics has been continually disturbed by the efforts of the Vatican to regain political power. In 1925 the situation became so acute that Premier Herriot, on January 23, issued this warning:

"Rome must cease its attempts to make of Catholicism a political party in France. Rome is trying to build Catholic parties everywhere. They have succeeded easily in Germany; they are now attempting a similar thing in Italy and France. Should they succeed, it would be a great misfortune for our country. The Pope has congratulated the Catholics for having organized in France. This is an intervention in French internal affairs. We are religious liberals. There is one policy and that is a policy of liberty and independence from the Vatican. Every nation is free, and we do not have to receive orders from the Pope."

The latest interference of the Vatican in French politics occurred in 1927, when Leon Daudet was excommunicated—although a devout Catholic and a long-time champion of his church—for refusing

*The Catholic Encyclopebia, Vol. XIV, Pages 100-101.

to carry out the instructions of the Pope in French politics. When Daudet died shortly afterwards the Catholic Church refused to give him Christian burial.

Of this action Robert Dell writes:

"If he (a Catholic) says that he agrees with our political principles, our reply is that he can prove it only by coming out of that organization (the Catholic Church) and that he should have no objection to so doing, for if he really agrees with us he is already a heretic and probably *ipso facto* excommunicated. And if he says, as Daniel O'Connell is alleged to have said, that he takes his religion from Rome, but not his politics, he is doubly a heretic, for he is guilty of the heresy condemned by Pius X under the name of 'political Modernism.'

"This heresy—that Catholics are not bound to obey their ecclesiastical authorities in political matters—was the theological ground of the recent condemnation of the *Action Francaise League* and its paper by the present Pope."*

A similar situation appears in all the Catholic countries of South America. There is not a single one of the Latin-American countries which has not at one time or another shown a vigorous opposition to clericalism as practiced there. The story of Latin-America's fight against clerical domination was recently told by J. Lloyd Mecham, of the University of Texas. Says Mr. Mecham:

"When the youthful nations of Latin-America undertook the direction of their own destinies, they were faithful to the religion of their fathers. Yet in a short time discord and disobedience began to make their appearance, and in Chile and in Argentine in the early 1820s the first attacks upon the Catholic clergy occurred."**

Mr. Mecham says that the reason for the enforcement of the Mexican laws by President Car-

* The Nation, July 3, 1929.
** Current History, January, 1929.

ranza was "the alliance of the clergy with the
opposition to the government." He observes also
that "the attacks upon the Church have not been
anti-religious but rather political in character."
In summarizing the situation in Mexico, he says:

"Beginning with the reforms of Rivadavia and ending
with the decrees of President Calles, most of the so-called
'sacrilegious laws' have not been based on anti-religion, nor
even anti-Catholicism. They were, with very few exceptions, measures designed to frustrate the exercise of political interference and influence on the part of the Roman
Catholic clergy. To accomplish this purpose the worldly,
not the spiritual, position of the Church had to be reformed. * * * A critical examination of the anti-clerical
legislation in Mexico from 1833 to the present time reveals
above all else a desire to take the clergy out of politics."

In closing he declares:

"The Catholic Church in Latin-America has come to a
parting of the ways. It must make its choice between two
roads: The first, adherence to the old pretentions, leads
to bitter disputes, with inevitable anti-clerical attacks and
consequent weakening of the hold of the clergy upon the
faithful. The second, recognition of the new order and
accomodation to the changed world by a complete sev-
erance of Church-State relations, leads to an active and
prosperous Church, which can enjoy once more the confidence and love of its communicants. If the Church sees
the light it saves a continent; otherwise, continued disaster
will be inevitable."

There is no need to extend this survey; the simple fact is that the Catholic Church is openly in
politics in every Christian country that is not
strongly Protestant. Clericalism is as well recognized a factor in the politics of all such nations as
are protectionism, militarism or any other political
movements. No man in those countries would
think of denying the political interests, purpose or
activities of the Roman Catholic Church.

CHAPTER XVIII

THE PRIESTS' POLITICAL PUPPETS

Denials of Catholic activity in American politics—Their acceptance vital to the Roman campaign—How they can be made
by sincere Catholics—The Papal method in politics—Catholic action controlled through the great secret societies—
The denials therefore purely Jesuitical—Patriotic interests
subordinated to those of the church—How Catholic minority uses "balance of power."

ALTHOUGH the political war of Catholicism
against Liberalism, and the struggle of the
hierarchy for political power, is open and recognized
throughout the greater part of the Christian world,
here in America it is constantly denied (though
not by the Catholic prelates) that Romanism "is
in politics." This denial is credulously accepted
by many non-Catholics, and doubtless even by great
numbers of Catholics.

It is made by Catholics who must be credited
with complete sincerity as well as by many whose
sincerity is most difficult to accept.

The whole social and political campaign of
Rome in America depends on these denials. Unless they are generally believed, Catholicism will be
confined to spiritual affairs; a wide realization of
her true methods and purposes might even lead to
political reprisals.

There are three explanations of these denials
which might justify even honest men in making
them. In the first place, it is a fact that in America
the Roman Catholic Church has so far been comparatively inconspicuous in politics. Any other
course would have been suicidal, for open political

activity by the Catholic leaders as such would automatically solidify the non-Catholic majority against them. They have been restrained, too, by the influence of American ideals on their own followers; there was obvious danger of rebellion if they attempted to exercise over them the kind of political compulsion which they apply in other countries. The contrast would have been too flagrant. Such political activities as the hierarchy has inspired have therefore been furtive; it takes pains not to disclose its true purpose even to Catholics whose patriotism is strong. In other words, conditions in America have forced upon the Catholic hierarchy the pose of aloofness from politics. Many Americans, including many Catholics, have not seen through this pose.

In the second place, as has been said before, Americans have not been sufficiently informed about conditions in other countries to know the general policy of the Roman Church. Since we have ourselves so largely escaped the political conflict which is common to the rest of the Christian world, we have found it difficult to realize that this conflict exists. For us, politico-religious controversy ended with the adoption of the Constitution. We have been anxious to believe the statements of American Catholics that it also ended for them at that time.

The best explanation of these denials, however, is to be found in the very special meaning given by Catholics to the language in which the denials are made. When a Catholic spokesman says that his church "is not in politics," he may not mean at all what non-Catholic Americans take him to mean. His own interpretation of his words, and a detailed statement of the Catholic Church's actual method of operation in politics, was published in 1926.

This statement was written by Count Guiseppi Dalla Torre, who is editor of the "Ossevatore Romano," the only paper directly controlled by the Vatican. He may therefore be considered as an unofficial spokesman for the Pope. Count Dalla Torre is also chairman of the "Azione Cattolica Italiana," an extremely interesting organization to which several references are made in the article. The organization corresponds in a general way with the Knights of Columbus and other Catholic secret societies outside of Italy, and its avowed purpose is to carry out policies of the Catholic Church in civil life. Pope Benedict XV referred to it as the "social branch of the Church," and Count Dalla Torre calls it the "social malitia of the Catholic Church," under ecclesiastical authority. The Count is therefore peculiarly well qualified to speak of Catholic political methods.

In his article he divides politics into two parts. As to the part which "concerns the art of government" he says:

"* * * because of the intimate connection between morality and religion,—which in the minds of believers are two inter-dependent terms,—we find that politics, which is also governed and disciplined by moral laws, is closely connected and interferes with religion and is therefore subject to another spiritual authority.

"According to Catholic logic, the Church, which is the custodian of religion, which interprets, teaches, and applies religious principles, which endeavors to bring morality and social life into conformity with its teachings, cannot ignore politics; neither can politics repudiate the guidance and the advice of the Church. * * *

"This can be summarized as follows: The Church does not exercise a political function; it exercises a moral and religious function; politics has a part in its program only when some political action reflects on moral and religious principles."*

This, of course, is the official Papal position with which we are already familiar. The Count tells us it is unchanged.

The second phase of politics he defines as "life, movement, the struggle among factions, and the development of their programs." Here he declares that the Church must stand aloof, "outside and above all political parties." He immediately proceeds to modify this doctrine, however, in the following statement:

"The Church therefore cannot descend into the arena of opposed parties, but it can take a stand against them when the rights of justice and truth are neglected or threatened. This, however, is not a case of political activity or party struggle, but the legitimate and dutiful action of the Church which always opposes injustice and error by whomsoever expressed or organized."

That is, the Catholic Church does go into party politics when it thinks wise!

Count Dalla Torre then proceeds to show how the Catholic Church, while "remaining out of politics," nevertheless directs Catholics in their political action. He says:

"Up to now we have spoken of the Catholic Church as such,—that is, regarded as the religious power existing beside the civil power in its own field of activity. But if we turn our discussion to the political parties themselves, and to the various currents of thought aroused by political activities, we come to a different and singular aspect of the problem, which is no less interesting. We no longer have to deal with the relations between Church and State, but with Catholic citizens in their relation to politics and parties. * * *

* The Forum, March, 1926.

"It is well known that the program of the last Popes, from Leo XIII to Pius XI, has called upon the Catholic laity to partake in a 'social action' the purpose of which is, under the guidance of the Church, to facilitate, often anticipate, and always integrate the aims of the sacred ministry. The laity was described by Pius XI as 'a quasi-participator' in the ministry, and Benedict XV referred to it as the 'social branch.' * * *

"While Catholic citizens in general are governed by so-called negative principles,—which means that they are not allowed to endorse and support anti-Christian programs,— the Catholics who belong to the *Azione Cattolica,*—that is, those who are members of special and independent Catholic associations,—have a purpose and a scope which is positive and which reveals the practical application of what has been said regarding the Church and its relation to politics and parties. * * *

"It does not abstain from political matters because, in the first place, being primarily an organization designed to mold the social conscience of the Catholic citizen, it must face politico-moral and politico-religious questions and indicate their solution; in the second place, because it is a defensive movement intended to safeguard the rights of the Church as well as moral and religious liberties, and must therefore enter the political field in which alone the defense can be operative, through legislation or legal representation, and in which, moreover, the most serious and decisive attacks and opposition are likely to originate. It would be absurd to reason otherwise, for then one would have to assume that the 'restoration of all things in Christ,' as set forth in the *"Omnia"* of Pius X, did not include the bringing of Christianity into public life."

In other words, Count Dalla Torre, unofficially the spokesman for the Vatican, very definitely interprets the commands of the Popes to mean political activity by Catholics in the interest of Catholicism. He lists the subjects on which this political activity takes place:

"The rights and liberties of the Church, the sanctity of the family bond, Christian education, and public morality are and will remain facts and problems of a moral and religious nature, even when their importance and urgency take them beyond the private or local jurisdiction of individuals and groups, and bring them into the scope of political institutions and State governments."

Count Dalla Torre cites two statements made by the present Pope in regard to this political activity as follows:

"The contribution, therefore, which you will bring to all political problems will be the best if you continue to be the best of Catholics."

"The *Azione Cattolica,* while not partaking in politics as such, intends to teach Catholics the best way of making use of politics. It offers the training demanded by every profession."

Count Dalla Torre further defines the purpose of the Catholic Church's secret societies as follows:

"In purely party matters the *Azione Cattolica* remains outside and above. Outside, because the triumph of its principles is not founded on the adoption of any specific political program; above, because its religious and moral character can bind together minds and energies which may be divided on material problems and party interests. The principles which govern the Church are extended therefore to this, its social vanguard. Its directors, like the Clergy, in order not to create a false impression as to the relation of the organization with the parties, have to abstain from active affiliation with any party. * * *

"In addition to its functions in forming the political conscience of Catholics, the *Azione Cattolica* exercises a defensive function through the action of individuals, that is to say, of 'militant' Catholics, who are not prevented from entering parties and who even find in them the only useful way of putting into practice the teachings of the *Azione Cattolica.* And in this case we may observe that a constant discipline binds the militant Catholic to the *Azione Cattolica* even in his political activities. * * *

"* * * through the supreme authority of the Catholic Church, and in its name by means of the *Azione Cattolica,* a practical and ideal function can develop without inter-

ruption, especially because the minds prepared in its ranks
can move and operate in the political field."

After all this the Count closes his article with
the standard denial; "the Church as such, with the
Azione Cattolica and with Catholics in general, does
not enter politics."

Here we have the whole story. The Catholic
Church is not in politics but its members are—organized by it, under its instructions, "bound by a
constant discipline." Priests and prelates do not
interfere in politics; they merely pull the strings
which send their political puppets into action under
their orders. Yet a Catholic believes that this fine-
spun and purely technical distinction justifies a
blanket denial of political activity by Catholicism!

There could hardly be a more complete statement than this by the Pope's spokesman, that
Roman Catholics in politics are subject to the
Pope's orders and are not permitted free will and
private judgment. This admission is almost unnecessary, since a Catholic's conscience is not only
trained but controlled by the Catholic Church and
would still determine his political actions, even if
he were allowed a technical freedom. But the
Catholic Church takes no chances and adds to its
control of conscience the direct political control
which Count Dalla Torre has described.

The Count reveals also the method of operation
of the Catholic Church in politics and shows another meaning of the assertion that it "is not in
politics" at all. This meaning is that it does not
join any particular party. That is, on all issues of
patriotism, prosperity and general public welfare
it remains aloof, ready to bargain with either side
and to throw support to that side which will pay
most heavily in the way of submission to Catholic

demands. In politics the voters whom the Pope can control work as Catholics but not as patriots!

In this country we are entirely familiar with this system. We know that any minority faction which can hold the balance of power between two major parties can often enforce its demands. We have seen special interests that could control either a balance in power of votes, or their equivalent in corruption money, dictate terms to both parties. We have seen it done by the saloon interests, and to some extent by their successors, the bootleggers, by the criminal element in large cities, by special financial interests. We have even seen it done by Catholics. We realize fully that by this means a minority is often able to impose its will upon an overwhelming majority.

Clearly, the Roman Catholic leaders realize this also, and have built their political policies to meet this situation. They are interested only in their own program and purposes—which, as we have seen, are hostile to American principles. For these policies they are prepared to take either side of any political question. There can be no doubt, for example, that if a Catholic had been nominated on the Republican instead of on the Democratic ticket in the 1928 campaign, the "Catholic vote" would have been Republican.

Thus, from the facts of European politics and from the explicit statement of the Pope's spokesman, we find that the Catholic Church controls the political action of its members in its own interests and regardless of all other interests. It does not permit a Catholic to be a patriot except so far as it benefits. What its purposes are in politics we shall see in our study of the conditions it imposed upon Italy by means of the recent Concordat.

CHAPTER XIX

PAPAL THEORY APPLIED TODAY

Pope himself disproves denials that Papal Theory is applied today—Lateran Accord enforces it on Italy—Carries out principles taught in American schools—The attempts to enforce
them also in Mexico—The claim to "juristic personality"—
Application in Italy shows present purposes—Re-establishes
temporal power and union of Church and State.

THE Papal laws on the relations of Church and
State and on the duties of Catholics as citizens,
and the instructions as to their political conduct,
are so clear and authoritative that it is surprising
any one should deny them or attempt to minimize
the opposition to Liberalism which they require.
Yet during the 1928 campaign and since many
Catholic propagandists, including Mr. Smith, have
denied that any conflict was possible between Catholicism and the modern State.

How much of their denials springs from their
own sincere ignorance, how much from their shrewd-
ly calculating on the ignorance of non-Catholics,
how much from political ambition or from Jesuitical
hypocracy, cannot be measured. Doubtless all factors are involved, but the peculiar attitude of
American Catholics toward this conflict will not
be taken up until a later chapter.

The immediately important point is that the
Pope himself, even before the echoes of the campaign
had died away, had given the lie to every protestation of his American apologists, and this to their
loudly expressed satisfaction. In the Treaty and
Concordat with Mussolini he showed the actual,
practical, modern attitude of the Papacy on almost

every point of the Roman policy toward the rights of nations and the liberties of citizens. At every point he established the theoretical, autocratic claims to supremacy just so far as he was able. If there is, as his American defenders claim, anything "medieval" or "outworn" or "from the limbo of forgotten controversies" in the Papal Theory today, it does not appear in these documents. They are a complete embodiment of theocratic autocracy in practical application.

However, it was not necessary for Americans to wait for the conclusion of the Lateran Accord, nor to look so far as Italy, to find complete refutation of the claims of Liberalism in American Catholicism.

They had before them the fact that all the doctrines of the Papal Theory are taught in American parochial schools and are laid down and supported in the Catholic Encyclopedia—an authorized and authoritative book of reference for all American Catholics. Surely it is hardly consistent with any claims of either Liberalism or Americanism for the American hierarchy to teach to American communicants doctrines so "inconsistent with the peace and safety of the State," as the following:

> *That it is "not lawful for the State to hold in equal favor different kinds of religion;"*
>
> *That it is not lawful for the State and the Roman Catholic Church to be separated;*
>
> *That toleration of other than the Roman Catholic religion is by favor or for expediency, and not by right;*
>
> *That intolerance is not merely the right, but the duty, of Roman Catholics:*
>
> *That the Pope has the right to annul American laws.*

Yet all these things are taught, not merely in the Encyclicals published in English, and in the Encyclopedia, but in the parochial schools. The following quotations are taken from the "Manual of Christian Doctrine," which has passed its 48th edition and so has reached at least a million Catholic children. It is official, bearing the *imprimatur* of Archbishop (Cardinal) Dougherty. It says:

"112. Why are the qualities of the Church superior to those of civil society, or the State?
Because the Church is a religious and supernatural society, while the State is temporal and natural. The Church is a universal, immutable, and an immortal society, while the State is particular, variable and temporal.

"113. Why is the Church independent of the State?
1—Because its origin, authority, object, and end are not from the State, but from Christ; 2—Because Christ willed that His Church, like Himself, should be independent of all earthly power.

"114. Why is the Church superior to the State?
Because the end to which the Church tends is the noblest of all ends.

"115. In what order or respect is the State subordinate to the Church?
In the spiritual order and in all things referring to that order.

"116. What right has the Pope in virtue of his supremacy?
The right to annul those laws or acts of government that would injure the salvation of souls or attack the natural rights of citizens.

"117. What more should the State do than respect the rights and liberties of the Church?
The State should also aid, protect, and defend the Church.

"118. On what is this duty founded?
On the obligation of civil society to profess religion. For, since nations come from the Creator, they owe Him, as nations, adoration, love, and obedience, just as do individuals.

"119. What then is the principle obligation of heads of States?

Their principle obligation is to practice the Catholic religion themselves, and, as they are in power, to protect and defend it.

"120. Has the State the right and duty to proscribe schism and heresy?

Yes, it has the right and the duty to do so both for the good of the nation, and for that of the faithful themselves, for religious unity is the principal foundation of social unity.*

"121. When may the State tolerate dissenting worships?

When these worships have acquired a sort of legal existence consecrated by time and accorded by treaties or covenants.

"122. May the State separate itself from the Church?

No, because it may not withdraw from the supreme rule of Christ.

"123. What name is given to the doctrine that the State has neither the right nor the duty to be united to the Church to protect it?

This doctrine is called **Liberalism.** It is founded principally on the fact that modern society rests on liberty of conscience and worship, on liberty of speech and of the press.

"124. Why is Liberalism to be condemned?

1—Because it denies all subordination of the State to the Church; 2—Because it confounds liberty with right; 3—Because it despises the social dominion of Christ, and rejects the benefits derived therefrom."**

* NOTE—The Manual, page 118, gives the following definitions:

"Heretics are such as, although baptized, reject one or more articles of faith taught by the Church, as Protestants.

"Schismatics are such as are separated from the Catholic Church, refusing to recognize and obey its lawful pastors." These are the people whom, it is taught, the State has the "right and duty to proscribe," that is, to outlaw.

** Manual of Christian Doctrine, Pages 131 and following.

This, in brief form, is the whole Ultramontane theory of the Papacy as applied to modern liberties. As the form in which it is written shows, it is no scholarly doctrine nor speculative philosophy, but is a law laid down for American children of small mental development. Surely this teaching, to such growing citizens, is enough of itself to disprove any claims to Liberalism on behalf of American Catholics!

If this were not enough to enlighten non-Catholic Americans, there is further disproof in the conflict between the Roman Catholic Church and Mexico, and the support given the Mexican hierarchy by American Catholics. To be sure the Mexican prelates always claimed that Mexico was "trampling" on the rights of the Church, but they meant only that it rejected Papal political rule. This is not a position that could be taken by anyone who believes in American principles. Even the Emperor Maxmilian, who failed to conquer Mexico, declared that he could not please the Mexican clergy and at the same time be a "just and liberal prince." In fact, the "trampling" consisted in an attempt to separate the Church and State, and end Papal Supremacy. There is no need to go at length into the controversy; the situation is sufficiently shown by the statement of William D. Guthrie, in an opinion written at the request of the Roman Catholic Hierarchy in America. He said:

"The Roman Catholic Church is not opposing the separation of Church and State in Mexico, provided that such separation be not a sham or a screen, and will leave the Church free to teach the Gospel, to educate children, and inculcate sound and true spiritual doctrine and moral rules of conduct, without dictation from or supervision by government officials."*

* New York Times, December 5, 1926.

That is, the Roman Church demanded a form of "separation" which would give her all the rights in education and politics demanded by the doctrine of Ultramontanism, and would conform to the theory of two co-ordinate jurisdictions. Further proof of this is found in Mr. Guthrie's denial that Mexico had any right to embody in her Constitution the provision that "the Mexican law recognizes no juridical (that is, juristic) personality in the religious institutions known as churches."

Let us pause a moment to consider this matter of juristic personality, as it is one which will shortly become important in the relations of the Roman Catholic Church and our own government. A "juristic personality" is a corporate legal entity—an artificial legal person—recognized by the law of the State. Usually it is that of a company or corporation, and it carries with it the right to hold property, appear at law, and perform other acts like those of any private person. It is created by the State and can be obtained only by conforming to the requirements of the State.

Now, what the Mexican Constitution provides is that churches have no such juristic personality, and none of the rights that go with them, unless these are enacted by law. What the Roman Church and Mr. Guthrie demand is that Mexico shall recognize such a personality without any authority from the State.

The practical effect of this claim by Rome was that, because of her insistence that she had a juristic personality independent of Mexican law, she would not obey the laws which required that churches submit to legal supervision, that priests be registered, and that the State must have a representa-

tive at certain religious services. All churches
except the Roman Catholic Church obeyed these
laws without difficulty or resentment. But the
Roman Church could not comply, for to do so
would have meant a surrender of her claim to
supremacy over the State.

That is, in defying Mexican law, the Catholic
Church was fighting to enforce its claim to supremacy. It is evident that if it could make good
its claim that it had an inherent juristic personality.
(that is, one which exists without authority from
the State) it would have an immense advantage
over all other churches. No other church claims
any inherent right to such personality; every one
derives its juristic personality from the express
assent of the State, and to this principle all other
churches give their full consent and approval. No
other condition is tolerable in a free State. If the
Roman Church could obtain the exceptional position it claims, it would thereby cut from under the
State all right and authority to provide perfect
civil equality for all churches, and thus to enforce
religious liberty.

Incidentally, the Roman Church has already
made the same claim under American law, and the
claim has been recognized insofar as its organization in the Phillipines is concerned. It is certain
to be one of the main points of conflict between
Romanism and the American government.

The fact that Rome rebelled against the Mexican laws, that it closed the churches and deprived
the people of religious instruction, and that it
even fomented armed rebellion against the Mexican
government, all rather than relinquish this advantage, should have been enough to show con-

clusively that it is still fighting for the enforcement of the whole Papal Theory. The fact that American Catholics supported it in spite of their protestations of Liberalism, should have been a sufficient lesson to American Liberals.

It is to the Lateran Accord, however, that we must turn for the latest and most complete lesson in the present purposes and practices of the Papacy. There is nothing theoretical about the Concordat. It definitely divides with the Italian State the civil government of forty million Italians. It very certainly does not in any respect go beyond the wishes of the Pope. It is—as nearly as he could make it— the embodiment of the principles he would enforce in modern government.

It is most enlightening. It had been nearly sixty years since any Pope had been able to rule any people directly. Much that was done by the last Pope who had this power has been forgotten, and the world has long needed to know what would happen in a State ruled according to the demands of modern Popes. The practical application of the Papal Theory to a nation had been confused by special pleas of the kind that marked the 1928 political campaign in America.

Now the Concordat has made Italy such a State —a government based upon the theory that the Pope is, by appointment of Almighty God, His sole representative on earth, infallible in matters of faith, supreme in matters of morals and conduct, independent of all human authority and subject to no human laws. Italy has become a nation ruled jointly by the Pope and the State; a living example of the political character of Roman Catholicism in practical operation. We are now able to set facts against such pleas as that of Archbishop Dowling that "so many conditions for its accomplishment are lacking in every government of the world that the thesis (of union of Church and State) may well be relegated to the limbo of forgotten controversies." "Conditions for its accomplishment" have proved *not* lacking in Italy. They may not be elsewhere, at present or presently.

When, during the recent campaign, American Catholics were asked to deny that they would support Papal Ultramontanism, men like Governor Smith replied that they fully supported the conflicting American principles (though they denied the conflict) and men like Professor Muzzey of Columbia said that "the Pope has been reduced from his sovereignty," "the medieval language in which he speaks is a gesture which is not enforced" and that "there is little cause to fear that the official pronouncements will take effect."

Thus Catholic apologists befogged the issue in many American minds. By the Lateran Accord with Mussolini the Pope has answered all questions by enforcing the full Papal Theory; American Catholics have approved almost unanimously. Thus the Catholics themselves have resurrected and defined the conflict for the modern world, have belied their own recent American propaganda and proved that their belief in Liberal ideas is limited to situations where they can benefit, and does not apply when non-Catholics might gain. We no longer need look to the past, or even to Papal documents, for full understanding of Catholicism. At last we have deeds, instead of evasive or obscurant words, and by its deeds we know the Roman Catholic Church of our own times.

The outstanding deed, of course, is the reassertion of the temporal and political power of the Pope through the creation of the Vatican State. The actual physical power gained naturally is of little importance: the Pope will have no army to use in political affairs. But two aspects of the Treaty which once more makes the Pope a temporal king are vital.

First is the re-assertion of the pontifical, political sovereignty of the Popes. This is the supposedly Divine Sovereignty, which the Pope claims over all Christians, and which he actually tries to exercise over the three hundred and thity million Catholics who are citizens of other nations. This Pontifical politico-religious sovereignty is the one which, under the Papal Theory, has the right to interfere in the affairs of all States, but is subject to no human law.

The re-assertion of this sovereignty proves that the historic claims of the Papacy have not been abated by one jot nor tittle; that they are not held as any idealistic philosophy, but that they are considered an immediate and Divine Right, to be asserted and enforced whenever and wherever it becomes possible. It proves that the Popes are not content with spiritual leadership, but are determined to wield political power. Romanists themselves proclaim this when they declare that the recognition of the temporal—that is to say, the political—power of the Pope is the vital point in the Treaty.

The second significance of the Treaty is that it gives the Pope—so far as Italy can give it—the power to enforce his will through politics, not only within Italy but internationally. Ever since Pius IX was driven from Rome by the armies of the

Italian republicans, the Popes have been working
with might and main to have their status as sovereigns restored, so that they would occupy by law
a place as a State among other sovereign States,
and not merely that of a religion among other religions. The archives of every chancellory in Europe are full of the records of these attempts—
Leo XIII even went so far as to support the French
republicans against his traditional friends the mon-
archists, in the hope that France would invade the
new Italian nation and give him back the Papal
States. The latest attempts were before the "Big
Five" at the Peace Conference of Versailles, and
before the League of Nations.

But what was refused by the European powers,
by the Peace Conference and by the League of Nations, has been granted by Mussolini alone. Under
the Treaty the Roman Catholic Church is now a
political power, with a purely temporal sovereignty
equal in international law to that of Great Britain
and of this country, and superior to that of Italy.

It is important, too, that by this Treaty there is
set up an alliance of despots, spiritual and temporal.
Mussolini stands for the denial of political freedom,
for reaction against all Liberal ideas and free government, in the same way that the Pope stands
against freedom in either religion, thought or government. But the absolutism of Mussolini is that
of the right of might; it is certainly temporary and
makes no overwhelming claims upon loyalty. It
will be changed in time with no violence to the
patriotism of Italians. On the other hand the
absolutism of the Papacy is that based on a claim
to Divine Right, and is maintained to be universal,
eternally unchangeable, and to demand the same

loyalty as is given to God Himself. It is natural that these two enemies of liberty should have allied themselves; it is typical of the Papacy that it should have used the temporary absolutism of Mussolini to cement the strength of its claim to eternal absolutism.

Thus in the Vatican Treaty the Pope has received from Mussolini a recognition of claims that have been rejected both in theory and in practice by every modern State, and a repudiation of the principle of "a free church in a free State" for which the liberators of modern Italy fought. Thus the temporal despot supports all claims of the politico-spiritual despot under the Papal Theory.

Far more than the subjection of Italians depends on this act. For the first time in centuries it marks a definite gain in political strength by the Papacy, for by it the Pope drives an entering wedge into the ideal and practice of human liberty, which had been growing on earth ever since Luther nailed his theses to the door of the church in Wurtemburg. For the first time since the massacre of the French Protestants on St. Bartholemew's Day and the repeal of the Edict of Nantes, he has crushed the liberties of a people. This Treaty marks the beginning of an actual return of the Papacy toward its medieval power; a start in the recovery of the ground that had been won from it in centuries of struggle by freemen. It is no wonder that the Roman Church rejoices. If one free nation can be subdued, why not others? Romanists see in this triumph a hope that they can destroy liberty in other peoples, and so march forward to complete sovereignty over the whole Christian world.

Chapter XX

THE PAPAL THEORY IN PRACTICE

Concordat measures subjection of Italians—State to enforce
Canon Law—Recognizes Divine Right of Roman Church—
Gives up right of freedom of religion—Enforces Catholic
education—Surrenders control of marriage—People given
no chance to pass on the Concordat—American Catholics
stultify their claims to Liberalism by endorsing suppression
of liberty—Aims of Romanism made clear.

ALTHOUGH the Vatican Treaty reveals much,
we must look to the Concordat to measure the
subjection which Mussolini and the Pope have
forced upon the Italian people. The whole document is based on the complete supremacy of Catholicism over the State. The Catholic religion has always been the official religion of Italy under the
Constitution, but it has never been enforced to the
satisfaction of the Popes. The Concordat agrees
that it shall be, through many specific provisions.

First of these is the official acceptance of the
Roman Canon Law by the Italian State, even to
the point of the enforcement of decisions of purely
ecclesiastical courts by the civil authorities. This
is a move toward the conditions under which the Inquisition delivered its victims to the "secular arm"
for burning, and although the Canon Law is more
or less recognized in most Catholic countries, there
is no other State which undertakes this extreme
medieval function under the supremacy of the Roman
Church. Of course there are many matters with
which the Canon Law does not deal, but from now
on, wherever Canon Law is laid down, Italy agrees
to accept and enforce it.

Along with this goes the recognition of the inherent juristic personality of the Roman Church—a matter with which we have already dealt in Mexico.* Italy does what Mexico refused—admits that the Roman Church has the right, without any grant of authority by the State and without the church's undertaking any duties to the State in return, to a corporate and legal existence. In this it accepts all the subjection which it has been shown was demanded of Mexico, surrenders its own rights, renounces the power to protect other religions, and gives to the Pope the right of decision in case of conflicts.

Under the supremacy of the church the first provision—and naturally so under the Papal policy—is the destruction of religious freedom. As Mussolini announced:

"The old liberal doctrine of separation between Church and State comes to be abandoned. We renounce considering the Catholic Church as a private association under common law, with religion a problem of individual conscience."

Article I guarantees to the Roman Church "free exercise of spiritual power" which, in view of what is claimed by the Popes under their "right of spiritual power," means sub-ordinating to the control of the Pope every other church and every form of belief or unbelief in Italy. Such toleration as is granted can only be that defined by Leo,** based upon expediency but not on right, and to be revoked whenever expediency permits.

It is true that Mussolini announced that other religions would not be interfered with, but there is

* See Page 214.
** See Page 132.

no legal guarantee of this and no recognition of any natural or moral right for them to exist. The Pope denies that they have such rights, and to grant them would be contrary to Canon Law and to other implications of the Concordat. Neither the Pope-King nor the Dictator would dare offend the whole civilized world by reviving the Inquisition or by driving dissenters out of Italy entirely, but their safety in future rests wholly in the hands of the Pope himself—their avowed enemy.

This contemptuous tolerance which he allows is far from religious freedom, as Americans understand it. The whole spirit of the Concordat, as well as the Roman dogmas, deny any liberty of conscience and bind the Pope and the Dictator to enforce Romanism so far as they dare. Thus the Pope, once more, applies in practice the Papal dogma of intolerance. This principle is among those declared by American Catholics to be pure theory or outworn gesture, but in Italy it is today in working order; quite clearly it will be applied whenever the Pope has the power and so far as he deems it expedient.

In spite of Mussolini's assurances, the Pope goes far with its enforcement under the Concordat. Certainly one of the essential factors in religious freedom is the right to bring up one's children in the faith of their fathers, and to assure freedom for future generations. The Pope has denied that right in Italy, both in theory and in practice. The Concordat provides for "religious instruction" in schools —that is, for the teaching of Catholicism with all its political and social anti-Liberalism.

Americans were assured by Catholics in this country that this provision would not be applied

to the children of non-Catholics. As Dr. Leo
Francis Stock, President of the American Catholic
Historical Association, stated in "Current History:" "There will be no religious coercion, since
pupils who are not Catholics will natually be
excused from Catholic instruction."* Dr. Stock
was mistaken. Signor Belluzzo, the Italian minister
for Public Instruction, sent out a circular regulating
the schools in accordance with the Concordat.
Teachers are to be trained by the ecclesiastical
authorities, who will decide which are fit to give
such instruction—in other words what teachers
may be promoted.

There is not a word in this circular allowing
any children of any kind to be withdrawn from the
religious instruction.** There are few Protestants in
Italy, a few more Jews; revolt against Papal rule
there has mostly taken the form of free-thinking.
There are millions of free-thinkers in the nation,
including many of the teachers; about 25 per cent
of the nation are not Catholic. Under the regula-
lations laid down the children of all three classes
must be trained in Catholic thought—the parents
may have religious toleration for themselves, but
there is to be no religious or mental freedom for the
children. And, under Roman law, even if some
concession should be made to Protestants and Jews
—which "expediency" may force upon the Pope—
the free-thinkers will be considered in law as merely
"rebellious children" of the Roman Church, and
therefore no freedom is allowed them or their children. Incidentally, these regulations also lay upon
free-thinking teachers a heavy price for continued
freedom; they must abandon their profession!

*Current History, April, 1929, Page 17.
** The Nation, July 3, 1929.

What this amounts to we may best realize if we imagine the outcry that would go up from American Catholics if Protestant religious instruction were made compulsory in our public schools, and Catholics were required to make their children attend the religious classes. Imagine the louder outcry if Catholic teachers were required to learn from Protestant ministers how to teach religion, and were then compelled either to teach it or to give up their teaching! The Pope's action in regard to Italian education shows clearly what is the purpose of the Roman Church in every country where it may get the power to enforce its ideals. Certainly this purpose is not in accord with American principles; certainly it shows no weakening or modernization of the Papal Theory. In actual practice the Pope has destroyed the religious liberty of millions of unborn children, deprived them of all right to free thought or to free search for truth, and made sure that most will become useful servants of the hierarchy. And he has done this to the children of Protestants, Jews and free-thinkers, as well as Catholics.

Religious liberty is still further suppressed by giving the Roman Church jurisdiction over all Christian marriages. This puts the whole control of all family relations ultimately into the hands of the Pope. Through this means it will even more effectively control the State, enforce the loyalty of its present membership and increase its numbers at the expense of the non-Catholic minorities.

Under the Concordat, it is true, civil law is still recognized for the marriage of non-Catholics, but no civil marriage of a Catholic is legally valid. Hitherto the State has required civil marriage even for Catholics; now under Canon Law marriage by any priest is valid, even without civil sanction. Undoubtedly in regard to marriage, as with education, free-thinkers will be considered Catholics, so that for them all freedom in regard to marriage is denied. An enormous pressure will be brought to bear even upon Protestants and Jews. The Roman Church declares that their marriages are mere "legal concubinage" and have no validity. It has the right to teach this to all Italian children—to teach non-Catholic children that their parents' marriages were not sacred—and to brand such marriages before the law!

Under the Concordat it is the Church courts which have the sole right to pass on the validity of any marriage, including those of all non-Catholics. The State is bound to enforce their decrees. Thus the Roman Church can, when it chooses, deny that any Protestant or Jewish marriage is valid; it can deny the validity of all the marriages which have taken place under the Italian civil law without priestly sanction, although they were valid when contracted. It can annul thousands of marriages which have been legal, therefore, at the mere request of either party. It can repeat a thousand times over all the usurpations of the rights of individuals and of other churches which marked the decision of the Rota in the Marlborough case.* It establishes a powerful social persecution of non-Catholics.

Another important fact about the Papal attitude shown by the Lateran Accord is that the Pope is actively involved in national politics—something which American Catholics have also denied. The

*See Page 95.

Treaty and Concordat constitute in fact a political alliance in national affairs. One proof of this is that Mussolini is given the right to veto the appointment of any Italian bishop if his political qualifications are not satisfactory, and that all such bishops are required to swear allegiance to Italy.

Another proof is that, in the election which immediately followed the signing of the Concordat, Catholic priests and laymen for the first time worked actively for Mussolini's candidates, and that these were elected by a majority of about 99 per cent.

The fact is that the continuance of the Concordat depends upon the continued power of Fascism. It is certain that one of the first acts of any Liberal government—which would be the only kind that could defeat Mussolini—would be to repeal the Concordat and restore the principles of freedom. It is probable that no such government, however, would seek to repeal the Treaty, which removes the long irritation caused by the Pope's fiction that he was a "prisoner in the Vatican," and by his opposition to the Italian government as a whole. So the Pope's interest in maintaining the Concordat forces him to support Fascism. Pius XI has gone even further—he has publicly warned Italy in his letter of June 5, 1929, that if the Concordat should be repealed he would revoke the Treaty, and thus again become a thorn in the side of Italy. Thereby he gives notice that he will punish Italy if it elects any government hostile to his policies—which means hostile to Fascism.

Finally, and not least important, is the consideration that all these Italian liberties were surrendered to the Pope without the consent of the Italian nation. In spite of the present strength of

Fascism, no one can for a moment believe that Liberalism in Italy is wholly dead, that the spirit of Garibaldi has utterly disappeared, that none of its citizens has any consideration for the rights of the millions of non-Catholics and the greater millions of unborn children. Yet Italian citizens were given no chance to pass upon Treaty or Concordat, and no one can claim that their formal acceptance by a Parliament selected almost to a man by Mussolini, in any way represents the opinion of the Italian nation. It may be that there are enough subjects of the Pope in Italy to have given a majority approval to the Accord, but no one knows. The significant thing is that neither Mussolini nor the Pope took any trouble to find out. Mussolini bartered away the people's liberty; the Pope joyfully accepted the betrayal. This, too, is logical under the Papal Theory, which disposes of the rights of the governed with the curt phrase "all public power must proceed from God."—i. e., the Pope.

The Accord with Mussolini has shown the real Papacy. It has again proved what most of the world already knew—that the Papacy never changes except to increase and define more rigidly its Ultramontane claims, purposes and laws. Even Catholics admit the growing demands of the Pope. Father Wilfrid Parsons, writing in "America," the Jesuit weekly, said for example:

"The Concordat which follows will appear to those who are not familiar with such instruments as a remarkable document. As a matter of fact there is much in it which is new, especially some matters peculiar to Italy, and *the regulations on marriage and education, which go far beyond former Concordats in their generosity* and will no doubt be a model for future ones with other States."

This "generosity," of course, consists in giving up human liberty to Papal control!

In short, the fate of Italy proves that, so far from
being more Liberal than before, the Papacy is less
so, that it is beginning to recover some of the
ground it lost after the Reformation and is magnifying its claims accordingly; that the Papal Theory
is a working program which the Popes constantly
extend and enforce by any and every means in their
power, regardless of the will and desires of the
people. It proves that today, as always, the Roman
Catholic Church, both in theory and in practice,
officially:

> *Refuses tolerance to any other religion except as a
> matter of temporary expediency;*
>
> *Denies freedom of thought, conscience or search for
> the truth;*
>
> *Deprives children of their right to free thought and
> knowledge;*
>
> *Interferes deeply in politics;*
>
> *Seeks control of all nations where it has a chance
> of success;*
>
> *Opposes all Liberal doctrines in all nations except
> where it may gain temporary benefit from them;*
>
> *Will use whatever power it can get to enforce its
> despotism and doctrines;*
>
> *Will control education and marriage so far as it
> can for this purpose;*
>
> *Will accept any violation of the rights of freemen
> by which it can benefit.*

The most dismaying thing about the whole affair to Americans is that American Catholics, who
in 1928 acclaimed Governor Smith's statement that
he believed "in the equality of all churches, all
sects, and all beliefs before the law as a matter of

right and not as a matter of favor," in the Spring of 1929 also acclaimed the Pope's violation of this equality in Italy.

They have given certain defenses for their approval of the Pope, to be sure. They claim that Italy has a right to make her own laws. That is true, but Italy did not make this one—the Pope and Mussolini made it. They point out that other countries maintain established churches. This is true, too, but not one of them attempts the tyranny or the denial of liberty which have been fastened upon Italy. Even if they did, the fact of one political crime would not excuse another.

They claim, finally, that the Concordat and Treaty affect Italy alone and are none of our affair. If this were true, there would be no reason for the rejoicing of American Catholics over the triumph of the Vatican! But it is not true in any way. The Papacy is an international and universal organization, and any triumph in one nation strengthens it for triumphs in others. But directly and immediately, with the present vast interchange and movement between nations, the suppression of liberty and of Liberal principles in one nation must in some degree tend to the suppression of them in all nations. From now on it is certain that every Italian who comes to our shores will be an enemy of American Liberalism. Thus in general and in detail, the whole cause of Liberalism has suffered. Is not that chiefly why American Catholics rejoice?

If liberty, and especially religious liberty, depend upon keeping the Roman Catholics from political power, then our American liberties are seriously threatened by Roman Catholic political activity. We cannot be secure so long as they hold, no matter with what temporary reservations, to the Papal Theory. What happened to Italy proves that liberty, to be safe, must rest upon the convictions of the whole people, and on their *full* loyalty to the ideal of equality, tolerance and liberty within the civil State. When a minority of the voters of any State is under control by an alien politico-religious sovereignty which denies the principles on which that State is founded, then it needs only the changing of that minority into a majority, to outlaw those principles as they have been outlawed in Italy.

American Catholics have shown their approval of this so far as Italy is concerned. They have endorsed the propositions of the Popes which have already been quoted. American Protestants are anxious to know whether this quotation from Leo XIII's Encyclical on "Human Liberty" expresses equally accurately their present attitude toward American principles:

"* * * although, in the extraordinary condition of these times, the Church usually acquiesces in certain modern liberties, not because she prefers them in themselves but because she judges it expedient to permit them, she would in happier times exercise her own liberty."*

The "happier times" have come for the Papacy in Italy. The Popes urge all Catholics to work for them everywhere. It seems that we in America are forced to believe that American Catholics will bring just this kind of "happier times" upon us here if they can.

* The Great Encyclical Letters of Leo XIII, Page 158.

CHAPTER XXI

THE POPE AND INTERNATIONALISM

Pope's new role as world leader for peace—Former supra-national
power of the Papacy—Its debasement to mere international
meddling—Recent instances of this in American affairs—
Lateran Accord gives Papacy the legal position of a nation—
Catholic rhapsodies as to Pope's impartiality—Facts of his
international interests—Boring within the League of Nations—
The Propaganda for diplomatic relations—Pope's ambition to
be world arbiter—Weakness of his claim to impartiality—
His alliance with Fascism a threat to America—Present
policy aims at restoration of medieval power.

THE single instance in which the Papacy seems
at first glance to have changed since medieval
times and to be more or less in harmony with the
high purposes of our own time, is in the international field. The present great desire for peace
and the claim of Catholics that the Pope can aid
in attaining it, make the international position and
policy of the Papacy so important as to deserve a
chapter to themselves.

The Roman Church insists that it is universal
and therefore impartial as between nations. There
was a time when at least the claim to universality
was justified, for under the Holy Roman Empire the
Catholic Church was in fact supreme throughout
Western Europe. At that time the church, claiming
divine authority over all men, and acting as the
political heir of Imperial Rome, delegated to temporal rulers that share which concerns purely civil
affairs, while reserving the right to intervene—as it
frequently did. This theocracy was later split up
into nations which, from the Catholic point of view,
really still belonged to the Holy Empire. The
Catholic Church holds that this theocratic empire

has never been rightfully impaired. The Pope has never admitted that his claim to moral authority does not give him complete right to control all temporal rulers—to be Ceasar as well as Pope.

Under the supremacy which began with the great Pope Gregory VII, Popes actually exercised a considerable authority over nations. Innocent III, for example, declared void the liberties which King John of England had granted in Magna Carta and which have become the foundation of political freedom. Sixtus V instructed Phillip II of Spain to send his "Invincible Armada" to destroy Protestantism and the growing freedom in England. This primacy disappeared for all practical purposes when the Protestant nations defeated the Catholic attempt to subdue them. From that time on the international relations of the Pope were merely those of a petty Italian prince, ruling an insignificant State, together with such slight moral influence over Catholic rulers as had been left by the spread of Liberal ideas. This influence could not be backed by physical force and was often without power.

Since that time the Papal international policy has hardly been worthy of a more dignified name than that of meddling. The Pope, to be sure, took part in the formation of the Holy Alliance, in which other European autocrats joined with him to prevent the further spread of Liberal ideas and democratic institutions. This project was defeated by the passive opposition of England and the active opposition of the United States. The proclamation of the Monroe Doctrine, with England's support, prevented the re-conquest of the Latin-American republics, which had been a chief objective of the Alliance.

Another instance of Papal international meddling came when Pius IX inspired the invasion of Mexico by the Austrian Prince Maximillian, supported by the soldiers of Napoleon III. The object was to bring Mexico once more under complete Papal control and undo the work of the revolutionary Liberal Juarez. This attempt was also defeated by the United States when the close of the Civil War freed the hands of the government and permitted us to warn France that we were again able to enforce the Monroe Doctrine.

The latest case of this kind which effects the United States was the attempt to force this country to intervene in Mexico in support of the Papal claims in that country. These, as set forth by William D. Guthrie, counsel for the Roman Catholic Hierarchy, include the supremacy of the church over the State, a juristic personality for the church independent of State law, the right to determine for itself what doctrines it shall teach and exclusive spiritual rights above those of any other church.

Two definite attempts were made by American Catholics to force action by this government. The most open and avowed was the great effort of the Knights of Columbus. This Catholic political organization demanded that our government should intervene in Mexico in defense of what it called "rights of conscience." This was a wholly un-American demand since Romanism actually insisted upon power to enforce its own conscientious intolerance, and there could be no possible excuse for American intervention in behalf of any alien power; still the Knights of Columbus had the right to petition Congress for anything they desired. This attempt failed because of the immediate outburst of non-Catholic opinion; an outburst which the Catholics have never quite understood.

Next in order came the attempt by the Holy Name Society, which professes to be purely religious. It sent a representative to Congress and in a secret hearing before a committee of the House threatened Catholic reprisal against individual congressmen unless intervention in Mexico took place. The record of this threat was kept from the public through Catholic influence. Other similar attempts were made to bring pressure by Catholic individuals. This agitation continued until the meeting of the American Episcopate, which in long and secret deliberation considered the entire anti-Catholic reaction which had been caused. It finally issued a letter which said that the Roman Church asked for no "human action" against Mexico, but which then went on to use every possible argument and appeal to inflame the minds of Americans against Mexico and so prepare the way for human action.

There was no reason for this letter except to turn public opinion toward intervention. It was, in fact, a propaganda of inflamation and an attempt to use the United States as a cat's-paw for Rome. The Roman Church issues such letters only when there is hope of producing action. A similar letter in Alsace almost caused a revolt against the French government on the school question. No such letter was issued here in regard to the persecution in Russia, although one was fully justified in that case.

The Catholic attempt to force American action in regard to Mexico was not finally abandoned until after the defeat of the Catholic candidate for president in 1928. One more abortive rebellion took place there but failed for lack of American support.

Thereafter the Catholic Church accepted the Mexican laws and announced that it would henceforth seek a peaceful settlement.

These instances go far to show the petty position to which Papal international politics had been reduced until Pius XI reached an agreement with Mussolini. Now, thanks to that agreement, the Pope has suddenly appeared in a new guise as the friend of internal peace, supposedly holding an unique position because of his supra-national status. This opens a new era in Papal diplomacy.

The world is seeking a way to insure peace without a sacrifice of rights, through arbitration, the League of Nations and the Kellogg Peace Treaty. The tendency is toward some such supreme tribunal as that described by Tennyson as a "parliament of man, a federation of the world." Catholic spokesmen claim that the Pope can aid greatly. The claim is plausible enough for shallow thinkers, since the ideal of a supreme power to bring peace and justice has long been voiced by the Popes. The claim falls on willing ears because it seems to accord with current aspiration.

In fact the Pope might help if it were not for one Catholic stipulation in regard to his supreme power which the Roman Catholics take pains not to mention. This is that the Pope holds inherent supremacy by divine right, and without reference to any human authority. Of course international law and international justice are "human authority," the Pope thus rejects the basis on which the world is acting; but so long as this one provision of Catholicism can be kept out of sight, his international claims commend themselves to all lovers of peace. His true position, however, is not international but supra-national, and he is seeking international power by expressing that desire for peace which is shared by all, and by neglecting to mention his claim to divine supremacy, which is the vital point in the whole situation and which is denied by all modern nations except Italy.

The fact that the Pope has any international political standing whatever is due to the creation of an actual temporal sovereignty in the Vatican City. By this means the Pope has become, in international law, a nation, with a right to apply for a seat in the League of Nations, to ask diplomatic relations with all other nations and so forth.

The creation of the Vatican City was hailed immediately by Catholics all over the world as a prelude to the Pope's becoming a supreme judge in international affairs. This was stated in the Pope's official organ, the "*Osservatore Romano*," by Count Dalla Torre, the Pope's official spokesman, as follows:

"The Catholic Church is not a national church, but a universal society and to the head of that society men of all nationalities owe the same spiritual allegiance."*

In this country it was set forth by Dr. Leo S. Stock, President of the American Catholic Historical Association, who said:

"But it is conceivable that he who now rules a spiritual kingdom of over 300,000,000 hearts will in time be considered as the ideal mediator in international disputes. Now that the temporal possessions have practically been surrendered, his position as arbiter would exclude all idea of hostility, rivalry, domination or conquest. His very humbleness should make his mediation acceptable. * * *

"With a government so politically weak as the Vatican City, the ordinary reasons for diplomatic intercourse will

* Time, March 18, 1929.

probably not exist. There are, however, other phases which may be given consideration. The dual nature of the Pope as civil ruler of his dominion and head of the Universal Church might conceivably *simplify negotiations with Catholic nations,* through diplomatic representation at the Papal court. Problems arising between the United States and Latin-American countries, for example, might more readily find settlement at the Vatican City."*

That is to say, the Pope will put *political* pressure on Catholic countries if we will deal with him! A little later Wm. F. Montavon, director of the legal department of the Catholic Welfare Conference, expanded the same views. He said:

"There remains, however, the fact that there has been added to the family of sovereignties a new member. How will she be received? The answer is already in evidence. The Holy See, even before the Treaty, was recognized as a sovereign, equal in rank with themselves, by a large number of States. The diplomatic corps accredited to the Vatican is already an important body. Its interest is not alone in problems of a higher order, problems of morality, of conscience, of culture. The Catholic Church differs from other Churches in being an organic body, world wide in extent, presided over by a central administrative head, the Holy See. Governments of non-Catholic as well as of Catholic nations, interested in the spiritual welfare of their citizens, have found it useful, even necessary, to be in direct relation with the supreme head of the Church.

"With the new freedom which will flow from the Treaty and the openly accepted sovereignty of the Holy See, it requires no flight of fancy to vision in Vatican City a diplomatic corps, composed of men not immersed in the intrigues and bargainings of a materialistic world, whose activities will centre around the higher interests of the soul and be devoted to the promotion of international peace, of justice, of the well-being of man based on international co-operation and not on international rivalry.

"Where is there to be found an atmosphere in which the spirit of conciliation between nations will thrive as it

* Current History, April, 1929, Page 16.

will in the atmosphere of Vatican City? In the perfect independence that comes from sovereignty, with no conflicting currents of a local character, political, economic, or social, to distract and divert the minds of men, Vatican City presents itself without peer as a place where controversies may be brought with confidence that here the disputants will be free in their discussion, able to find in the Holy Father a friend worthy of their trust, eminently fitted to reconcile divergent views and aid them in the just solution of their differences."*

It must be remembered that the Papacy did not preserve peace when it was supreme. Also, that some nations will consider that not even peace is worth "international co-operation" *under Papal Supremacy*. Moreover, the truthfulness of this beautiful picture must be considered in the light of the fact that the Papacy has definite temporal interests all over the world, a rather definite alliance with Fascist Italy and certain other political friendships as well as a natural partiality for Catholic countries; also, that the Pope and his subjects would consider him a judge with divine powers superior to any human law and free to decide just as he pleased. Finally, since the enforcement and enlargement of Papal Supremacy come before all other considerations with him, it can be expected to control all his judgments. Therefore, we must believe that any "judicial" power given the Pope would be used to cripple Liberalism and weaken Liberal nations.

It has been both stated and denied that the Vatican would demand a seat in the League of Nations. So far all independent States as small as the Vatican City have been denied admission, but no statesman doubts that if the Pope should apply he would be admitted because of his influence on the Catholic

* Current History, July, 1929. Page 544 and following.

powers. The discussion has been an attempt to find out what the effect of such an action would be on public opinion.

It is likely, also, that the Vatican recognizes the difficulties which would confront it as a member of the League. First, it would make it practically impossible even for the most adroit apologists of the Papacy to claim any distinction between its spiritual and political authority. In view of the open political activities of the Papacy in so many countries, however, this would have little influence. Second, the League often has to deal with countries divided in their religious faith. In these countries almost every important political question has a religious implication and any decision by the League would effect the religious situation in that country. If an agent of the Pope were involved as a member of the League it might seriously complicate the Papal policy.

Most important, perhaps, is that if the Pope became a member of the League it would greatly hamper the movement to make him "the ideal mediator in international disputes." As a member he would be in some degree bound by the actions of the League, in spite of his rejection of all human authority, and his freedom of action would be greatly hampered. By remaining outside the League, he would be able to asseverate his claim to impartiality and supremacy.

Whether or not the Pope remains outside the League, there is no question that the hierarchy is seeking all possible influence inside the League. A revelation of its attitude—and of the political interests of Romanism—was made in an article by the Jesuit Wilfred Parsons.   Speaking of the activities of the League he said:

"The Catholic traveler is naturally curious to hear how all these various organizations affect the Church.   It is clear at the outset that since their activities cover practically every branch of human welfare, they must cut across the religious, cultural, humanitarian, missionary and educational life of the Church at many points.   And such, I was informed, is the very interesting and somewhat alarming fact.   *The Church is working in almost all of the fields which the League of Nations has taken for its own.*   Moreover, in nearly every case, it is the moral aspect of life, not merely the political, with which the League is dealing in its various branches.   The problems of childhood, of population, of marriage, of woman and child labor, the white-slave trade, the narcotic plague, slavery, alcoholism, college and university life—the League of Nations is working over every one of these and many more besides, and so is the Church.

"When one asks the natural question, just how much legitimate influence does the Church exercise in all these discussions of the League, one comes across some very remarkable facts.   The Permanent Secretary of the League itself, Sir Eric Drummond, is a practicing Catholic.   Many of the delegates in the Assembly and Council are Catholics, some of them practicing.   Practically all the auxiliary commissions and committees I listed above have Catholic members on them.   Moreover, each one of these bodies possesses what are called "assessors," or technical advisers, and many of these assessors are Catholics also.

"Are these Catholics active?   The traveler is likely to be nothing if not persistent, once he hears a fact like this.   Here again one gets a shock.   In many cases these Catholics could not be active if they liked.   They are merely delegates; they merely bear a message from their Government and their duty is to see that that message is heeded.   Whether the message is consonant with Catholic principles or not, is not their affair precisely.   That point is settled in the Cabint at home, and how the Cabinet settles the matter depends almost altogether on *the degree of Catholic influence brought to bear on it by the Catholic*

voters in each country. I wondered how much alive to this fact are the Catholics in the various member nations of the League, particularly the Catholic countries. Very little can ultimately be known to give a definite answer to my question until that fact is established. But a good deal of the world's immediate future depends on the answer that is made.

"There is, however, one class of League servants who could, if they would, exercise a very considerable influence to see that right and reason and Christian (Catholic) principles prevail, or at least are heeded. This is the class of assessors, who come from the great national and international beneficent societies. It is in their deliberations that the final decisions of the League have their germ. It is difficult, however, to discover just how widespread is the play of Catholic principles here; ***to judge from what has come out of the League, the picture is not entirely discouraging.*** But imagine the responsibility of Catholics in countries which are members, to see that they are properly represented!"*

If this description and assertion are even partly truthful, it will be seen how enormous may be the Pope's influence on the League of Nations through his control of the consciences of its Catholic officials and through his control of the citizens of the nations which those officials represent.

The demand of American Catholics that this country should exchange ambassadors with the Pope burst with great vigor and then subsided with almost equal suddenness, probably because the propaganda had over-reached itself in so many respects. It included a vast amount of half truths and actual lies which were very promptly found out. It had declared that England always maintained an ambassador at the Vatican, although the truth is that she has had one there only since during

* America, March 9, 1929, Page 523.

the World War, when Papal intrigues with the German powers forced her to seek diplomatic protection in that way. Catholics also said that before the fall of the Papal States in 1871 this country had a minister there. There is a grain of truth behind this. We had, not a minister, but a consul-general, sent to the Papal States to represent American business interests. We have never had any diplomatic relations with an infallible pontifical sovereign, and we can not do so without violating the principle of the separation of Church and State.

Another line which the Roman propaganda took was shown in the following quotation from a clip-sheet sent by Rome's press agents to newspapers:

"In view of the fact that the United States controls the destinies of millions of Catholics and that not infrequently questions of administration arise the settlements of which could be expedited by direct negotiation, as a practical matter it might be to the advantage of the United States to have its spokesman at the Holy See."

This statement betrays the whole situation. It shows that the Papacy seeks diplomatic relations with America, not in the interests of the Papal State, but as an international financial organization and for the purpose of affecting its subjects who are living in the United States and of being able to represent them as a whole before our government and to bring pressure to bear upon our government in their name. Now, under American law there can be no such thing as a dual citizenship or loyalty. If a Catholic is legally a subject of the Pope he cannot be an American citizen. If he is an American citizen, then no foreign power whatever has any right to represent him or any interest of his in any dealings with our government. There can be no question concerning "the destinies of millions of Catholics" in this country which the Vatican or any foreign power has any right to take up with our government through diplomatic channels. When Catholics in this country plead that their being here requires diplomatic relations between our country and the Papacy, they admit that they stand in a relation to the Vatican which definitely compromises their relation with America as citizens.

This country cannot enter into diplomatic relations with the Pope, therefore, without conceding his right to political rights over American Catholic citizens and thereby surrendering to him a large part of American sovereignty. Fortunately, since the visit of the Papal Legate to the President, it seems certain that this demand of the Catholics has failed. We may be certain that the result would have been very different if we had a Catholic president! This fact and the fact that American Catholics felt justified in demanding diplomatic relations, show how curious is their understanding of American principles.

One of the most important phases of the international Papal policy based on temporal sovereignty is the plan to become a rival of the World Court as supreme arbiter of the world in international relations. From all quarters come rosy pictures of the great force for peace which the Pope would be as a supreme judge to nations. It would be hard to concoct a more absurd scheme, especially on the point made by Mr. Stock, that the Pope would be particularly fitted to handle the problems arising between the United States and the Latin-American countries which are Catholic.

This country conducts its international relations under international law and we expect any issue which comes up to be adjudicated under that law. But the Pope does not recognize international law as binding upon him in any way—international law is one form of "human authority."

Worst of all, the Pope has subjects in every civilized country, and through the interests of his subjects he would be a party to almost every international issue. Could he be expected to hold an even scale of justice between a Protestant country like the United States, England, or Germany and a Catholic country like Spain or Italy? Moreover, in Austria, Poland and the Balkans, both Italy and the Papacy have aggressive policies which would be inevitably involved in any disputes arising there. Finally, the Pope by his compact with Mussolini has quite definitely allied himself with the interests of Fascism. All this is in addition to his own desire to establish his own political supremacy!

Would the Pope decide on questions affecting the interests of subjects of the Catholic nations, and particularly of Italy, in the interest of abstract justice? Or of Italy? Or of the Papacy? And as to all Catholic countries: Whose interests would their own representatives support when they came before the Pope? Jugo-Slavia has sent a Roman priest as its minister to the Vatican. Does he represent his country or his Pope? Or is he in fact to become part of the diplomatic body at the Vatican which aims at world control?

Another point—in "Current History," for April, 1929, John Hearly, who was assistant to Thomas Nelson Page when the latter was Ambassador at Rome, gives evidence that during the World War the Vatican protected men who were active German spies. In case this country became involved with any Catholic nation, could we expect anything but that every Papal agent in this country would act as a spy for our enemies? And what could we expect from our own Catholic citizens? We know that the Papacy maintains that its own interests impose on Catholics claims and duties superior to those of their own country.

We have not yet covered the whole of the Pope's ambitions in the international field. As with his relations to individual nations, so in this, the true position of the Vatican is revealed in his Treaty with Italy. Article II of that Treaty declared that Italy expressly agreed to recognize the supernatural claims of the Holy See in international relations. Thereby Italy accepts the supremacy of the Pope so far as its contacts with other nations are concerned, and binds itself to carry out in the international field the policy of the Vatican. It is true that by Article XXIV the Pope agrees that he will not take part in *temporal* disputes between States unless the contending parties request it, but by this very provision the Pope reserves the right to intervene at his own pleasure in disputes which are not temporal, that is, which involve morals. International law is international morals. So we have an alliance between the Pope and the Dictator which definitely and openly is intended for operation in international affairs. The impact of this alliance upon the civilized world may become tremendous.

In the first place Italy has committed itself to a policy which must be rejected by every non-Catholic nation. No State can assent to sovereignty of any kind in the Pope in international relations, nor can recognize his right to participate in them without the surrender of its rights by assenting to Papal

Supremacy. In the second place, the Treaty agrees that Italy will support the Pope internationally "in conformity with its traditions and with the demands of its mission in the world." Many of the darkest pages of history spring from these "traditions and demands."

More important, as a result of this Treaty we must henceforth consider the Papacy as an ally of Fascism in international affairs as well as in Italy. This has a definite danger for America. Mussolini has publicly announced his hostility to this country—not while he was negotiating debts and loans, to be sure, but in earlier utterances. He pictured America as a materialistic monster that must be destroyed. He declared that control over both trade and culture was swinging to us, and that for the salvation of Europe this must be stopped. He predicted war between us and Japan and went out of his way to be friendly to Japan. He forecast another world war by 1935 and demanded an Italian army of 5,000,000 and a vast air fleet, but did not say against whom he intended to use it. Finally, as late as June 6, 1928, he said to the Italian Senate:

"American initiative seems determined to conquer Europe. * * * It is impossible to foresee to what point the bow of American desire for power will be bent, **or what resistance it may encounter.**"

There is no need to repeat the evidence that the Papacy also looks with hostile eyes upon America as the most powerful Protestant State.

We may be sure, too, that the allied absolutists will stir up Latin-America against us and against the Monroe Doctrine. Opposition to this Doctrine is a policy of Mussolini's through the Fascist societies he has established in Latin-America; it has been a policy of the Papacy since the days of the Holy Alliance.

The whole tendency of this new Papal program was set forth by Robert Sencourt. He said:

"There can be no question of the Pope's determination * * * to do everything possible to solidify peace in Europe along the lines of what he has from the first declared to be the motto of his reign: 'The peace of Christ in the reign of Christ.' In the autumn of 1926 he instituted the new feast of 'Christ the King,' and it would only be reasonable to expect that this movement, in which the Pope has already shown himself so vigorous in the matter of the *Action Francaise,* would find its completeness in new definitions as to a supernal and sovereign law between and over nations. No one who is watching the development of either religion or politics can ignore the extraordinary possibilities presented by the fact that *the Pope has in his own view openly emerged on to the eminence of the spiritual law-giver of Christendom.*"*

Thus it is clear that the Pope, in his new international policy, is still further strengthening the political application of the Papal Theory under necessary adaptions to modern international relations. He is not attempting, as yet, to exercise the same direct power as that by which the ancient Popes deposed kings, but his policy aims at the same results. It is based on the same principles. He has set up the same political alliance with Italy that made the Holy Roman Empire and the Holy Alliance infamous; he has won a promise of international support for the "traditions and mission" that drenched the world in blood. He has claimed a position which no non-Catholic State and no non-Catholic citizen of any State can grant him without sacrifice of their own rights by an admission of Divine Papal Supremacy.

* The Atlantic Monthly, June, 1929.

Part III

The Conflict in America

CHAPTER XXII

THE NEW IMMIGRATION

Catholic issue brought by immigrants of the last generation—
The change in immigration since 1890—Difference in adap-
tability of different races—Old forms of selection of the traditional American type disappear—Counterfeit "assimilation" which does not include even an understanding of Americanism—Resistance to American ideas stimulated by the
Roman hierarchy—The un-American character of American Catholics shown at the Eucharistic Congress—How the
new immigrants involve America in the World Conflict.

WE come now to the question which is vital to
Americans: How does the political conflict between Romanism and Liberalism affect this nation?
In all the Christian world outside America the
struggle between the autocratic principle of Papal
Ultramontanism and that of human liberty based
on the Protestant philosophy is recognized as constant and vital. In most countries the conflict is,
indeed, less violent but no less real than it has been
during the past centuries. An observer so well informed as Hilaire Belloc declares that it is again
increasing.

This country, however, had been almost immune
till recently. There had been at three different
times outbursts of anti-Catholic feeling but these
were chiefly religious and largely local; they scarcely
affected national politics. The situation today is
very different; opposition to Catholics has changed
from dislike to their religion to distrust of their
patriotism; even charges of prejudice and bigotry
have not prevented many intellectual leaders from
sharing this distrust; and the issue has been solidi-

fied, clarified, dignified and established in our national thought by a presidential campaign.

In this form—as a political and not as a religious conflict—the issue has been raised by the new type of immigrants who began coming in large numbers about 1890. The few Roman Catholics in this country before that day had presented no serious problem and had to a large extent adopted the mental attitude of Americanism. The "Catholic vote" in politics hardly existed until the new immigration had come in sufficient force to effect local elections. It did not become of national interest until they threatened to hold the balance of power in a national election. Now, however, their eight million votes may easily determine the result in future national campaigns at any time when non-Catholics are divided.

The danger to Americanism is that these recent immigrants would attempt, in such a case, to enforce Catholic ideas on the country. Few non-Catholics will deny that if such an attempt had any serious chance of success it would become necessary for them to drop other political differences and unite against it. It was fear of this that caused so many Democratic Protestants to vote for Herbert Hoover. Catholics seek to retain the tolerance and win the support of non-Catholics by denying the reality of this danger.

The question is, then, how much of this World Conflict of two vast, opposing philosophies of civilization the new immigrants have brought with them from Europe. They are about nineteen-twentieths of all the Catholics in America. In their old homes they were both mentally and politically in harmony with Catholic philosophy.

Certainly they have been changed to some extent by their stay in America. Most have adopted our language, our clothing and many of our customs. On the surface many of the third, or even of the second, generation can hardly be distinguished from Americans of the older stock. But we are not certain—we are very doubtful—whether this change has gone much below the surface. There is no evidence that it has gone far enough so that they now accept the American instead of the Catholic philosophy and ideas, or that it will go so far in another generation or two—or ever. Yet, unless they have thus fundamentally changed, we must expect them to maintain here the same opposition to the Protestant Liberal idealism which characterizes Roman Catholics outside the United States— 90 per cent of the total membership of the church. In other words, until these new immigrants have been Americanized they will be hostile to Americanism; the conflict is too deep-seated for compromise.

The question of Americanization did not arise until after 1890. Till then the vast majority of the immigrants had justified our trust that all men desired the freedom this country offered, and that America could assimilate all comers. In those days most Americans believed that revolt against spiritual or political despotism was universal to humanity; they could hardly conceive of any voluntary acceptance of the Catholic philosophy; they assumed that people were held under autocracy only by force. Since our own ancestors had left Europe in protest against European tradition, we took it for granted that all who came had the same mental attitude.

In fact this had been so, and most of those who

came before 1890 were absorbed without difficulty. Andre Siegfried thus states the situation:

> "Between 1880 and 1890, when the second wave of Germano-British immigration was being assimilated, the results appeared more or less satisfactory. The regular American type was being evolved. On a British foundation were superimposed layers of Germans, Scandinavians, and Irish and a sprinkling of Jews. The whole mass was strongly impregnated with Protestantism, for even the Catholics and Jews seemed to adapt their religions to the Protestant outlook. In their boundless optimism, the Americans were confident that all this composite humanity would finally be absorbed, physically and morally, without leaving any appreciable or dangerous residue."*

A little over a generation ago, however, several changes in conditions caused a change in the character of immigrants. America had become wholly settled, pioneer hardships had ended and we had begun the era of intensified production which soon made our prosperity seem almost miraculous to Europeans. The old form of selection had brought to this country only those moved by the vigor of their revolt against European conditions to disregard danger and hardship. From this time on immigrants came seeking, not freedom, but prosperity.

Because of this there was a complete change in the sources of immigration. Earlier immigrants came largely from the most progressive nations; they were those whose protesting attitude out-ran even that of Protestant peoples. The new migration came from less progressive countries—from those where economic distress was great. Therefore the shift was from the Protestant to the Catholic countries. How great was this shift is shown by

* America Comes of Age, Page 10.

the following table, giving the percentage by decades from each section of Europe:

IMMIGRATION

	Percentage	
	Nordic	*Latin-Slav.*
1860-70	98.4	1.6
1870-80	91.6	8.4
1880-90	80.2	19.8
1890-1900	48.4	51.6
1900-10	23.3	76.7
1910-20	22.8	77.2

The single exception to this general description were the Jews. The two and one-half million immigrants of that race were, in truth, fleeing from religious persecution.

Upon arrival in this country, also, the new immigration met conditions very different from those of the pioneer period. The process of selection by survival, which had marked the frontier days, had ceased. They did not, as had previously been the case, scatter over great stretches of territory and mix with others of different parentage. Instead, they settled almost entirely in homogeneous colonies either in the great cities or in certain industrial regions, like the mining camps of Pennsylvania. Finally, their numbers had so increased that there was no need for them to mix much with other races, and the amalgamation which had previously been unavoidable was stopped. Indeed, many earlier arrivals who, as Dr. Siegfried points out, had begun to adapt themselves to the American outlook, backslid when these new arrivals offset American influence.

Hence, the great bulk of recent immigrants have been almost impervious to American ideas. In truth, American ideas scarcely reached them; many kept their own language; most kept their own ideas and if they adopted American words for those ideas it did not change their mental outlook.*

A Catholic writer states the difference clearly:

"Whenever Catholic and Protestant get into controversy, either publicly or privately, the Catholic is at the disadvantage of not knowing the other fellow's mind. Consequently, while apparently talking logically in English, they are actually talking in two different languages which neither of them understands."**

This is true—and depressing! Yet all American ideas and all our institutions are built absolutely upon the American meaning. It seems that the Catholic cannot understand enough about Americanism to be able even to discuss it intelligently!

Nor does the European Catholic accept the civic responsibilities of freedom. As Dr. Siegfried remarked: "the feeling of social obligation is typically Anglo-Saxon—that is, Protestant."

This instinctive resistance to American ideas has been carefully stimulated by the Roman Catholic hierarchy. It knows that any Roman Catholic who becomes at all Liberal is lost to the church. No sincere priest could view without distress the spectacle of any Catholic adopting the American ideas of freedom and human rights. Moreover, the financial welfare of the Papacy is directly involved, for the Vatican has been very largely supported by contributions from this country.

* See Page 170 and following.
** America, September 21, 1929; Page 560.

The extent to which assimilation has been opposed by the Catholic Church is stated thus by David A. Orebaugh:

"At the outset it seems fair to remark that the rank and file of American Catholics are wholly at a loss to understand Protestant distrust of the papacy. They are encouraged to attribute it to sheer bigotry and fanaticism. Subjected from infancy to the rigorous discipline of the Church, they have no adequate conception of Protestant principles, ideals, and habits of thought. Even though born in America, they do not have, nor can they be expected to have, the same outlook on modern life and institutions—particularly democratic institutions—that their Protestant neighbors have.

"Prevented from sharing many of the beliefs and theories of Protestants, they cannot acquire any sympathetic appreciation of the Protestant background and point of view, and their opportunity to become acquainted therewith is limited. The affiliation and fraternization essential to mutual understanding are discouraged by the Church.*

The result has been that these peoples of the new immigration have been exceedingly difficult to assimilate, and to a large extent have not been assimilated at all. Some reasons for this were summed up by Dr. Siegfried as follows:

"Without considering the natural and often brilliant abilities of these many races, we must admit that from the American point of view the new immigrants were not the equal of their predecessors. The early settlers had come to exploit virgin soil and had borne all the risks and toil of a creative work. They were the real pioneers. The newcomers, recruited in their very homes by the immigration agents, were attracted by a wage level that seemed high in comparison with the mediocre standard of living of southeastern Europe. Instead of heading for the great spaces of the West, they now congregated in the Atlantic ports or in the industrial and mining centres of the East—

* The Forum, July, 1929.

truly a bewildered and inarticulate crew existing on the margin of the original civilization!"*

Dr. Siegfried lays particular emphasis on the religious factor in immigration, saying:

"From the religious point of view the change was even more striking, for the majority of the immigrants were no longer Protestants. There were Jews from Russia or Poland, and Catholics from Italy and the Slav countries; and altogether their material and moral assimilation was slow and difficult. They formed solid indigestible blocks in the lower quarters of the big cities, and even when by the second generation they had acquired an American veneer, they were out of sympathy with the spirit of the country and the Protestant and Anglo-Saxon traditions laid down by the Fathers of Independence."*

He traces the resistance to assimilation by the new immigrants directly to the Catholic Church saying:

"In every case the resistance to assimilation comes from the Church, which scarcely conceals its hostility to the efforts of the Puritans to change the mode of living of the country by means of the law."**

In regard to the Catholic priests he remarked that "they are naturally in no hurry to see them (their parishioners) welded into the Anglo-Saxon uniformity," and again "they are nearly all against Prohibition and in favor of a popular Sunday. In this they show that they are * * * good politicians."*** And also: "he would have brilliant possibilities if unfortunately he did not have the soul of a politician and if his footsteps were not forever dogged by materialism."****

* America Comes of Age, Page 7.
** Ibid, Page 23.
*** Ibid, Page 50.
**** Ibid, Page 52.

A striking description of the mental attitude of American Catholics today was published in the "Forum" in an article by Stanley Frost describing the Eucharistic Congress which was held in Chicago in the summer of 1926. He says:

"Through all and all the time there kept intruding facts, actions and ideas which are utterly at variance with the American tradition.

"Most obvious was the physical fact that the people were, with very few exceptions, anything and everything but Americans. Irish mostly, French Canadians, Poles, Slovaks, a few Germans—a score of races. It was comparatively seldom that any English was heard in the crowds, and then usually with an Irish brogue or an accent of some other kind. The programmes were printed in thirteen languages! The atmosphere, the languages and the faces were all those of Ellis Island perhaps, but certainly of nothing more American than that.

"This was particularly noticeable in the processions of the clergy. It added greatly to the color of the spectacle, and brought pride to many of those who watched. 'The Church Universal' was a comment heard more than once as the ranks marched past. It is a proud boast—but not an American boast. The Americans of a few decades ago, and most of them even today, have been content to confine their universal brotherhood to oratory.

"Hardly less obvious, and bearing more directly on the significance of the Congress, was the reverence with which the prelates were hailed on all occasions, and the many signs of respect and subjection which were constantly shown. This certainly is foreign to the admitted American trait of independence, but it may be argued that it is no reverence to any human person, but an obeisance to certain men and objects as symbols of Divinity. That argument, however valid, does nothing to establish any harmony between these worshippers and the American traditions; for the men who made America denied vehemently the right of any intermediary between them and their God, and never accorded more than respect to their ministers. Certainly their natures had small place for such outward forms of reverence.

"There was noticeable at Chicago, too, a difference in the very form and expression of piety from that common in what 'American' communities remain in America. A suspicion grew that there might be a racial difference even in spirituality between these peoples, largely of Alpine and Mediterranean types, and the more northern stocks who preceded them here. But another idea took shape as the sacramental procession passed; there was to be seen there a distinct likeness in the faces of all the prelates. Race differences showed, and differences in character and spirituality and zeal, but above them all was an unmistakable likeness. Every one had been stamped, it seemed, with the seal of The Church Paternal. They might be humble or high in power, but all were part of a great paternalistic system. America, it has been said, is individualistic.

"This point of view takes quite literally such remarks as that of Robert J. Casey who, in the Chicago Daily News, described the cardinals as 'overlords of the greatest dynasty left in the world.'

"Surely there can be no question that it was to escape from dynasties of every description, more than any other one thing, that drove to this continent the men who made the America of all but the last few years, and just as surely they would have resented bitterly the fact that any such display as the Eucharistic Congress was held upon the soil they helped to win, and would have denied vehemently that there was anything 'American' about it!

"So, for all the beauty and the fineness of the great gathering at Chicago, and for all its spiritual values, one fact stands out: it was alien and foreign to America as America has been, and even as America is today."*

In fact, the only "American" thing about the Eucharistic Congress was the tolerance given it by non-Catholics!

Although the Roman Catholic propagandists were active at the time this article was printed and it was published in one of America's most influential magazines, no Catholic attempted to dis-

* The Forum, September, 1926.

pute the description it gives. Indeed, they could not do so with any chance of success, since the testimony of European Catholics as well as of American Catholics, and the common knowledge of the nation, all agree that this new immigration has not been Americanized. It was the realization of this fact which led to the Immigration Act in 1924; an act that was deliberately intended to check Roman Catholic immigration, even though this was not openly admitted by Congressmen. This law, however, cannot change the alien character of Roman Catholics already here. Dr. Siegfried says on this point:

"The danger of a numerical inundation is past * * * it is quite a question whether the measures against foreign penetration have not been taken too late, for these heterogenerous seeds will continue to grow once they have been planted."*

The American nation, then, must face the fact that the European Catholics of the newer immigration have refused to become a part of it. They are not of the same stock as the men that built America and established its mental outlook. They were not actuated by the same motives and were not subject to the same process of selection or survival. Whether because of race instincts or of training they not only fail to accept American ideals—they refuse them. Their church encourages this refusal and cultivates their natural tendency to remain apart from the American nation.

They have not become Americanized; more, they do not understand—nor show signs of wishing to understand—American principles and ideals. Nor does the record of the past two generations—or of

* America Comes of Age, Page 129.

four or five generations in the case of the Irish and the French Canadians—give us any encouragement to hope for a change in the future.

On the contrary, since these newer immigrants did not leave Europe to escape its despotic conditions; since they have no resentment against these conditions nor the philosophy which underlies them, they will naturally and inevitably endeavor to transplant them here. This means, in brief, that they will attempt to turn back the whole current of American idealism, thought, and progress.

They have brought with them to America, in proportion to their numbers, all that is involved in the World Conflict between the Papacy and human liberty.

CHAPTER XXIII

AMERICAN "LIBERAL" CATHOLICS

The assumption that American Catholics differ from others—
Facts opposing this idea—No such claim made officially—
The evidence of some Liberalism—Difficulties of judging
this evidence—The absurd talk of an American Pope—Catholic prophecies of the conflict with Americanism—The loss
of spirituality because of emphasis on politics.

THROUGH all discussion of American Catholics
runs the idea that they differ from those of the
rest of the world. Obviously they want this believed; the reactionary policy and political activity
of Roman Catholicism in other countries are so clear
that non-Catholic Americans could not trust the
loyalty and good citizenship of American Catholics
if they were known to share this attitude.

It is a curious fact, however, that this idea has
never been expressly stated by any Catholic writer
so far as can be learned. Throughout their writing
runs the standard phrase "American Catholics"
with the clear implication that they are entitled to
be judged upon a different basis from others, but
they nowhere tell what the distinction is, nor how
it is accepted or even tolerated by the hierarchy.

During the 1928 campaign there was an instance
of this in Alfred E. Smith's open letter to Charles
C. Marshall. Mr. Smith said, "These convictions
are held neither by me nor by any other *American*
Catholic so far as I know," but he did not explain
how American Catholics could reject any part of
the general law of their church, nor how their
church could tolerate any such disobedience.

Thus, there is no clear and precise statement on

this vital point, which provides the only basis on which Catholics may claim fitness for American citizenship, agree with American principles, or be trusted in politics. If American Catholics are different, if they expect us to accept their Americanism because of this difference, surely we are entitled to such a statement. So far, however, we are forced to base our conclusions upon indirect evidences.

Certainly it is not true that the mass of the Catholics here differ mentally from others. No sane man can claim that the French Canadians, the Polish colonies like that in Detroit, or the inhabitants of New York's "Little Italy" have in any mental way differentiated themselves from their kinsfolk. The description of the Eucharistic Congress by Mr. Frost, quoted in the last chapter, was a statement of a well known situation but in no way a discovery. All Americans know that these great masses of Catholics have not assimilated— know it so well that their immigration was restricted because of the fact.

There are, however, Catholics of long American ancestry and of those intellectual and individualistic types of minds which are restive under the Catholic system and which were responsible for the Protestant Reformation. Such minds will appear from time to time and cannot be suppressed even by Catholic education. America is particularly favorable to their development.

Their importance can hardly be overstated, for they are the hope of the Americanization of Catholics. Certainly no movement toward Liberalism can fairly be expected from Catholic prelates. They are a part of a vast system and must remain loyal to it. The only chance for an Americanization movement inside the Catholic Church comes from the possibility that the Catholics of independent minds will win effective leadership. Their position is worthy of careful study.

It is impossible for any Protestant to judge how wide-spread is the discontent inside the Catholic system. We hear mutterings. Several letters to the newspapers after the restoration of Papal temporal power contained such statements as this:

"As an American Roman Catholic myself, I want to say that I heartily concur in their disapproval as do thousands of other American Catholics and many thousands more throughout the world."*

A similar statement appeared in an anonymous article in the "Atlantic Monthly" in April, 1928. The writer, a Catholic priest, after declaring that the Catholic Church was guilty of "medieval thinking" said:

"Many know that something, to them unfathonable, is radically wrong with the system."**

Other Catholics wrote to the "Atlantic Monthly" that this article showed "a potent levening of modernism" and was "assurance that—some day —the Catholics of America will be Americanized." The most suspicious American can have no doubts about such men as these; if they represented Amercan Catholicism there could be no conflict!

Non-Catholics must hope that this movement is widespread and will prove powerful, but we must confess our inability to judge it fairly. There are immediate and vigorous replies to all such articles,

* R. B. Costello, N. Y. Telegram, August 17, 1929.
** Atlantic Monthly, April, 1928, Page 675.

re-asserting the solidarity of Catholicism. We cannot, either, judge these. All that can be said is that there is some stirring of Liberal thought inside the Catholic Church; nevertheless there are certain facts concerning this and similar internal movements from which we can draw some conclusions as to the probable result of the agitation.

Our difficulties in estimating the present importance of the movement are two. First is its furtiveness. The writer of the article in the "Atlantic" did not dare to use his name, as he said, "for obvious reasons." One of the reasons certainly was to avoid ecclesiastical punishment. Another was fear of social ostracism. A like secrecy marks other publications along the same line. It is quite possible that the movement is far more widespread than it appears; it is also quite possible that it is pitifully weak.

Our second difficulty is the great complexity of Catholic propaganda. Even those most familiar with the methods of modern publicity campaigns cannot be sure how much of it may be taken at face value. This does not mean that we question the sincerity of the Liberal Catholic writers, but there is doubt of their persistence if and when the Papacy takes action to suppress the movement. There is even a possibility that the hierarchy may be encouraging them because of the present situation. There have been previous similar movements inside American Catholicism, with a suggestive relationship to anti-Catholic feeling: in each case signs of Liberalism inside the Catholic Church appeared at a time when anti-Catholic agitation was important; in each case they continued without rebuke so long as the outside agitation lasted; in each case they convinced many Protestants that there was nothing to fear from Catholicism; and finally in each case they were promptly and completely suppressed as soon as the anti-Catholic agitation died. It is possible that this is coincidence, but it inclines non-Catholics to be cautious in accepting—not the sincerity—but the importance of the current Catholic Liberalism.

One recent suggestion that is clearly propaganda is the frequently voiced prophecy that we may shortly expect an American Pope. The fact is that no American citizen can become Pope. It is doubtful whether any American citizen could be a member of the Curial government, since all residents of the Vatican City are automatically political subjects of the Pope. Under American law dual citizenship is not recognized and an American citizen could no more become king of Vatican City than he could become king of England.

Aside from this absurd pro-Catholic propaganda, however, there are serious and sincere evidences of Catholic desires to be American. Most notable was an article by E. Boyd Barrett, entitled 'Will American Catholics Secede from Rome?''* Mr. Barrett is a former Jesuit priest and at the time of writing was a member in good standing of the Roman Catholic Church.

He says that the "race consciousness of American Catholics" is being aroused and that "they are hurt to the quick by suspicion of divided allegiance." He declares there is a widespread "forget the Pope attitude" and traces this back to Bishop England, who announced in 1827 that "he would not allow the Pope, or any bishops of our

* The Forum, August, 1929, Pages 89 and following.

church outside this union, the smallest interference with the humblest voter at our most insignificant ballot box." He quotes Father McClorey as declaring that American Catholics would fight the Pope in case of a war between America and the Papacy. He even points out that most Catholic populations at one time or another have been driven into conflict with the Vatican by their patriotism. He says that "to reconcile pure, unadulterated Americanism with the Encyclicals of Pius XI and Leo XIII is impossible," and that Pius XI emphatically and dramatically institutes measures "which American Catholics, as good Americans, simply cannot accept." Because of these things Mr. Barrett predicts that American Catholics "will begin to regard as inevitable a sad leave-taking from the Eternal City." He goes on:

"A few days after the Lateran Peace was signed, the editor of 'America' wrote: 'The merest suspicion that he (the Pope) is the cat's-paw of any national government in anything he says or does would be fatal to his spiritual influence.' In due time it dawned upon him—and it must be evident to everyone who studies the Treaty and Concordat—that it would be impossible for the Pope to escape being 'the cat's-paw' of Mussolini, at least in some matters. And so, in later republishing his statement in book form, he cautiously amended it. Now it reads: 'The merest suspicion that he (the Pope) is the cat's-paw of any national government in anything that he says or does *in his spiritual apostolate* would be fatal to his influence.' There could be no better proof than the amending of this clause that American Jesuits, like other Americans, recognize that a door has been opened to Mussolini to enter in and influence the government of the Church.

"Cardinal Cerretti sees, as a result of the Lateran Peace, 'a new era in the history of the Church,' and Bishop Schrembs, 'far-reaching results, not only for Italy, but for the world at large.' Both prophecies are vague and neither will be belied if the future reveals the Lateran Peace to have been a disguished declaration of war upon Americanism and the starting point of a great schism. * * *

"The dawning of the schism will no doubt test the independence of American Catholics regarding the terrible threat of excommunication. This threat made the insurgent Catholics of Rhode Island waver and collapse. But in their revolt the issue was one of purely local interest, and no ecclesiastical support was forthcoming. Had the whole Catholic population of America been involved, had race-consciousness been aroused, and had bishops and priests joined hands with the schismatics, the fear of excommunication would have counted for little.

"As to the probable course of the impending Western schism, it is infinitely hazardous to guess. In all likelihood there will be a preliminary period during which, under the rule of a 'Patriarch of the West'—a native-born bishop, resident of this country and conceded by Rome in deference to urgent demands from the American hierarchy—the American Catholic Church will become a truly national institution. Thereafter, some economic or social factor will suffice to sever the ever-weakening bond between American Catholics, imbued with the spirit of independence, and Roman Catholics, gathered in defense of the archaic battlements of the Vatican City."

Another evidence of internal revolt against the Papacy is the anonymous series of articles in the "Atlantic Monthly" running from January to May, 1928. The "Atlantic" stated their author to be a priest. He does not go so far as Mr. Barrett but does attack the Papal system at many points. He gives particular emphasis to the extent to which temporal power has driven out spirituality. He says:

"If Christ had intended to establish a Church fashioned after the kingdom of the Caesars, He would certainly have called Herod or Pilate, not the poor fisherman Peter, to be its first head. If He had intended to found a school of theological science, He would have called some of the

Greek or Roman philosophers, whose teachings have since been adopted, to watch over its early destinies."*

And later:

"This beautiful teaching of love, which is the soul of the Christian religion, has become a dead letter. It is not even deemed worthy of a place in the catechism. Charity has been debauched. It has been converted into an organized system in which the giver is honored and the receiver is stigmatized."**

All through the article it is a shepherd of souls who is speaking; one who has no concern with politics. Nevertheless a few of his remarks touch it. He says: "This confusion of politics with religion * * * is a confession of weakness on the part of the Church." And again: "For an American to obtain a bishopric today it is practically necessary either to have a friend in the Vatican or at least to be an alumnus of a Roman theological school."

These are the most important recent evidences of Liberalism inside the Catholic Church. They have received no support from any prelate, although they have not, either, been officially denounced. They are a cause for hope. But this would be much more true if they were the first of the kind that had occurred.

* Atlantic Monthly, 1928, Page 548.
** Ibid, Page 671.

CHAPTER XXIV

ROME'S EASY VICTORIES

Earlier movements for Americanization of Catholics here—Their
rise and fall in parallel with anti-Catholic agitation—The
encouraging start of the Paulist movement—Americanism
drowned out by new immigration—The movement crushed
by Leo XIII—Submission of "Liberal" Catholics—Rome's
opposition to patriotism—The Pope's power to suppress
Americanism among Catholics—The possibilities of revolt.

THE fact which chiefly causes pessimism in
regard to the present Liberal movement among
American Catholics is that it is the fourth of the
kind and, so far as appears, is less vigorous than
the three which proved wholly futile. In only one
did the Pope find it necessary to take any action
whatever.

The first came shortly after our Revolution.
The Roman Catholic Church in America had been
subordinate to London, but the Revolution broke
this connection. After some delay, John Carroll
was made prefect apostolic of the thirteen original
states, as a body distinct from that of England.

The Catholic Year Book tells briefly the story
of this first attempt at freedom:

"Already the question of foreign jurisdiction had arisen,
and the new superior in 1785 urged that as Catholics were
not admitted to any office in the State unless they re-
nounced all foreign jurisdiction, civil or ecclesiastical, some
plan should be adopted by which an ecclesiastical superior
might be appointed 'in such a way as to retain absolutely
the spiritual jurisdiction of the Holy See and at the same
time remove all ground of objecting to us (Catholics) as
though we (they) held anything hostile to the national
independence.' "*

* Catholic Year Book, 1928, Page 112.

There is no record available as to what, if anything, the Holy See had to say about this proposal, nor does the opposition noted seem to have been organized. The American Catholics of that day, however, showed symptoms of infection with American free ideas. For example, the Roman Catholic Church in the city of New York took the position that it had a right to choose its pastor and dismiss him at its own pleasure and several other churches joined in resisting the authority of the bishops. This, of course, was promptly suppressed. At this time, too, every effort was made to incorporate Catholic immigrants into churches where English was spoken, but by 1789, when the anti-European furor relaxed, this practice had begun to be abandoned.

The second Americanization movement appeared in the Catholic Church under the leadership of Bishop England, who has already been mentioned. About 1820 there began to arrive in New York considerable numbers of Irish Catholics whose resistance to Americanism was intense. In politics it took the form of hostility to native Americans as office holders, and mobs paraded the streets with banners reading "Shall Americans Rule Us?—Never!" This brought about the first vigorous anti-Catholic agitation in this country. It was at this time that Bishop England appeared. This movement lingered in an unimportant way for a few years and died out when the agitation quieted.

Anti-Catholic feeling was revived following the Catholic influx of 1848-9 when the Know Nothing movement took place, and again Catholic prelates showed signs of Americanism. There was enough of this spirit among them so that at the Vatican Council of 1870 seven American bishops voted against the dogma of Papal Infallibility. When these bishops returned to America they found the anti-Catholic agitation of the A. P. A. at its height and, although they made the "sacrifice of conscience" required by the acceptance of infallibility, they took part in the most strongly Liberal movement the Catholic Church in America has ever seen, which finally resulted in the "heresy" of Americanism.

The first leader of this movement was Father Isaac Thomas Hecker, who founded the order of the Paulists. Its object was to justify Catholicism to a non-Catholic world. He was a native-born American with no interest in medieval theology or ancient ritualism; he undertook to bring the Catholic faith into harmony with American thought and life. The number of the Paulists was never large but their influence was out of all proportion to their number and they had the support of many of the leading prelates, including Cardinal Gibbons, Archbishop Ireland, Archbishop Keane, and Archbishop Spalding.

Due largely to their influence, Catholicism in this country showed distinct American tendencies and many of their publicly announced principles and purposes were entirely in harmony with the best American thought. Cardinal Gibbons praised the separation of Church and State, Bishop Spalding endorsed the public school system, and Archbishop Ireland, admitting that the Catholic Church had been alien, declared that it must cease to be such. No fair-minded man can deny that the Americanism of these Catholic leaders was above suspicion and beyond reproach.

They met opposition as vigorous and active as was seen in any quarrel within the Catholic Church over the question of the language in which the parochial schools should be taught. The Catholic Church on the whole has always preferred teaching its schools in little used tongues, and especially in dialects into which the writings of Liberals have not been translated. To this day in France local schools are taught in the dialects of Brittany, Flanders or Alsace—pupils who know only these dialects cannot possibly read any important writings containing any modern thought.

At that time the Catholic clergy in America were holding a similar policy and teaching their schools in foreign languages in order to prevent the pupils from being contaminated by American ideas. The single exception was the Irish, and the Germans and other Catholics accused them of "Americanism," by which name the movement was shortly known. The anti-Americans even demanded that the Catholic Church in this country should be divided according to European races, with bishops and priests of like race and language with the majority of their parishioners. The greatest achievement of the Paulists was to defeat this movement and establish English as the proper language for American Catholics.

Following this victory, the "Americans" founded the Catholic University in Washington for the further spread of their doctrine and the training of Catholic teachers who should be American in spirit. This was the culmination of the movement.

The result was an enormous decrease in anti-Catholic feeling in the United States and a great increase in the respect and confidence given to Catholics by liberal-minded Americans. With leaders such as these and with the Americanization of the

Catholic Church preceding so rapidly and successfully, it appeared that American principles and institutions had nothing more to fear from American
Catholics. If this movement had been allowed to
continue it is perfectly safe to say that there would
have been no Catholic issue today. The Americanization of Catholics caused the collapse of the A. P.
A. movement and established a widespread tolerance
for Catholics which lasted without a break for
nearly thirty years.

The movement was not allowed to go on, however, and its chief effects were wiped out even while
the confidence it had inspired continued. Two
things contributed to destroy it. One was the vast
influx from Europe. It seems entirely possible that
if the Catholic Church in America had been allowed
to develop as other American churches have, through
natural increase, we should have seen a thoroughly
American form of Catholicism which might possibly have liberalized the entire Catholic Church.
But American Catholicism was overwhelmed, sub-
merged and drowned by the immigrants. They
came in such numbers, bringing with them their
own teachers and leaders, that they promptly took
possession of Catholicism in America and made
sure that it would preserve its identity with the
Catholicism of Europe. Most of the Catholics already here followed their lead and abandoned
Americanism.

Even more important was the action of Leo XIII.
In two Encyclicals Leo struck at American ideals,
declaring them anti-Catholic, and so suppressed
the entire Americanism movement. The first of
these Encyclicals was written on January 6, 1895,
and was in general merely a letter of praise and
encouragement for the Catholic Church in the

United States. Even in this pleasant document, however, Leo took pains to attack American principles. He said, for example:

"For the Church amongst you, unopposed by the Constitution and government of your nation, fettered by no hostile legislation, protected against violence by the common laws and the impartiality of the tribunals, is free to live and act without hindrance. Yet, though all this is true, it would be very erroneous to draw the conclusion that in America is to be sought the type of the most desirable status of the Church, or that it would be universally lawful or expedient for State and Church to be, as in America, dissevered and divorced."*

Leo also took pains to rebuke tendencies toward political independence. He said:

"We ardently desire that this truth should sink day by day more deeply into the minds of Catholics—namely, that they can in no better way safeguard their own individual interests and the common good than by yielding a hearty submission and obedience to the Church." (Page 330)

He did not in this letter repeat his direct attacks upon Liberalism, but he did advise Americans to read the Encyclicals which contained these attacks and govern themselves accordingly. Finally he warned against any contact with non-Catholics, saying:

* * * rather, unless forced by necessity to do otherwise, Catholics ought to prefer to associate with Catholics, a course which will be very conducive to the safeguarding of their faith." (Page 332)

Shortly after he had written this Encyclical, Leo struck more directly against the Americanism movement. The University at Washington had been founded to give education in American principles among Catholics and its rector was Archbishop

* The Great Encyclical Letters of Leo XIII, **Pages 323** and following.

Keane, who had become the leader of the movement. In September, 1896, Leo simply notified him
that he had been removed; no charges were preferred, there was no hearing on the question, Archbishop Keane was given no opportunity to defend
himself. No one can doubt that this action was
taken because of the Liberalism of the views which
the Archbishop held and taught. By this action
Leo stopped the Americanism movement at its
source.

The way in which the Liberal leaders among the
Catholics responded to this action of the Pope is
extremely suggestive and exceedingly discouraging.
There were a dozen prelates in America who had
declared that Catholicism and Americanism could
be reconciled and who had shown vigorous and
intelligent patriotism. Certainly in any other
church these men would have voiced at least criticism or regret at Leo's action. Not one of them did
so, though this action of the Pope's was not of the
kind which Catholic dogma decrees to be infallible.
It was merely an executive action and not an *ex
cathedra* statement of principles. The acquiescence
of the American Catholics shows how far the Papal
authority extends beyond the letter of the Roman
dogma.

Archbishop Keane, the man most directly affected, read to the students of the Catholic University the letter removing him from office. When
he had finished he added this abject statement:

"I do not ask reasons; I beg you, my friends, and you,
students, do as I have done. Do not ask why the Holy
Father has done this. It is sufficient that he has done it
for it to have been done wisely and well."*

* The Ku Klux Klan, Page 185.

The prelate next most prominent in the Americanization movement was Archbishop Ireland of St. Paul. He was a close friend of Theodore Roosevelt and it is common knowledge that his Americanism was the only thing that prevented his being made a cardinal. Yet he also made complete submission in a sermon in Washington a year after the removal of Archbishop Keane.*

It was in January, 1899, that Leo dealt the death blow to the Americanism movement and to all Liberalism among American Catholics. In an Encyclical on "Americanism in Religion" he took the work of Father Hecker as his text. He thus defined the doctrine he was about to attack:

"The principles on which the new opinions We have mentioned are based may be reduced to this: that, in order the more easily to bring over to Catholic doctrine those who dissent from it, the Church ought to adapt herself somewhat to our advanced civilization, and, relaxing her ancient rigor, show some indulgence to modern popular theories and methods."**

In his attack on this doctrine he says:

"The rule of life which is laid down for Catholics is not of such a nature as not to admit modifications, according to the diversity of time and place. The Church, indeed, possesses what her Author has bestowed on her, a kind and merciful disposition * * *." (Page 443)

"But in the matter of which we are now speaking, Beloved Son, the project involves a greater danger and is more hostile to Catholic doctrine and discipline, inasmuch as the followers of these novelties judge that a certain liberty ought to be introduced into the Church, so that, limiting the exercise of vigilance of its powers, each one of the faithful may act more freely in pursuance of his own

*See Page 78.
The Great Encyclical Letters of Leo XIII, **Pages 442 and following.

natural bent and capacity. They affirm, namely, that this is called for in order to imitate that liberty which, though quite recently introduced, is now the law and the foundation of almost every civil community." (Page 444)

"Hence, from all that We have hitherto said, it is clear, Beloved Son, that We cannot approve the opinions which some comprise under the head of Americanism." * * *

"For it raises the suspicion that there are some among you who conceive of and desire a church in America different from that which is in the rest of the world. One in the unity of doctrine as in the unity of government, such is the Catholic Church, and, since God has established its centre and foundation in the Chair of Peter, one which is rightly called Roman, for where Peter is there is the Church." (Page 452)

With this Encyclical there ended all advocacy of Liberal opinions among American Catholics of any importance. So far as can be learned there has not since that time been a single American prelate who has dared to defend American principles. During the last campaign there were in circulation a number of quotations from prominent Catholics endorsing American principles, but it was notable that in order to find these, Catholic propagandists had to go back to the time of the old Americanism movement. Archbishop Ireland, for example, was quoted; he is long dead and recanted before he died. Cardinal Gibbons was quoted, but his remarks in endorsement of American principles were made in 1887!

Thus in this, the most vigorous, best led and most sustained effort that has ever been made to introduce Liberalism into the Roman Catholic Church in America, the issue between Americanism and the Vatican was fairly joined and Rome's victory was complete. Since that day the anti-American strength of the Roman Catholic Church has been re-enforced enormously from overseas,—from about six million in 1890 to above twenty-three million today—and there is not to be found in the hierarchy today a single man ranking with Gibbons or Ireland, with Spalding or Keane. If under such leadership as these men gave and at a time when the Catholic Church in America was still largely composed of native Americans, the movement could be so easily destroyed, what hope can non-Catholics have that such a movement as Dr. Barrett suggests could be successful today?

Three things must be taken into consideration. In the first place, the Roman Catholic Church must automatically oppose any strong national spirit among Catholics. In other countries beside this, Catholics have at times undertaken to put the Catholic Church in tune with patriotism. These tendencies have always been fought by the Papacy. On this subject the Encyclopedia Britannica says:

"These aspirations have been proclaimed with especial emphasis in France, in Germany and in the United States, but are everywhere met with a blank refusal from the Ultramontane side. For Ultramontanism fears that any infusion of a national element into ecclesiastical life would entail the eventual independence of the people in question from Papal control, and lead to developments opposed to its Papalistic mode of thought. It endeavors, therefore, to undermine all aspirations of this nature and, its own tendency being essentially international, strives to ensure that national sentiment and national interests shall not find over-zealous champions among the clergy."*

In the second place the Papacy holds two tremendous weapons to prevent the success of any such movement. The first is the weapon of excommunication. Non-Catholics have seldom realized the great value of this weapon to the Papacy,

* The Encyclopedia Britannica, Vol. XXVII, Page 572.

but it is two-fold. In the first place, the threat of excommunication usually will bring any Catholic to terms and force him to accept, at least outwardly, the orders of the Vatican.

But excommunication has another effect, and one that is almost more important. By it the Pope can instantly eject from the church any man who holds opinions which the Papacy disapproves. Every opportunity for him to agitate his opinions or educate Catholics is automatically closed.

Thus, if any does resist the Pope, he nevertheless cannot by any possibility bring to his support any body of co-religionists or set up inside the Catholic Church any opposition to any idea, policy, or plan which the Pope proposes. It is this use of the power of excommunication which has for so many hundred years prevented any reform in the Catholic Church and which can prevent it indefinitely. So long as the Pope holds this power, the Catholic Church cannot be changed against his desires.

The Pope has a second weapon against the Catholic Church in America which—in the last resort— could be even more sweeping than excommunication. This is the power to remove any priest or bishop at his own pleasure. It was this power which stopped the Americanism movement by the removal of Archbishop Keane; it is in full force today. Each Catholic priest and prelate holds his place at the simple pleasure of the Pope. If any one of them should attempt leadership toward Americanism, he could be removed instantly. If at any time the Pope should desire the American hierarchy to adopt a policy more vigorously anti-American than the one it now pursues, he would have only to remove the present prelates and replace them with men exactly to his own taste.

There remains the possibility suggested by Mr. Barrett* that the American prelates would themselves lead a revolt against Papalism. This is to be hoped for; yet we cannot forget that of one hundred and fifty prelates who voted against Papal Infallibility, only two refused to make "the loyal sacrifice of conscience" and accept it. It does not seem reasonable to expect any greater independence on an issue that does not go so deeply into faith and conscience—and after sixty years of Ultramontane teaching and selection of leaders!

The Catholic Church in America, then, is less American than at any time in its history; no movement toward Americanism may be hoped for from its hierarchy. At the same time the Papacy is more powerful in fact and in theory than it has been since the foundation of this nation. We must face the truth that so far as the Roman Catholic Church in this country is concerned it will in all things meet the desires of the Pope. It will never be more Liberal or more American than he wishes. If at any time it shows any tendencies toward adaptation to American thought, the Pope can bring it into subjection with a single stroke of his pen.

Yet this does not mean that there is no hope for a spread of Americanism inside the Catholic Church. We have seen that there are stirrings which we cannot measure. It is impossible for Catholics, in spite of all their church may do, to live in a free country without being infected to some degree by the principles of freedom. We may trust that even the Popes, counseled by wise politicians, would not

* See Page 269.

attempt an enforcement of doctrines which would cause a revolt among their subjects in this country. What we cannot do is to guess at what point such a revolt would take place.

We must expect, then, that any liberalization of American Catholics will be led by men outside the hierarchy, and not inside it. Even a full schism is possible without a sacrifice of the Catholic faith, in spite of all the present power of the Pope. Few people, either Catholics or Protestants, know that there exists a Catholic Church which is recognized by the Vatican as having true bishops and priests and yet is absolutely independent of the Pope. This church sprang up in 1870 among the Catholics who rejected the dogma of Papal Infallibility. It has never been strong but it has throughout the world some 200,000 members, of whom perhaps one-tenth are in this country. It is within the bounds of possibility that American Liberal Catholics should increase in number, abandon the Papal Church and join this one.

This, however, is little more than a pious hope. The situation which we must recognize is the permanent anti-Americanism of the Roman Catholic Church in this country and of all its loyal subjects—an anti-Americanism whose activities and practices are limited only by expediency.

CHAPTER XXV

ROME'S CAMPAIGN IN AMERICA

Roman attitude controlled by need for opportunism—Influence of American ideals forces policy of temporary equivocation—The real meaning of Catholic "endorsements" of Americanism—Catholics as well as Protestants often misled—How the hierarchy meets danger of Americanization—Feudal discipline maintained—Reverence for the prelates—Teaching of Ultramontanism—Opposition to co-operation with non-Catholics—Solidarity in politics—Control of publications.

WE come now to the heart of our problem, the position of the mass of Catholics in America. Our previous inquiries have all been to enable us to understand this. We have seen that the Catholic Church, in its root principles and by many specific definitions, is hostile to the principles upon which our American government is based; that throughout the world it carries this hostility into practical politics in the endeavor to supplant Liberalism everywhere with the supernatural autocracy of the Papacy; that there is no ground for believing in any important difference between Catholics in America and elsewhere; and finally that four attempts of American Catholics to compromise with Liberalism have been easily and completely suppressed.

Nevertheless, it is true that the Roman Catholic Church in this country seems at first glance to occupy a position different from that of Romanism in the rest of the world. What we must determine is whether the difference gives us any reason for hoping that America may escape the world conflict between the two forms of civilization.

The strategic situation of Catholicism in America is governed by two main factors. The first is that the Roman Church here considers itself in a hostile environment. It does not believe that the neutrality of our government is real; it sees an implacable enemy in our public schools and it holds that, as Hilaire Belloc says:

"* * * this material strength of governments, coupled with and supporting the far more important effect of Nationalism as a spiritual power, forms everywhere an obstacle to full Catholic life."*

The position of the Church he states thus:

"* * * the recognition of the truth (so unpalatable to most men today, and especially to those of the Protestant culture), that *the Catholic Church must either rule society or be ruled in Her own despite.*"**

That is, the Roman Church is hostile to Americanism and assumes that America must be hostile to her. Certainly there is much truth in the assumption. American civilization is built, as we have seen, on Protestant ideals. In this country the Catholic Church is confronted by a majority of at least five to one that is always latently hostile and that could become actively so if it saw a need. No one questions the devastation it could inflict upon American Catholicism if it became aroused. The Roman Church here is surrounded by a Liberal spirit which, if not counteracted, will destroy the Roman Catholic state of mind even if it makes no attack on the Catholic faith.

The second fact in the strategic situation is that this public spirit induces in American Catholics a tendency toward Liberal ideas. The American hierarchy is in command of forces which are somewhat questioning and somewhat sullen. They are not,

* Survivals and New **Arrivals, Page 118.**
** Ibid, Page 124.

indeed, anywhere near rebellion against Catholic teachings but they are considerably astray from that unquestioning obedience demanded by the Papacy, and they must be handled with caution.

In these circumstances the strategy of the Catholic Church in America is inevitable. It is in no position to meet a direct issue, since its own forces are somewhat untrustworthy and its opposition is overwhelming. Therefore, it must avoid causes of open dispute; it must do everything possible to placate, allay, disarm, and chloroform the opposition. It must attempt to create a deluded American "state of mind," so that there will be no attack upon Catholicism, and so that the old American spirit can be more easily destroyed if Romanism ever finds a chance to attack. At the same time Romanism must hold together its own forces, prepare them to respond to a call to arms when the opportunity arrives. This is the most elemental strategy; it is the course that would be taken by any man with even half sense unless he had an obsession for martyrdom.

The most obvious way in which this is shown is in the protestation of endorsement of American principles, inconsistent though these endorsements are with the doctrines of the Catholic Church. We heard many of them during the 1928 campaign, most notably the long letter of Alfred E. Smith to Charles C. Marshall.

We have seen that such endorsements today come from laymen only; that the prelates quoted along this line are long dead. But what of the seeming Liberal statements of the former prelates? A non-Catholic cannot but wonder how any men so well informed as they were as to the law laid down by the Popes could express the opinions they did. It is worth while to examine them at some length to find out just what these prelates were trying to accomplish, and how it was that their statements did not bring sharp rebuke from the Vatican. Let us take what is probably the most definitely Liberal of all these statements, one made by Cardinal Gibbons in 1887 and previously quoted. He said:

"American Catholics rejoice in our separation of Church and State, and I can conceive no combination of circumstances likely to arise which would make a union desirable to either Church or State."*

That sounds entirely Liberal and as if it were intended to be a blanket endorsement of the principle of separation of Church and State.

Note, however, that it is limited by the word "American," implying a distinction, denied by the highest Roman authorities, between American and other Romanists. Cardinal Gibbons' complete submission to Pope Leo XIII, who vigorously demanded separation of Church and State, makes us wonder whether he did not here take refuge in the Roman Catholic doctrine of "mental reservations." Any Catholic may conscientiously do this except when, as Mr. Smith did, he expressly disclaims reservations. Cardinal Gibbons had not, when he made this statement, so declared himself.

To make sure just what this amazing doctrine is, here is the justification and explanation of it in the Catholic Encyclopedia:

"Writers of all creeds and of none * * * admit the doctrine of the lie of necessity, and maintain that when there

* Governor Smith's Letter to Chas. C. Marshall, Atlantic Monthly, April, 1927.

is a conflict between justice and veracity it is justice that should prevail. The common Catholic teaching has formu-lated the theory of mental reservation as a means by which the claims of both justice and veracity can still be satis-fied. * * * It was commonly admitted that an equivocal expression need not necessarily be used when the words of the speaker receive a special meaning from the circum-stances in which he is placed, or from the position which he holds. Thus, if a confessor is asked about sins made known to him in confession, he should answer: 'I do not know,' and such words as those when used by a priest mean: 'I do not know apart from confession,' or 'I do not know as a man' or 'I have no knowledge of the matter which I can communicate.' All Catholic writers were, and are, agreed that when there is good reason, such expression as the above may be made use of, and that they are not lies. Those who hear them may understand them in a sense which is not true, but their self-deception may be permitted by the speaker for a good reason.''*

To avoid what the Encyclopedia so aptly calls "self-deception," we must examine Cardinal Gib-bons' statement with particular reference to the "circumstances in which he was placed" and the "good reasons" he might have had as a Romanist to "permit" self-deception by American Protestants.

Cardinal Gibbons at the time of this statement was in the same strategic position as that of the American hierarchy today. He was primate of his church in a nation where, if union of Church and State should come about, it would be hostile to his church, since it would be necessarily Protestant. Except for the separation of Church and State, his church could hardly have existed here. Its con-tinued prosperity depended then, as it does now, upon non-Catholics being convinced that it was not opposing American principles and that there was no danger of conflict between it and our government.

* The Catholic Encyclopedia, Vol. X, Page 195.

It is no reflection upon his character to ask whether all these circumstances did not allow him to add in his own mind a special meaning to his words, so that their actual meaning to him and all Catholics would be about as follows:

"American Catholics rejoice in our separation of Church and State (note that he did not, even with mental reservations, say 'believe in separation of Church and State') since in America we could not possibly make the State subservient to our church and it is only this separation that permits us to prosper here as a church, and I can conceive of no combination of circumstances likely to arise which would make a union desirable to either Church or State until the time comes when we can unite the Roman Church to the American State with the Roman Church in admitted supremacy."

Mental reservations like this would explain the apparent conflicts between American prelates and the Pope, and between different Roman spokesmen. They would explain, also, how these conflicts end so suddenly when the Pope speaks, and why they leave no aftermath. They would explain, in the last place, how it happens that so many Americans have come to credit the Roman Church with Liberalism so far as America is concerned in spite of the Pope's pronouncements. The American prelates are carefully "permitting" our self-deception.

So these statements can be given no weight as showing the attitude of the Roman Church toward what it calls Liberalism, which includes all American principles of liberty, equality, separation of Church and State, and freedom of conscience. We must continue, because of the doctrine of mental reservation, to accept the word of the Pope as the final authority for American Catholics.

What, then, do these apparently Liberal state-

ments of American Catholics actually mean? It is
clear that they mean nothing so far as Liberalism
is concerned; nevertheless they do have a meaning.
It is that the leaders of Catholicism in this country
are diplomatically trying to camoflage their real
convictions, trying to make the best of a situation
which they consider bad and are not trying to change
the situation—even though it is contrary to their
principles—so long as a change would injure them.

There has not been a word uttered by any American Catholic that I can find which can be taken as
a pledge that the American Catholics will not
overthrow American principles the minute that they
can benefit thereby. Their slogan today is "Make
America Catholic." If they do, we must believe
that they would suppress liberty here as it has been
suppressed in Italy. They approve of tolerance and
Liberalism from us to themselves; even with the
utmost of mental reservations they do not pretend
that they would ever permit it from themselves to
us. Their whole attitude toward American Liberalism today may be summed up in a quotation
whose source I have been unable to trace:

"We demand from you those liberties which your principles require you to give us, since you have the power, but
which our principles will require us to refuse to you whenever we get the power."

The rulers of Catholicism today deny those
liberties to mankind in every country where they
have power. They do not specifically say that they
will use the rights we give them to destroy our
own rights; they could not be expected to warn us
in the circumstances. But there is no need; their
purpose has been fully stated by their Popes; it is
implied in the whole position of the Roman Church,
it is enforced where possible, and they do not deny it.

How many American Catholics realize that this is the position of their church it is impossible for anyone to say. Doubtless the number who do not is very large. In the first place the vast majority have no interest in such questions at any time; they are not analytical and many of them could not understand the conflict, no matter how carefully it was explained to them; they will follow whatever leadership is strongest at any moment. Doubtless many more Catholics have been deceived by the seemingly Liberal statements of Catholic leaders, just as non-Catholics have been.

There is danger to the Roman Church in this situation; the danger that a considerable portion of their membership—and the most vigorous and intelligent portion—would revolt once the conflict with Liberalism and Americanism was made clear to them. It is this danger to Romanism which is the greatest hope of non-Catholic Americans in the present conflict. The American hierarchy is laboring with desperate energy and great skill to offset it.

In the first place it maintains in America a church discipline in some respects more rigid than anywhere else. This is condemned by the Catholic priest who wrote "The Catholic Church and the Modern Mind." He says:

"In no other country of the world, perhaps, has the hierarchy preserved the spirit and the methods of feudalism as have the bishops of the United States. * * *

"Feudalism was an unpopular and a degrading system of government. It contained none of the political elements that tend to develop the individual. It was a system in which the masses of the people were bound to the will of one man in a serfdom which was but a step removed from slavery. 'No system,' writes Guizot, 'has ever in France, remained so odious to the public instincts. * * * You will find the feudal system considered, by the mass of the population, a foe to be fought and fought down at any cost.' (History of France, Volume I, Pages 230 and 231.)

"The Catholic bishop is still given his feudal title, 'Your Lordship.' At ordination the newly made priest kneels, as the serf once knelt before his feudal lord, his two hands held between the hands of the bishop. Then the bishop says 'Dost thou promise me and my successors reverence and obedience?' The answer follows: 'I promise.' In these later days the oath against modernism is generally demanded after ordination just as it is required of seminary and university professors at the beginning of each academic year. * * *

"The newly ordained priest has now bound himself to reverence and obey his bishop. Little does he dream of the future humiliations this step may entail. * * *

"The bishop feels that he is responsible to God for the lives of the priests who have promised to reverence and obey him. Not satisfied with the reverence and obedience shown by devoted children to their parents, he, (the bishop) demands those external signs of fealty and honor which the feudal lord required of his serfs.

"When the priest, or any of the faithful, greets His Lordship, he must kneel before him and kiss the episcopal ring upon his hand."*

Later he remarks:

"The Church fears individuality and personality in her members. There is always the danger of heresy, the danger of insubordination."**

Along with this goes the feudal and un-American system of personal reverence, almost of worship, for the "princes" of the Church. We had an enlightening example at the Eucharistic Congress, when the Papal Legate was accorded an ovation such as has never been given by America to its greatest men—such as could never be given by men

* Atlantic Monthly, 1928, **Pages 542 and 543.**
** Ibid, Page 549.

holding American principles to any man. This reverence is enforced with all the power of the church. No longer ago than 1928, in Rhode Island, certain Catholics dared to bring suit against their bishop on the charge that he had misused the church's funds. They were excommunicated for it.

By means such as these the Roman Catholic Church cultivates the habit of submission in her American subjects. As the priest wrote in the "Atlantic Monthly:" "fear, moral and religious fear, prompts the Catholic to kiss the foot or the hand of his ecclesiastical ruler * * * Ecclesiastical dignities have so magnified the self-importance of their holders that these latter have come to substitute their will for that of the people."*

Surely the American hierarchy need have little fear of mental independence from those who submit to this feudal system!

The American hierarchy also teaches all the doctrines of Ultramontanism under the Papal Theory, even though it does not insist upon them in public. The teachers may not explain either to the mass of their own people or to non-Catholics the full meaning of these doctrines, but the foundations are laid for their use whenever it becomes strategically possible. Proof of this is that all the quotations from Catholic sources used in this book have been printed under the authority of the church for the instruction of American Catholics. They might be multiplied indefinitely. The Catholic Encyclopedia, an authoritative book of reference for Catholic students, lays down all these doctrines.

As evidence let me cite the article from the Catholic Encyclopedia on the Inquisition. It is

* Ibid, Pages 547 and 549.

too long to reprint in full, and since my own summary would certainly be considered unfair by Catholics, let me quote again the Catholic writer in the
"Atlantic Monthly." He says:

"The writer first shows that the killing of heretics was,
in the first five centuries of the Church, considered as
opposed to the spirit of Christianity. * * * *

"Of the Spanish Inquisition he says, 'Its excesses were
largely due to the fact that in its administration civil purposes overshadowed ecclesiastical.' Yet Pope Innocent IV
in a bull says, 'When those adjudged guilty of heresy have
been given up to the civil power by the bishop or his representative, or the Inquisition, the podesta, or chief magistrate of the city, shall take them at once, and shall, within
five days at the most, execute the laws made against them.'
Moreover, he directs that this bull and corresponding
regulations of Frederick II, quoted above, be entered in
every city among the municipal statutes under pain of
excommunication, which was also visited on those who
failed to execute both the Papal and the imperial decrees.

" 'Nor could any doubt remain,' continues the author
in the Catholic Encyclopedia, 'as to what civil regulations
were meant, for the passages which ordered the burning
of impenitent heretics were inserted in the Papal decretals
from the imperial constitutions. The aforesaid bull remained thenceforth a fundamental document of the Inquisition, renewed and re-enforced by several Popes, Alexander
IV (1254-61), Clement IV (1265-68), Nicholas IV (1288-92),
Boniface VIII (1294-1303), and others. The civil authorities, therefore, were enjoined by the Popes, under pain of
excommunication, to execute the legal sentence that condemned impenitent heretics to the stake. It is to be noted
that excommunication itself was no trifle, for, if the person
excommunicated did not free himself from excommunication
within a year, he was held by the legislation of that period
to be a heretic, and incurred all the penalties that affected
heresy.'

"In the end, the zealous writer accuses non-Catholic
writers of bigotry in condemning the Inquisition."*

* Atlantic Monthly, 1928, Page 673.

Such is the teaching given to American Catholics by the American hierarchy. It is carried down into the elementary schools, as was shown in the quotations from the "Manual of Christian Doctrine" already cited. It includes deliberate falsification of American history. It can have but one result: no person who receives "Catholic education" can have any true understanding of American principles, and each pupil is mentally prepared to accept their destruction and the imposition of Papal Autocracy whenever the American hierarchy can accomplish it.

The American hierarchy has further organized a "quarantine" to prevent American ideas reaching its subjects. It makes every effort to maintain the solidarity of the Catholics, it prevents their mixing with non-Catholics and it combats vigorously any possible infection of American Liberal principles.

How successful this effort for solidarity has been is shown in the political activities of the Catholics. It is of course denied by the Catholics that there is any such thing and Catholic prelates usually avoid appearing personally in political matters. The open endorsement of Governor Smith by Catholic prelates was an exception; on the whole they admit activity in politics only when there is some definite interest of the church at issue. Nevertheless the Catholic Church here has the Knights of Columbus and the Holy Name Society for use in politics as "social militia," as described by Count Dalla Torre.*

The most enlightening instance of Catholic solidarity in politics is shown by the career of Governor Smith; it requires an immense credulity to believe that the continued success of this representative of a corrupt Democratic political machine

* See Pages 204 and following.

should have won so consistently in a Republican state without the solid support of Catholicism. Certainly without it he would never have been nominated for the presidency. Certainly, too, his presidential campaign shows the use of Catholicism as a political force; there is no other explanation for the raising of the Catholic issue both in the Democratic National Convention in 1924 and in his speech at Oklahoma City in 1928.

A detailed study of the operation of the Catholic Church in American politics was made in Massachusetts in 1925 by Mrs. Kate Sargent. Some excerpts from her report follow:

"The exercise of Roman influence in public affairs occurs chiefly in educational legislation; and there it has proved a serious stumbling block to progress. * * *

"Any movement toward improvement in public education hits the Church in three ways: it reinforces that control of education by civil authorities which is contrary to the Catholic idea; it develops a liberal thought which in every generation has proved a danger to the Church's control over its followers; and by raising the standard of the public schools, it constrains a like improvement in the parochial schools.

"The non-Catholic citizen, who judges proposed measures on their merits alone, is frequently startled and astonished at the points where Roman Catholic opposition breaks out. Measures that are most carefully worded so as not to injure religious sensibilities may prove antagonistic to Roman Church policies, and are then bitterly attacked. A study reveals that their enactment would encroach upon what the Hierarchy regards as its own special preserves in education. * * *

"One of the most amazing fights in the history of education took place in 1919,—amazing because the bitterness it engendered still rankles fiercely, and yet the general public knew nothing of the facts, owing to the excessive 'discretion' of the newspapers * * *."†

† The Forum, November, 1925, Pages 731 and following.

The issue came over projected general reforms in the public school system. The story is too long and complicated to repeat in full; the essential point is that these reforms had been recommended by an official board which included Catholics and that these had approved the reforms, apparently without consulting the church authorities. Mrs. Sargent describes some of the incidents of this fight and gives in detail the methods used by the Catholic hierarchy—the flood of inspired letters from school children, coercion of legislators, instructions from Catholic prelates as to political organization and deliberate misrepresentation of the purpose of the legislation proposed. In closing her description she says:

"Not one Protestant voter in thousands ever knew of the sectarian opposition, or ever heard of the parochial school letters. Of the two concurring Catholics on the recess commission, one at least suffered severe discipline for his independence of thought and action. This man, a public official of unassailable honor and recognized abilities, was defeated for the State Senate; an anonymous paper was circulated against him in his church, wherein he was characterized as a renegade; and his business suffered. He has since removed from his old district and now resides in a suburb which is a Protestant stronghold.

"It is by no means the contention in this article that the influence of the Roman Church is always on the wrong side of the question. The purpose here is merely to indicate, by a few examples, the extent to which the Church, fundamentally a religious institution, wields power in secular affairs."*

Mrs. Sargent describes a similar fight by the Roman hierarchy to defeat the child labor amendment. The action in this case was carried on by Catholic women. The situation was a peculiarly interesting one because two Catholic politicians had

* The Forum, November, 1925, Page 737.

endorsed the amendment before the Catholic Church decided to oppose it. These were Mayor James M. Curley of Boston and United States Senator David I. Walsh. Mayor Curley recanted absolutely; Senator Walsh made no public repudiation but was forced to keep silent.

One more case of Catholicism in politics is cited by Mrs. Sargent. Two politicians of adjoining counties, one a Catholic and one a Protestant, were indicted on charges of conspiracy to extort money through threats of prosecution. The Protestant was tried and convicted; the Catholic was then tried and was found guilty unanimously by five justices, two of them Catholics. Nevertheless the Knights of Columbus raised the cry of religious persecution; the convict was publicly "vindicated" by the concerted action of the Catholics and received 76,000 votes when he ran again for the office from which he had been ousted.

All activities of this kind of course aid in maintaining the solidarity of Catholics as against Americans.

Even more effective is the Catholic press. It is completely under control of Ultramontanism at all times and in all ways, not only on religion but on political topics. It avows this openly. Probably the most fair-minded of all Catholic publications is the "Commonweal," whose purpose is to commend Catholicism to non-Catholics, yet it makes this frank statement:

"We of the Commonweal have tried our best to chart and guide our course in relation to practically *all the social topics and problems* discussed by us in the light of the authoritative and inspiring doctrine laid down in that document (a pastoral letter of the American hierarchy to define teachings). We know that other Catholic journals

have done the same thing and that a very considerable number of our most influential clergymen and teachers have made
the bishops' joint pastoral the principal text-book of many
sermons and writings and much school work. But we also
think that much more should be done to diffuse and make
operative the great and helpful social and intellectual
benefits of that document."*

Thus is Catholic thought controlled, thus are
Catholics prevented from sharing in the purposes,
the ideals, and the principles of the nation at large.
We hear many complaints of propaganda appearing
in the non-Catholic press and they are only too well
justified, yet here we have a press openly avowing
that it does not attempt to think for itself. It is
clear that the American hierarchy's effort to
maintain the solidarity of Catholics is highly
successful.

* The Commonweal, September 11, 1929.

CHAPTER XXVI

THE PURPOSE OF ROME'S SCHOOLS

Parochial schools intended to prevent American education and assimilation—A quarantine against infection of Liberalism—Catholic writers set forth this purpose—Reasons for antagonism to public schools—Little emphasis on schools in Catholic countries—Parochial school campaign intensified since Smith's defeat—Roman law newly proclaimed and enforced—Pope's latest Encyclical re-states Roman Church's extreme position and hostility to Liberal education—How the parochial school provides recruits for anti-American campaign.

THE most important and successful of all the measures taken by the American hierarchy to prevent the spread of Liberal ideas, to maintain the strength of its political army, and to recruit soldiers for it, is the establishment of its vast parochial school system. This is the foundation and the culmination of the whole campaign. It may be merely a coincidence, but it is a fact, that since the defeat of Governor Smith for the presidency in 1928, there has been renewed activity along this line, and renewed pressure on parents. This movement began with the leading American prelate—Cardinal Hayes of New York—and has received direct support from Pope Pius in a long Encyclical.

Both to its own communicants and to non-Catholics, the prelates justify the parochial school system on the gound of the need for more religious instruction than can be given children in the home or by the church directly. There is enough merit in this plea to win the sympathy, or at least the consent, of all religious-minded people.

When we look at the matter closely, however, we find that religious instruction is not the chief purpose of the parochial schools. Nowhere else has the Roman Church developed schools to any such extent as in America. The illiteracy of the Catholic countries is notorious and is due chiefly to the failure of the Roman Church to provide education—of which it has had full control. Yet in those countries the need of moral training is as great as in America.

There are special reasons why the parochial school has been so vigorously pushed here. The key appears in a statement made by Hilaire Belloc when he says in speaking of the public school that it "is now the strongest political instrument of our time." He goes on:

"It is strange how long it took people to wake up to the situation. Even now the most of men have just begun to speculate on its possible use for certain definite ends of propaganda. But the great religious quarrel in France, the change worked by the elementary school in Britain, the recurrent agitations in the United States against public grants for the schools of a religious minority, have begun to make the latent power of the system apparent.

"The wisest observers now clearly perceive that if compulsory elementary universal instruction be captured and used to a certain end, it can completely transform the character of all society. When we remember that the system is supported and confirmed by the ever-increasing network of public examinations, all taking the same history, geography and philosophy for granted, the formidable character of this new thing should be sufficiently apparent.

*"Therefore, the inevitable conflict between the Catholic and the non-Catholic conceptions of human nature, life and destiny, cannot but make the elementary school their battlefield."**

A little later he says in regard to the public schools:

* Survivals and New Arrivals, Page 161.

"Any philosophy not of the machine must suffer, and in case of so distinctive an entity as the Catholic Church—a thing distinct from all the rest of the world, understanding and penetrating, yet separate from, the world—the hostile character of such a machine should be self-evident.

"I am proposing no solution, I am making no prophecy; but I am stating an issue which none, I think, can, upon consideration, deny. The elementary school, mastered by the lay State, and imposing its instruction by compulsion, is of its nature hostile to the Faith, whether hostile intention be present or no."**

When we remember that this is the only country in the world in which any considerable number of Catholic children would be exposed to the principles of Liberal education if they attended the public schools, the reason for the great development of parochial schools is self-evident. They are intended as a defense against Liberalism in the public schools. Their purpose is not to give religious instruction so much as it is to prevent instruction along lines of American principles. They are a quarantine against the spread of liberty.

We have already seen the un-American political instruction which is given in these schools; they are hot-beds of Ultramontanism. Further testimony is found in the "Atlantic Monthly" articles already referred to. The anonymous priest says:

"It is not generally known that the Church school is, par excellence, an American invention. Nowhere else in the whole world is ecclesiastical education pursued so relentlessly. Zeal for religious education in this country is unbounded. The fiery young archbishop of a venerable See declared in his inaugural sermon, 'The Catholic school is the salvation of the Church in America. The policy in this diocese will be *school first, church second.*' * * *

** Ibid, Page 162.

"Parents are often threatened with eternal perdition if they fail to send their children to God's schools. * * *

"Eight years of daily catechism in the parochial school do not suffice to make our youth safe from the seductions of modern life. They might be contaminated if allowed to attend public high schools. It is a confession of weakness. * * *

"The Catholic Church is ever on the defensive against the Protestant movement. This is manifest especially in her educational effort. Her schools abound somewhat in mathematical ratio to the prevalence of Protestantism. She is not so zealous for schools in Catholic countries.*

"Where are the parochial schools of Spain and the South American countries? No Mexican Indian ever received eight years' daily instruction in the catechism. There is also the land of the Popes. There are no parochial schools in Italy. * * *

"The American Catholic Church seems to be tending toward the heresy of religious intellectualism. It is an elusive heresy, the mother of rationalism. America has ever been a wayward child of the Church. * * *

* * * zeal for dogmatism has grown great in the so-called Protestant countries. Among the Catholic nations there remains a popular indifference to dogma that is striking. In this particular, America is the direct antithesis to the old Catholic countries. Obviously American Catholic doctrinalism is not based on ancient tradition. Such intellectualistic teaching was not considered necessary for salvation by the historic Church. We must not forget that for fifteen centuries there was no popular instruction such as is given in America today. If, then, this intense instruction is not necessary for salvation, it must be demanded for other reasons. * * * (Page 163)

This writer argues at length that in the parochial school spirituality has been sacrificed, as well as moral training. He closes his article with this statement:

* Atlantic Monthly, Feb. 1928, Pages 158 and following.

"There is but one quality that proves the excellence of a religion. It is the excellence of the lives lived by its devotees. When the American bishops cease their school-building crusade and begin the work of developing Christian character, there will be hope for the Church in America." (Page 166)

Although the parochial school campaign has been active for many years, and intense since 1890 when the danger of the Americanization of Catholics was at its height, there was an even greater insistence upon it following the defeat of Governor Smith. This corresponded with renewed Catholic activity in many lines—notably newspaper and radio propaganda, and apologetics directed toward non-Catholics by means of inter-denominational conferences.

The most vigorous utterance on schools came from Cardinal Hayes of New York, on August 4, 1929. In a pastoral letter he wrote:

"At a recent convention of the National Catholic Educational Association, the slogan was 'Every Catholic Child in a Catholic School.' *Parents are not free in this matter. Their strict duty is to send their children to the only school that can preserve the precious jewel of their Faith.*"*

This utterance was made the text for a vigorous propaganda in Catholic publications all over the country. Typical of this were two articles by the Jesuit Father Paul L. Blakely, and they are important because of the present predominance of the Jesuits in Romanism. Among other things he said:

"After many years of contact with Catholic schools and Catholic parents, I am still dumb (if that is possible) with amazement, and a certain chagrin, when I meet Catholics who have never heard that the duty to which Cardinal

* America, August 31, 1929, Page 496.

Hayes refers, is set forth with emphasis in the law of the Church. * * *

"It must be brought home to them that to send their children to some Catholic school, is, most emphatically, not a pious devotion, like taking off one's hat when passing a church. They must be taught that it is a 'strict duty' which, if neglected, renders them liable to another old-fashioned thing, to wit, hell fire. Then, it may be, they will consent, albeit grudgingly, to obey the Church's positive command in this matter.

"I may speak foolishly, but I cannot help thinking that all of us, priests as well as the educated laity, have been far too mealy-mouthed about this obligation. * * * Ten centuries hence the law * * * will be as mandatory as it is today, and as peremptory as it was ten centuries ago."*

Father Blakely confirms all that has been said about the true political purpose of the parochial schools in this statement:

"Upon the maintenance of the Catholic schools depends, humanly speaking, the future of the Catholic Church in this country, and the survival of at least some remnants of Christianity (meaning Catholic principles) *in our legal codes and our public life.*"**

The position of the Catholic Church was brought up to date, and the American campaign for parochial schools further stimulated, by the Encyclical of Pius XI, published on January 11, 1930. In this he re-asserts the supreme right of the Roman Church to control all education, carefully limits the rights of the State, and insists that every State should support the Catholic schools from general taxation. He denounces public schools as hostile to Romanism. The key-note of this Encyclical is the following:

"No perfect or even adequate education can exist which is not Christian education."***

* America, August 31, 1929, Pages 496-7.
** Ibid, Page 497.
*** Translation from the New York Times, Jan. 19, 1930.

In this and all other of the Pope's remarks, it must be remembered that to him and all Catholics, "Christian" means "Catholic." He goes on:

"Education belongs pre-eminently to the Church for two supernatural reasons which God Himself conferred exclusively on her and which, therefore, are absolutely superior to other reasons of a natural order.

"The first reason is the explicit mission to teach entrusted to the Church by its Divine Founder. * * *

"At the same time as a mandate to teach, Christ conferred infallibility in educative work on His Church. * * * The Church, therefore, has the independent right to judge whether any other system or method of education is helpful or harmful to Christian education. * * * Nor can the exercise of this right be considered undue interference, but precious maternal care on the part of the Church to safeguard her children from the grave dangers of doctrinal moral poisons. * * * As for the scope of the Church's educative mission, it extends over all peoples without any limitation. * * * her educative mission extends also to the non-faithful."

The Pope places the right of parents to control the education of their children next after that of the Roman Church, and before that of the State. He says:

"Families, therefore, have directly from God the mission and therefore the right to educate their children, which is an inalienable right because intimately bound up with family duties, which are prior to any claims by civil society or by the State and therefore inviolable by any earthly authority."

He declares that it is the duty of every State to support Catholic education:

"* * * it is the duty of the State to respect the supernatural rights of the Church over Christian education. * * * Principally it is the State's duty to encourage the education and instruction of youth in all ways and in the first place by favoring and helping the initiative and work of the Church. * * * However, it is clear that in all these means for promoting public or private education and instruction, the State must respect the native rights of the Church and families over Christian education, besides observing distributive justice."

What he means by "distributive justice" is supporting the Catholic schools from public funds. He says:

"* * * the State ought more reasonably, and can more easily, provide schools by giving free rein to the initiative and work of the Church and the family and by helping them with adequate subsidies."

Further on he declares that distributive justice "requires" that Catholic schools shall be helped by public funds. He allows the State a very limited right in education:

"* * * the State may reserve for itself the institution and direction of preparatory schools for some of its departments, and especially for the militia, provided it takes care not to injure the rights of the Church and families."

He re-asserts most emphatically the absolute duty of Catholics to send their children only to Catholic schools, as follows:

"We repeat and confirm their (previous Popes') declarations, together with the prescriptions of the sacred canons by which attendance at non-Catholic, neutral or mixed schools or of schools, that is to say, indifferently open to Catholics and non-Catholics without distinction, is forbidden to Catholic children and can be tolerated only at the discretion of Bishops in special circumstances of place and time and under special precautions. * * *

"The fact alone that religious instruction is imparted (often with too much parsimony) is not sufficient for the schools to be considered as conforming with the rights of the Church and Christian families and worthy to be frequented by Catholic scholars. For a school to be acceptable it is necessary that the whole teaching and organization of the school, namely, the teachers, the curriculum and the books, be governed by the Christian spirit under the maternal direction and vigilance of the Church."

Finally the Pope avows the civil and political, as well as the moral, purposes of Catholic education, in the following statement:

"Christian (that is, Catholic) education comprehends the whole sphere of human life, both earthly and spiritual, both intellectual and moral, both individual, domestic and social * * *."

Roman Catholic leaders in America, led by Cardinal Hayes, immediately tried to soften the effect of this pronouncement on those who believe in the American system of education. They claimed in the first place that the Encyclical was not directed against American conditions, but was general in its purpose, and in the second, that the Church recognized the rights of the parents as coming above all others.

The first claim is only partly true. Certain parts of the Encyclical were doubtless inspired by the quarrel of the Pope with Mussolini over Italian education. But there are certain other parts, including all those which have been quoted, that can have little or no application in Italy, but that do apply directly, and chiefly, to America. Such are all his remarks about distinctively church schools and the evils of public schools. As has been shown, parochial schools exist almost exclusively in Protestant countries, and are far more developed in America than anywhere else. No amount of explaining can set aside the direct and immediate application of the Pope's teachings to American conditions.

As to the prior rights of parents over their children, Father Blakely explains that the Roman Church can admit them without injury to itself or loss of authority, since it rules the parents! He says:

"* * * the laws and minor regulations which the Church has seen fit to adopt, in no wise infringe upon the right of parents to control the education of the child. Undoubtedly that right is theirs. * * * But no one can claim any right to do what is wrong. * * * As supreme in Faith and morals, she (the Church) demands that she be consulted in the education of the child, and that the law which she ordains to safeguard both parent and child, be fully obeyed. In no sense does she invade, or usurp, or destroy the right of parents to control the education of the child. But she does defend the equally undoubted right of the Catholic child to receive an education that is truly Catholic, and she does insist that parental right cannot include the right to do something that is wrong—namely, to bring up the child as a pagan."*

This, in plain English, means simply that the parents have the "right" to do what the church tells them, and nothing else. Father Blakely fails to explain by what reasoning Rome also enforces her laws against the wishes of the Protestant parent in case of mixed marriages, or of millions of free-thinking parents in Italy nor how she justifies taking a child away from its parents, and bringing it up a Catholic, as was done with a Jewish boy in the last year when the Papacy had the power to perpetrate such an outrage.

Such is the Roman educational campaign—the corner stone of its anti-Americanism. It preserves its children from contact with American Liberal ideas; it brings them up to complete hierarchial subjection; it prepares them to carry on its anti-American struggle.

When all these activities of the Romanist hierarchy in America are considered, their purpose be-

* America, September 7, 1929, Pages 520-21.

comes obvious. There has been no recession from the extreme Ultramontane doctrines of Papalism, though they have been kept in the background. Vast numbers of American Catholics do not realize the meaning of the training they are given—the Catholic legislators described by Mrs. Sargent did not Nevertheless, the foundations for Papal and hierarchial supremacy are carefully laid.

With the whole Catholic population of America the hierarchy is preparing, as it did with these legislators, a basis on which it can secure the acceptance of its authority when it desires, and the enforcement of claims which it now allows to lie dormant. It is doing this by making sure that Catholics have trained consciences upon which Papal Ultramontanism may safely rely. Thus, in America today, the Roman hierarchy is drilling an army—unified, disciplined and blindly submissive—that can be used against American Liberalism if ever the "strategic situation" changes. This is true even if many or most of its members do not realize the purpose in view.

CHAPTER XXVII

THE DELUSION OF SECURITY

The menace of disunity because of Romanist policy—The attempt to undermine and pervert Liberal American principles and the institutions based on them—Effect of these menaces already serious—A chief cause of increasing lawlessness—Threatened points of conflict—Catholic predictions of strife and victory—Increasing Catholic aggressiveness due to increased numbers—Survival of Americanism depends on elimination of Papalism from politics.

THE record of Catholicism under the Papal Theory is now complete. From the first vague movement toward the supremacy of the Roman See a thousand years ago, through the autocracy of the Middle Ages and the long fight against human liberty, through the triumph of Ultramontanism which marked the renewed strength of the Papacy half a century ago, down to the present increased aggression, including solidarity and opposition to Liberalism in America, the record shows not only unwavering consistency but re-invigorated encroachment in our own days.

Always there is a vast chasm between the philosophy, the social practice and the political purposes of Romanism and those of modern Liberalism. The modern policy of the Papacy, instead of closing the chasm, is laboring to widen it. Whatever tendency there is among Catholics to adapt themselves to modern thought and conditions comes in spite of the opposition of their spiritual leaders.

These conditions cannot be questioned by any sincere and informed person; nevertheless there are many who attempt to convince us that they hold no menace and present no problem. They can give no reason except their own incurable optimism. There can be no logical basis for their reassurance, in view of the fact that one-fifth of the American people are radically opposed to the ideas fundamental to our national thought and institutions. There are some 23,000,000 persons holding the philosphy and submitting to the discipline of Catholicism. They hardly understand American Liberalism but must oppose it so far as they do understand, and must fight its practical working out in social and governmental institutions.

It is idle to pretend that there is no menace in such an opposition; those who suffer this delusion are of the same type as those who assured us in 1913 that there could never be another great war! This is a conflict based upon convictions which are fundamentally religious, whether those who hold them consider themselves religious or not, and religion is as vital a force in human life and as pregnant a cause for strife as any that is known. As Hilaire Belloc says:

"Religion is at the root of all culture, and societies differ more from difference in religion than from difference in any other factor. It is more powerful than race, far more powerful than physical environment."*

It is certain that this conflict presents a vital problem, for it must not only cause many struggles over social and political policies, but a deeper danger in loss of national unity.

There is no need in this day to argue the necessity for unity of mind in any nation which is to be strong. The subject has been too thoroughly covered by one of the greatest of modern psychologists,

* The Contrast, Page 147.

Professor William McDougall. He defines nationhood as follows:

"* * * the essential condition for lack of which any
such people would fall short of nationhood (is) * * * such
mental organization as will render the group capable of
effective group life, of collective deliberation and collective
volition. * * * A nation is * * * a population * * * possessed
of a national mind and character."*

He also declares that the religious differences
among European peoples are "clearly due to the
assimilation of the form of the religious and ecclesiastical system to the innate tendencies of the
people"** and that "innate mental constitution,
and therefore race, is of fundamental importance in determining mind and character."***

In other words, the strength of a nation depends
upon the unity of the national mind; this in turn
depends upon the religion and racial characteristics
of the individual members of the nation.

America was settled by kindred races, imbued
with similar ideals of personal liberty and public
service. There was no problem of unity so long
as immigration came from races holding those
ideals.   But we now realize that there has been practically no assimilation whatever, so far as fundamentals go, of most immigrants since 1880. The
introduction to Dr. Siegfried's book says of this:

"The influx of Latin and Slav immigration that swept
across the Atlantic during the twenty years before the War
now threatens to alter the very composition of the American race. Against this the descendants of the original

* The Group Mind, Page 141.
** Ibid, Page 160.
*** Ibid, Page 164.

Anglo-Saxon Puritan stock are defending themselves with grim determination.''*

Even the Irish, many of whom are now Americans of several generations, have not been assimilated in the sense of becoming American in their outlook on life. Of all these Dr. Siegfried says:

"Assimilation only begins to be troublesome with the Catholics.**"

Thus racially and mentally our national unity has already been destroyed by Catholics. They do not think as we do, feel as we do, nor share our principles nor our purposes individually, socially, or politically. So long as this condition lasts national unity is impossible. This discord is constantly fostered and aggravated by the Catholic hierarchy.

Another menace caused by the twenty-three million Catholics in America is to the permanance of our fundamental ideals. Rome inculcates in its followers a system of thought which is implacably hostile to them. The whole strategy of American Catholicism forbids any direct attack, but Romanism seeks to accomplish its purpose indirectly. By a hundred clever methods it is "whittling away" at American ideals, underminding the foundations of national thought, confusing our logic and baffling our purpose. It has already rendered non-Catholics' understanding of their own purposes vague and contradictory, and has confused the whole issue. In time it might seriously pervert every American ideal.

Its similar indirect attack upon religious Protestantism is also important because, as we have seen, the ideals of Protestantism and of American

* America Comes of Age, Page vi.
** Ibid, Page 23.

patriotism are so very closely allied. In regard to this situation, Dr. John Moffatt Mecklin, in a book which was an attack on the Ku Klux Klan, says:

"Again in the matter of religious liberty and toleration the devout Catholic pursues an opportunistic policy. The Klansman has foolishly allowed himself to be jockeyed into a position in which he is, in actual fact, the opponent of tolerance while his Catholic adversary is really its champion. It is the logic of circumstances, however, rather than devotion to the principle of toleration, that determines the Catholic attitude. The devout Catholic, for whom the immediate practical problem is his status in American democracy, has no other choice than to champion religious toleration. For he is well aware that the principle of religious toleration has been of incalculable value to him in finding a foothold in a country essentially Protestant and traditionally prejudiced against all things Catholic.*

"Now when we throw together in a free democratic society two types of religion, one of which accepts religious tolerance as a vital principle of society, the other as a mere matter of expediency and hence to be repudiated when circumstances require it, we get a very interesting situation. Tolerance for Baptist, Methodist, or Presbyterian means a fair field and the right to compete with other sects for the religious loyalties of men. Tolerance for the Catholic Church, not necessarily intentionally but in actual practice, means merely license for carrying out the logic of a theocratic autocracy. Protestantism thus finds itself in competition with a church which does not accept the rule of a fair field except as a matter of expediency, that does not treat the various forms of Protestantism as legitimate rivals but as erroneous and dangerous deviations from the true faith and therefore to be eradicated." (Page 198)

"Under these circumstances Protestant antipathy to Catholicism does not seem wholly without justification. These facts must be honestly faced before we condemn offhand the anti-Catholicism of the Klan." (Page 199)

Since Americanism is beyond question an outgrowth of Protestantism, and religious equality is

* The Ku Klux Klan, Page 196 and following.

a political principle, this Catholic attitude toward Protestant ideals has distinct political importance.

Still another menace from Catholicism is its effect upon the stability of our national institutions. As has been shown, these institutions have been developed from and are adjusted to our own national genius, based on Protestant idealism. They are therefore automatically repugnant to the devout Catholic. In the same indirect way in which Catholicism attacks American ideals, it is also undermining the embodiment of those ideals in social and political institutions. It is doing this in two ways:

First, by the change which it is bringing about in our national mind through the injection of the European mentality against which our fathers rebelled, from which they escaped, and with which our institutions are out of harmony;

Second, through the importation of European problems and causes of friction which our institutions have escaped by avoidance, and with which they are not equipped to deal.

We have already seen the effect of this in several different ways: an increased tendency toward paternalism, persistent attempts to nullify the Constitution, refusal to accept civic responsibility, resistance to the national conscience, and particularly in a mental as well as an actual refusal to obey moral laws. The refusal is serious enough; the fact that Catholic inmates of penal institutions are out of all proportion to the number of Catholics in the country is so important as to deserve more attention than can be given here. It has become even more serious since Catholic intellectuals defend disobedience to law. The Jesuit weekly, "America," declares:

"In all this business of the passing of the Volstead Act, we can see a host of rascals and hypocrites. But we can see no law. For law is, pre-eminently, a rule of reason, adopted by competent authority, for the common good."*

Similarly Father John A. Ryan argues:

"The ethical proposition laid down by Senator Borah to the effect that it is never right to violate civil law, that a constitutional amendment is always morally binding until it is repealed, are false propositions. * * * There are exceptions. * * * If they buy liquor they can feel assured that they are violating no civil law; if they make it and keep it for their own use, then he can have no fear that they are transgressing any moral law."**

With such statements from Catholic leaders it is no wonder that Catholics are being crowded into our penitentiaries!

The attitude of the Roman Catholic Church itself toward lawlessness has been well illustrated in two great American cities and, indeed, in others. New York and Chicago very nearly hold the pre-eminence of corruption in America and both are under predominantly Catholic governments. Upon their officials Catholicism must be able to exert its utmost influence. Conditions in both cities are notorious, yet in neither has the Roman clergy shown any sign of attempting to bring home to the Catholic officials their responsibility for these conditions. If the Roman Church has spoken it has been in a whisper. If it has taken any stand in favor of decency and in opposition to corruption, this stand has been kept a deep secret. Yet Chicago is the city honored by the Eucharistic Congress and New York police and firemen sprawled in the mud to kiss the hands and the feet of the Pope's legate to that Congress.

* America, March 2, 1929.
** The Commonweal, April 3, 1929.

The reason for this Catholic lawlessness was stated by Dean Inge of St. Paul's, London, in the following appraisal of Catholicism:

"On the whole it can hardly be denied that it has been a failure. It does not seem to have raised the moral tone of society in the countries which have adopted it, except perhaps in such Arcadian communities as Oberammergau and in some very limited circles living an old-fashioned life under priestly direction. It has shown all the defects of despotism—a costly and luxurious central government, necessitating heavy taxation and the ruthless suppression of all movements toward freedom.

"This kind of oppression is peculiarly searching and tyrannical under a theocracy because it lays its hands not only on overt acts, but upon all liberty of thought. * * * An acute conflict of loyalties is set up between Church and State; *no Catholic is more than conditionally a patriot, and the conditions are of the political and not of the moral order.* * * * Conscience is stifled; and the Catholic is curiously impervious to that lay morality which, with all its defects, generally embodies the best features of a national character. These defects are, of course, not in any way connected with the Christian religion; *they are the defects of theocratic autocracy in its Catholic form.*"*

These dangers are mostly invisible and intangible, matters of the spirit and of thought. It is easy to deny them or to ignore them, it is easy to be blind to their menace if anyone so desires. We believe in free thought and free speech; therefore it is even possible for shallow "Liberals" to tolerate the Catholic propaganda on these grounds so long as they refuse to see that it is founded on denial of free thought and speech to Catholics themselves, and aims at a denial of those rights to all men.

They have the excuse that Catholics are at great pains to avoid the appearance of any conflict. They

* Outspoken Essays, Second Series, Page 111.

do this by what Dr. Mecklin calls "opportunism," but what may as fairly be called "hypocrisy." In many superficial ways Catholicism has adapted itself with marvelous Jesuitry to American civilization; nevertheless it has not in any degree modified its essential theocratic, politico-religious principles and structure, nor its fundamental objection to Liberalism. So long as this remains true the conflict can be ignored only by those who are either mentally blind or who blind themselves with a baseless optimism.

There are other menaces which are entirely tangible and which have already brought Catholicism and Protestantism into direct conflict; still others may cause open warfare at any time.

So far the chief struggle has centered about the public schools. The Roman Catholic Church, being what it is, must oppose them. It forbids children to attend the public schools; nevertheless it attacks and tries to control them. It has prevented the reading of the Bible and revised the histories. Thus, even while insisting upon its right to teach its children what it wants, it has succeeded in preventing us from teaching our children in our schools what we want. It is to be noted, too, that this activity of the Roman Catholic Church has been directed particularly against religious teaching; it has been from first to last an exhibition of intolerance by the one religious body which most loudly demands and most seriously needs toleration.

Moreover, the Roman Catholic Church has tried, again with much success, to capture our public schools through forcing into them Catholic teachers. It maintains many Catholic schools for the training of public school teachers. One has only

to look at the school system in any city which is
controlled by Catholic governments. There is not
today, for instance, a single Protestant in the dozen
foremost positions in the New York City schools
and every New York City teacher knows that Protestants cannot hope for important promotion. Catholic educators boast that in New York the graduates
of the Catholic normal schools are far more successful in obtaining teaching positions than are the
graduates of the normal schools supported by the
State!

Here is already a direct and open conflict, one
definitely incited and led by the Roman Catholic
clergy. It has not become violent only because
Protestants are not fighting back. How real it is
will appear if we imagine what would occur were
the situation reversed; what a deafening outcry
would arise if Protestants, although in the majority,
should try to forbid the religious teachings of the
Catholic schools or to force Protestant teachers
into those schools! Yet Catholics have done both
those things to us!

Of course we will not attempt either, but it is
possible that many American states may adopt laws
forbidding the teaching of such anti-American doctrines as are contained in Catholic textbooks. If
they do, there will surely be a tremendous outcry
and a violent conflict.

Certain other conflicts have previously been
touched upon. The list includes many subjects.
Some will probably never go beyond the political
field but others will definitely require Catholics to
choose whether they shall obey the laws of their
nation or of their Pope. In the list must be put
all the following subjects:

IMMIGRATION. The Catholic Church opposes immigration restriction because it wants recruits from abroad and it uses a definite influence in politics on this subject.

PROHIBITION. This invades Rome's claim to all control of morals, and is most seriously opposed by Catholic leaders, who encourage their followers to violate the law. They have not, however, urged them to resist the law.

MORAL LEGISLATION OF ALL KINDS. The same opposition is extended to apply to any law affecting morals. Catholics habitually resist any laws for the preservation of the Sabbath and violate such laws if they are adopted. They would unquestionably take the same attitude toward similar laws on other subjects. The censorship of indecent literature is a current example.

BIRTH CONTROL. Regardless of our personal attitude on this subject, it must be recognized that there is a definite possibility of certain American states passing laws which would commit the state to work along this line. If such a law were passed any Catholic official would be forbidden by his church to carry it into effect. Here for the first time we pass the line between passive and active resistance to American law.

EUTHANASIA. This, like birth control, is another extreme illustration, but no one can say that it is impossible. It is the name given to the proposed practice of ending the lives of incurable idiots, lunatics and babies that are hopeless monstrosities. This practice is being widely advocated and might be adopted by some states. Any Catholic would be required by his religion to resist any such law.

For a Catholic, even today, it is permissible under Canon Law to burn a heretic alive but it would be murder to end a useless, dangerous or monstrous life.

EUGENICS. Conflict on this is quite likely to arrive. There is already wide advocacy of laws which would forbid the marriage of any two persons unless they have been certified by proper medical authority as being physically fit to have children. Under the Canon Law neither a Catholic priest nor a Catholic person who desired marriage could obey such a law nor any other law restricting the birth of children—fit or unfit.

MIXED MARRIAGE. A situation still more likely to arise will come from passage of laws forbidding the Catholic practice of requiring that children of mixed marriages be committed by contract to the Catholic religion. Such laws as this, aiming to secure the religious freedom of the children, would be entirely in line with American principles and will almost certainly be adopted in some states. A Catholic priest would be forbidden by his church to obey, and direct conflict and resistance to law would certainly arise the moment that such a statute went into effect. The same would be true of any law requiring the Catholic Church to recognize the validity of civil marriages. The Church does not do so, but the direct issue this raises against the authority of the State has never become acute. A provision forbidding the Catholic Church to teach that civil marriages are invalid, however, would certainly make it so.

INTERNATIONAL AFFAIRS. There are possibilities of serious conflict here, although we may hope that they are remote. There is evidence that during the World War the Vatican protected German spies in Italy because of its sympathy with Austria. Quite certainly, if this country were engaged in war with a nation which the Vatican favored, the Roman hierarchy in America and all who followed its orders would give what protection they could to enemy agents. If this happened, as is possible, American Catholics would be required to face the ultimate test of loyalty.

These are all danger points. On which one the direct conflict between Catholicism and American law will first arise it is, of course, impossible to predict. That it is inevitable is asserted by Catholic writers as well as Protestants. William Thomas Walsh, for example, says:

"Any or all of these problems—unless the majority accepts the Catholic view, as it ultimately will because that view is right—could lead to a serious impasse."*

That is, Mr. Walsh declares that Catholics will refuse to accept American law on any such conflicts. Mr. Belloc, in a quotation cited once before, says that the conflict is inevitable:

"But no one can know the United States without admitting that when the conflict shall there arise, an equilibrium will not be established or preserved, for the conflict will be novel and will seem monstrous. On the one side you have a plain affirmation that the law is the law and must be obeyed, and indignant surprise on the rejection of what seems so obvious and universal a rule. On the other, you will have, as you have had throughout history, resistance to and denial of that rule."**

In this conflict American Catholics will almost certainly have the open political leadership of the Catholic hierarchy, but the conflict does not depend

* America, July 20, 1929.
** The Contrast, Page 165.

on this leadership any more than Catholic opposition to American ideals depends on the political leadership of the hierarchy. The conflict would go on even without this leadership, since at all points it springs from the mentality—perhaps from the racial character—of the Catholic population. Conscience and the point of view which the Papacy has so carefully implanted through many generations can be depended upon to maintain the war of Papalism against Americanism.

The power of the Romanist campaign in America does not even depend wholly on numbers, although numbers are important in a democracy. Thanks to the immigration laws we need no longer fear an inundation of Catholicism from abroad. Even the high birth rate of Catholics, of which their leaders have boasted and from which they had predicted ultimate domination, is dropping rapidly.

The fact that the Catholics have become a powerful minority, however, has caused a change in the tactics of the hierarchy here. Until recent years the Catholic leaders have usually been content to maintain their own religious freedom, but the increased numbers of the last few decades have brought a greatly increased aggressiveness.

This shows in two ways. The first has been the development of vigorous and widespread propaganda, which has taken many forms. By far the least dangerous of these is the openly Catholic press. Much more effective is the pressure brought to bear upon publications which are not supposed to be Catholic, through secret Catholic ownership or the influence of the Catholic advertizers. This form of propaganda effects equally fiction, the stage, the movies and the radio. An example is the treatment of clergymen by these agencies; Protestant clergymen are constantly being lampooned and attacked but there has not been in years any depiction of a Catholic priest which was not complimentary. There is bitter irony in the fact that this Romanist propaganda depends on the American principle of free speech which Catholics oppose. In Italy, under Catholic control, any similar anti-Catholic propaganda would be vigorously punished.

The second form of Catholic aggressiveness is shown in politics. Through the use of the "balance of power" Romanism brings pressure to bear upon both parties by threatening to throw all its strength to whichever party will most fully meet its demands. The success of this policy is proved by the extent to which Catholic voters—though a minority—have succeeded in imposing their desires upon the vast majority of non-Catholics and in the tremendous power of the "Catholic vote" in almost every campaign. This is possible, of course, only because Protestantism is divided and unorganized while Romanism is a militant and unified organization. This condition will remain so long as non-Catholics refuse to recognize and face the menace of Catholicism. It will become impossible the moment that non-Catholics unite.

Thus Americanism is threatened from many directions by the presence of our twenty three million Catholics. The danger menaces almost every point of American life—our civil order and our principles, our schools and our national unity, stability of our institutions, free speech, law observance, majority rule, public regulation of morality and even international policy.

Taken together, these attacks upon Americanism and attempts to subvert it threaten to bring about a vital change in the nation, to transform its spirit, its beliefs and its purposes. This threatened transformation was clearly foreseen by Mr. Belloc in a passage already quoted. It is set forth by Dr. Siegfried in the following, which places the blame squarely on the present policy of the Catholic Church:

"The Catholic Church is, therefore, the natural rallying point of those who are being jostled by Americanization, and whose customs are being trodden under foot. In championing them the Church runs the risk of going to extremes in opposition to the genuinely humane spirit of Americanization, and also of sharing the exclusiveness of the races it is trying to protect, such as the Irish, the Germans, the Italians, the Poles, and the French-Canadians. Thirty years ago that great statesman, Cardinal Gibbons, steered the Catholic Church into a very different path. He wished it to take its place among the national institutions of the country, not as an Irish or German influence, but as simply and essentially American. In the face of bitter resistance he set out to break up the nationalist groups within the Church itself, but since his death, Catholicism has reverted to its previous type, and again become the religion of the foreigner. * * * In the great cities of the East and Middle West, and even in the Far West, this traditional alliance between the Irish and the Catholic priests gives the religion a medaeval aspect which is both primitive and pathetic."*

Dr. Siegfried sums up the situation in a statement that has already been quoted:

"Is it possible to contemplate a United States that is neither Protestant or Anglo-Saxon? This is the aim of an opposition which, however, is not constructive and resists only by instinct. And yet they persist."**

To non-Catholics, as Mr. Belloc says, such a change would be a monstrous perversion. For three

* America Comes of Age, Pages 50-51.
** Ibid, Page 146.

hundred years America has followed unhesitatingly the path of human freedom, of denying any Divine Right to Pope, king or aristocrat. Americanism has become the supreme embodiment of the Protestant ideal; the future development and fulfillment of that ideal are inseparably bound up with the destiny of this nation. Such embodiment as its principles have found in Europe could hardly survive their destruction here. If the great purposes of the Reformation, of Liberalism and of human progress are to come to fruition, it must be through the preservation of the Americanism of our fathers as it has inspired this nation until now. In this is the key to the destiny of humanity.

Yet the preservation of liberty, where Roman Catholics are concerned, depends upon keeping them from political power. When they have power they destroy liberty as they have destroyed it in Italy. If they should win power in America, they would destroy our rights as they have destroyed the rights of the Italians. Even short of this, whatever influence the Roman hierarchy and its followers may be able to exert in our mental, social, civil or political life, must inevitably be used against American Liberal principles—to cripple, thwart, pervert and ultimately to destroy them if possible!

The menace of Catholicism in America is no less than this—it aims to stop this great experiment in the erection of a civilization built upon human rights; to cut off at the roots its purpose, its principles, its splendid achievement, its half-won fulfillment and its infinite promises.

Under the influence of Catholicism America might become great in some other form of civilization but it would not be the American form. If Catholicism wins we may be sure that with its victory government of the people, by the people and for the people will have perished.

We cannot prevent this great and vital conflict. We can hope to do no more than to avoid weakening our own position against the day when that conflict shall become acute, to prepare our own forces, and perhaps, to some extent, to weaken the position of our enemy.

CHAPTER XXVIII

LIBERAL PARALYSIS AND ITS CURE

Rome well prepared for the conflict—"Catholic Action" the beginning of direct attack—American Liberalism weak, confused and divided—Rome's success depends on continued
paralysis of Liberals—Failure of toleration to solve the problem—Need of detailed interpretation of the Constitution as
to application of American principles—The Liberal objectives: to clarify the issue; check anti-American teaching;
force Romanism into equality with other churches; enlighten patriotic Catholics; arouse liberal-minded Americans—The final result certain.

IT remains only to take account of the strength
that can be mustered by both sides in the titanic
conflict between Catholicism and Liberalism which
is impending in America. Romanism, as we have
seen, is fully prepared. It has succeeded almost
completely in saving its followers from any con-
tagion or even understanding of Liberal American
ideas. It has maintained an iron discipline and
forced the acceptance of dogmatic Ultramontanism.
It has permitted little weakening of the solidarity
of its 23,000,000 people. It has prepared them to
give full obedience whenever the time may come
that it feels able to make a direct attack upon
Americanism, and in the meanwhile to follow its
lead in all preliminary maneuvres.

Recently Rome has begun to swing them into a
definitely offensive campaign, abandoning the defensive attitude which it had so long kept. The
symbol of the reinvigorated aggression of the Roman
Church throughout the world is the movement
known as "Catholic Action," described by Count
Dalla Torre.* It has been put to work in every

* See Page 204 and following.

Christian nation and in every field of conflict, but especially in politics. Its purpose is to control Catholic thought and influence non-Catholic thought through organized campaigns in every possible line; to control every Catholic in politics by enrollment in such organizations as the Knights of Columbus and the Holy Name Society; to emphasize the differences between Catholics and all other people, and to constitute in them a body of effective propagandists and fighters. The name is well chosen, for the movement stands for organized, vigorous, devoted, persistent and aggressive "Catholic Action" in social, civic and political life.

This movement is fast taking form in the United States and is providing that leadership for the anti-American campaign which Dr. Siegfried found lacking a few years ago. It is the first step toward making effective use of the solidarity and subservience which the hierarchy has so carefully cultivated. With this Catholic solidarity at last active in its attack on Americanism, several results may come. One is certain—a bitter struggle. It might end in the destruction of the American idea of Liberalism and Catholic control of the nation. It may, short of this, undermine our ideals and pervert the course of national development. It may, and it certainly will for a time, confuse national purpose and impede national progress. Whatever the final result, we shall be fortunate if the conflict can be settled without serious disturbances.

So long as Catholic Action remains aggressive the conflict cannot end unless American Liberals surrender their own ideals. While it lasts all the influence of American Catholicism will be thrown against the success of our civilization, or of any civilization based upon human liberty. If Americanism is to be preserved, if it is to be protected against open aggression and subtle perversion, there must be organized a definite and active campaign in opposition to Catholic Action. Without organized resistance, without a Liberal counter-attack, we may be sure that in time the autocratic theocracy of Rome would win the struggle and liberty would be destroyed.

Yet American Liberalism is pitifully weak to meet the attack, and is even less able to organize a counter-offensive. Partly this is due to its own internal dissensions, partly to over-confidence based on past victories and long safety, but chiefly to the confusion of thought which Catholicism has already succeeded in creating. The achievement of the hierarchy in building up its anti-American army in a free country is a tremendous one, but is not to be compared with its amazing success in paralyzing American Liberalism. It almost seems, at times, as if the old-time Liberalism, the Liberalism which was aggressive in defending and extending human liberty both for itself and all the world, were wholly dead.

We have, to be sure, a movement which has stolen the name. But this modern Liberalism, so-called, has little in common with the old. It has never understood the essentials of the preservation of liberty; has hardly even learned in what liberty consists. It is based very little on conviction and much on indifference; it willingly tolerates anything, however evil, which does not attack it, but is utterly intolerant of reasoned opposition. It is often completely perverted into a pursuit of license. It sees a menace to individual liberty in moral laws, but none in the destruction of individuality by the parochial schools; it condemns the restriction of immigration, but advocates restriction on the birthrate of native Americans; it is horrified at censorship of indecency but not at censorship of thought by the Pope; it tolerantly renounces religion, but intolerantly abuses those who profess faith; it tolerates priestly control of voters, and reviles attempts of ministers to exert influence; it ridicules conscience, loyalty and patriotism. It is a "Liberalism," not of principle, but of supreme egoism, of sensuality and materialism; at best mandlin and utopian. There is no health in it.

Yet because of its name it still holds the support of many who believe in that name but have not stopped for analysis of its present debased meaning. It, too, has thus contributed to the paralysis of true Liberalism, and is almost as much an enemy of American principles as is Catholicism.

In spite of this weakness there is no need to despair of the future of true Liberalism nor of its ultimate victory against Romanism. Indeed, the question that confronts us today is not so much what means to take to insure this victory, as the choice of means which will succeed with the least possible strife, injury and resulting bitterness. This is true because there is one great weakness in the Roman position, in spite of all its strength. That weakness is:

The success of the Roman Catholic campaign in America depends wholly upon the continued paralysis and inertia of American Liberalism.

History proves this conclusively. Rome has never won against anything like even numbers of the northern races imbued with the desire for freedom. It took more than a century to destroy the French Hugenots, though treachery, torture, bad faith and the abilities of the greatest French king were used against them, and they were never a tenth of the nation. The subservience and lack of initiative which Rome must instill into her people if she is to control them are a fatal weakness in any real conflict!

The vast majority of Americans are inherently Liberal-minded; they will become irresistably aggressive the moment they see their liberties threatened. They have in our democratic institutions the machinery both for defense and victory. They need only to be aroused; and they will arouse themselves whenever the issue comes home to them.

This, therefore, is the objective toward which we who are already awake must direct our efforts— to make the issue clear.

The first need is to free the minds of the paralyzed Liberals of the idea that our American principle of toleration can provide a solution for the conflict. It did postpone it for a century; we had all hoped that it was a permanent panacea, but its failure is already evident, for the conflict has re-appeared. Let there be no misunderstanding: toleration *as a principle* remains as strong as ever, but toleration *as a preventive of conflict* has not been enough to bring the peace we expected from it.

The reasons are obvious once the situation is faced. Religious toleration is based on the same principle as a truce in war—an agreement by both sides to avoid aggression. It fails, as a truce fails, unless it is faithfully observed by both sides. It has failed in this instance because the religious truce is not observed in politics by the Roman Catholic Church. It will continue to fail so long as Catholicism persists in dogmatic intolerance and political aggression against American principles—and this will be until it has reversed the whole course of its history and abandoned its pretensions.

The practical effect of toleration in America, therefore, is to give to Catholics a great advantage over non-Catholics. They interpret it as giving them the right to suppress freedom in their schools, to practice intolerance themselves, and to carry on a politico-religious campaign. Catholicism not merely violates the truce; it demands in the name of American principles which it rejects for itself, that non-Catholics not only keep their own pledge of inactivity, but "tolerate" the Catholic refusal to do the same.

This does not mean that we must abandon the principle of toleration; far from it. Such a course is unthinkable. Even if we could bring ourselves to revert to the religious persecutions of two hundred years ago, we know that they would be futile and would intensify instead of healing the discord. But we could not; our own principles forbid. Complete and unhesitating toleration must be given to the Catholic religion—as to all others—both for the sake of expedience and for our own peace of conscience.

But when we examine the failure of toleration we see that it is neither complete nor fundamental. It has failed at one point only and when this single point has been safeguarded we may safely maintain the principle unchanged.

This point is an accurate definition of what matters may justly claim immunity because of religious toleration. The failure of toleration to function, most of the present confusion, and much of the success of the Romanist campaign, has been due to the fact that there has been no sharp line drawn as to where tolerance should begin or stop. The principle is new in human thought, and with typical human laziness we have allowed it to remain vague. In general we have allowed each religion to choose for itself those matters on which it could claim religious tolerance, and have respected the claims of each.

To be sure at times the public conscience has revolted, as in the case of Mormon polygamy and the spreading of contagious disease by faith healers. These revolts, however, have dealt each with a single abuse and have not gone to the root of the problem. What is necessary is a clarification of the whole question, so that we may know definitely how far the cloak of religion can be spread. Certainly it must cover all relations between men and their Maker and all beliefs which are held merely as a form of faith, such as the Catholic worship of saints. Just as certainly it cannot cover criminal actions, however strongly they are supported by religious beliefs, such as the human sacrifices of Voodooism. Between these two extremes lies an undefined middle ground, and it is here that the conflict in regard to toleration rages—a conflict that has been raised by the demand of the Roman Catholics that their political campaign against American principles be tolerated in the name of religion.

This conflict can almost entirely be ended by the simple process of definition of rights. There has been no standard by which the political activities of Catholicism could be measured against American principles. It is true they are based on ideas and purposes which the Popes declare to be religious, and it is natural enough that Catholicism should make all the use it can of religious toleration in their behalf. If there had existed any definition of the extent to which toleration may be stretched to cover "religious" activities which are hurtful to the body-politic or to other citizens, none of the confusion and little of the conflict would have arisen.

This definition must come from the conscience of the American people and no one may presume to anticipate their verdict. It is possible, however, to suggest some of the details in regard to which definition is necessary. For example:

How far may a church go in teaching disloyalty to the American government as a religious principle?

How far may it go in inculcating opposition to the principles on which our government is founded?

May it advocate disrespect to American laws and the American Constitution?

Shall it be allowed to teach that there is any human authority superior to that of the government on any law?

Can it be allowed to organize political machinery on a religious basis?

May it use its spiritual authority to coerce voters or members who are in public office?

Finally, how much of these activities must be accepted by citizens of other faiths, or of no faith, without opposition or criticism, on grounds of religious toleration?

It cannot be pretended that answers to these questions, definitions covering this conflict, can be worked out easily or without hot debate. Unless they are worked out, however, the principle of religious toleration itself will break down under the load of purely political questions which are being thrown upon it.

Such a process of definition is entirely in harmony with American principles and customs; it has been necessary with almost every one of the guarantees embodied in the Constitution. These were of necessity stated only in the most general terms; they could not be enforced in practice till they had been given detailed definition through legislation, and careful interpretation through judicial decision. The same process must be applied to the right of religious freedom. The conflict will only be finally ended when we have added to the principle of tolerance, specific Laws of Toleration.

It is so with all other matters involved in the conflict. The practical application of the known principles must be worked out and made statutory. So long as the dispute remains in the fog and misunderstanding which now surround it there can be no hope for permanent religious peace.

The outcome for which American Liberals must work throughout the conflict is the re-creation of unity of national mind and character in America. This *must* be the result if national strength and progress are to continue unchecked. It can be brought about—unless through the suppression of Liberalism—only by the conversion of Catholics to American principles. But the basis for any such conversion must be clarity of thought and accurate definition of principles, so that Catholics may understand exactly the political philosophy we offer them. This requires, in addition to a definition of religious toleration, a codification of the rights and duties of churches under the principle of the separation of Church and State. Some of the questions involved are:

The legal position of all churches in respect to the State, to their members, and to each other, together with their duties toward the State and the precise limits of their right to political activity either directly or through religious power over their followers.

The rights and limits of power of churches over the marriage and education of their members.

The rights of children to religious freedom and the conflicting rights of parents or churches to limit such freedom.

The relative powers of the churches and the State in regard to the validity of law and the duties of citizens.

The rights of the clergy to organized political authority over the members of their churches.

In general, we must make Catholics know the American meaning of freedom, equality and Liberalism, and the reasons why we believe in them!

It has not hitherto been necessary to define these rights, because so long as all important American churches were Protestant, the Protestant understanding of the principle of separation of Church and State was universally accepted. Since the Roman Catholic Church challenges that definition, it has now become a duty of the legislative bodies to let the country know whether or not the historic meaning continues in control.

When these definitions of American principles have been worked out, it is obvious that there must follow legislation to prevent the teaching of anti-American definitions to immature minds in the

primary schools. The principle of freedom of
thought and speech certainly does not mean that a
few men should be able to close the doors to free
thought and free discussion in the minds of millions
of children. We cannot allow this "freedom" of
suppression any more than we can allow "freedom"
to any man to impose bodily slavery on others.

Also, we cannot allow an unrestricted right to
anyone to inculcate in immature children resistance to the moral principles on which our government and social institutions rest. This obvious rule has been clearly stated by one of the leading Catholic writers, Gilbert K. Chesterton, in an
article on "The New Tolerance." He said:

"* * * every Commonwealth is in fact founded on a
moral philosophy * * * some scheme or figure must run
through the whole pattern; it cannot be merely patched
with a totally different pattern * * * the social authority
does reserve a right to defend its moral order against certain extremes of destructive differentiation."*

This is perfectly good sense, and American
Catholics must expect that it will be applied against
them so far as their campaign is destructive of
Americanism. The moral order upon which America is founded is based upon the Protestant idea of
human liberty, and the nation has ample and just
authority to defend itself against Catholic attack
through the teaching of anti-Liberal principles
in its schools. It has been repeatedly held by the
courts that the right of free speech does not cover
the preaching of rebellion; similarly, there can be
no question that the Catholic conflict is so vital
as to make teaching children anti-Americanism in
the name of religion a practice "contrary to public
security."

* America, July 27, 1929.

Under this principle there are certain Catholic teachings which so obviously have no claim to religious toleration that they should be forbidden even before the definitions suggested have been reached, since they are "inconsistent with the peace and safety of the State." It is not tolerable, for example, that millions of Catholic children should be taught the following:

That it is not lawful for the State to hold in equal favor different kinds of religion.

That the State may not lawfully separate itself from the Church.

That tolerance of religions other than Roman Catholicism is permitted by the State not as a right, but as a favor or for expediency.

That the Pope has the right to annul any American law.

The inconsistency of such teachings in America is so great that when Charles C. Marshall asked Governor Smith his opinion in regard to them, Mr. Smith indignantly declared that he "never heard of any such stuff being taught." The evidence is conclusive that "such stuff" is being taught, and no American-minded person can deny that this should be stopped. If it were not taught, no Catholic would be interested in laws forbidding it!

To take this course of the definition of American principles and the prevention of their being taught to immature minds—full freedom of discussion among adults must not, of course, be hampered—would have many advantages. It would not prevent the conflict; that cannot be escaped. In fact, for a time this course would certainly seem to increase the struggle. It would not do so in fact but it would bring it into the open and force it upon public attention. This, in itself, would be worth while.

The initial advantage would be that the Roman Church would be forced either into conformity with American principles or into open revolt—which is not conceivable. This would mean, first of all, religious disarmament. All other American churches long since disarmed for political conflict by accepting the principles of toleration and religious equality, and by drawing a line between religion and morals and politics. Catholicism alone refused, and this has given it the political advantage which it is now exploiting. If we are to have permanent religious peace, Romanism must accept a status no better nor worse than that of all other American churches. If it will not, others must arm themselves again, and progress will be set back by two centuries!

Catholicism would be forced, too, to stop its teaching of anti-Americanism and permit the Americanization of its members. The future generations of Catholics would almost automatically be assimilated if their priests allowed it, and thus inevitably the conflict would come to an end. The teaching of Romanist theocracy in the parochial schools is now making future friction inevitable—that is its purpose.

In the meanwhile we cannot safely entrust any important political power to Roman Catholics. We know that in politics and the administration of office many of them would be controlled against American principles, either through "giving ear to the bishops and the Holy See," or indirectly through the operation of priest-trained consciences. It is true that there are some Catholics against whom this charge does not lie, but since non-Catholics cannot know with any certainty which they are, and since Romanism is carrying on the campaign it does, we must distrust them all.

Another great advantage of a definition of American principles is that it would make clear to many Catholics the present position in which they have been placed by their church. There are millions of them—perhaps even a majority—who cannot understand why their Americanism is questioned and are bitterly resentful. This is natural; they do not know the vast gulf which separates political Catholicism from American principles. They do not realize that the two are mutually hostile. Indeed, they do not know what American principles are or mean. They think of themselves as good Americans; definition of principles would enlighten them; we may confidently hope that many of them would become Americans in fact. It is a national duty to show them what true Americans believe, and try to bring them to accept Americanism.

This implies no assault on their religious faith. It does not touch the *spiritual* leadership or authority of the Pope. It is a purely political education and conversion that must be sought. In fact, such a change would almost certainly benefit spiritual Catholicism, for there would be fewer priests who, as Dr. Siegfried says, "have the soul of a politician" and more who were truly pastors.

The greatest advantage of this course is that it would hit political Catholicism at its weakest point by arousing Liberal minded Americans. Our weakness is neither in our numbers nor in the strength of our convictions, but in our blindness as to this particular danger, and in our division over minor matters. Catholicism is alert and united. We have no clear understanding of our share in this conflict— we are not even all convinced that this is a conflict!— while Catholicism is planning for it under strict discipline, directed by a supreme authority with carefully matured objectives and strategy.

In spite of all this, Catholicism is winning ground not so much because of its own strength as because of our blind sloth. The defense of Americanism rests, of course, with those who see the danger through all the confusion. There is encouragement in the fact that so many saw it in 1928, but discouragement in the further fact that so many believe the danger ended with the defeat of Mr. Smith.

The great need today, therefore, is that more Americans shall see and face the Catholic issue as an immediate menace. When enough do so, there can be no doubt of the result; it will not require more than a third of the Liberal-minded Americans to make this sure. And it is because clarifying the issue and ending the confusion through definition of American principles will arouse such Americans, that this course offers so much hope.

Let me repeat; American Liberals will rise to meet the issue once it is made plain; many Catholics will refuse to support clerical anti-Americanism if they realize the purpose of the hierarchy; the whole Romanist campaign in this country will crumble if that church is forced to accept equality with other churches.

The sooner this can be done, the better; for the longer the Liberal awakening is delayed, the more violent will be the result. There is no possibility that this nation will ultimately submit to the destruction of freedom. The Roman campaign of propaganda, subversion and political aggression can at the most win only temporary and partial success. But if it should succeed that far, so that American citizens suddenly awoke to find their liberties actually restricted, it is to be feared that the reaction would cause such bitter enmities as to revive conditions of two centuries ago. After that the closing of the breach would be impossible for generations.

The course suggested would prevent the impending conflict from going to extremes. Rome has infinite patience but little heroism and leads no forlorn hopes. The Pope wants no religious war; he knows the result from painful experience. The hierarchy does not break its head against solid walls, but hopes for them to crumble. The aggression of Romanism here has come only since it believed its increased numbers and non-Catholic indifference gave it a fighting chance for success. The moment that non-Catholics are aroused, and still more if priestly political control of Catholics weakens, at that moment Romanism will know that further aggression would be not only useless but dangerous to itself, and it will relapse into the kind of watchful waiting that characterized it before 1890.

Indeed, if this should happen, the hierarchy might find itself once more in danger from anti-Catholic agitation, and it would then almost certainly permit the movement for acceptance of American civic principles which in the Nineteenth Century was led by Cardinal Gibbons and Archbishop Ireland, and which disappeared with their deaths from American Catholicism. Then, but not till then, would we again be on the road to the assimilation of the new immigration, and the re-creation of national unity of mind.

It is certain, of course, that every step in this direction will be bitterly fought. Already Catholics have denounced "The Protestants' Ambition to Run the Country."* The program suggested is an expression of exactly that ambition, if we include as "Protestants" not only members of Protestant churches but all Americans of the Liberal tradition. We who believe in Liberal principles *do* intend to run the country. America was born of Protestantism, reared in it, has grown great upon it, and we do not intend that it shall now be perverted. We are determined that it shall remain "predominantly Protestant and Anglo-Saxon."

There are many difficulties in the way, since it will be in truth, as Mr. Belloc said, a "monstrous" struggle. But those difficulties will be met, for as the conflict becomes open and clear it will draw upon all the best thought and the highest consecration of Americans. We can fight for freedom as well and successfully as did our forefathers, if we find the need. And, if the issue be honestly faced, no man can evade the great truth that this conflict will determine whether Catholicism can force Americans back into the bondage of the Dark Ages, or whether this nation shall continue to lead that march of progress and human freedom which Martin Luther started four centuries ago.

When American Liberals once see that truth, the result, though it may be costly, is sure.

* Extension Magazine, July, 1928.

THE END.

Anti-Movements in America

An Arno Press Collection

Proceedings of the Asiatic Exclusion League, 1907-1913. 1907-1913

Beecher, Edward. **The Papal Conspiracy Exposed.** 1855

Beecher, Lyman. **A Plea For the West.** 1835

Budenz, Louis F. **The Techniques of Communism.** 1954

Burr, Clinton Stoddard. **America's Race Heritage.** 1922

Calhoun, William P[atrick]. **The Caucasian and the Negro in the United States.** 1902

Ministers of the Established Church in Glasgow. **A Course of Lectures On the Jews.** 1840

Dies, Martin. **The Trojan Horse in America.** 1940

Dilling, Elizabeth. **The Red Network.** 1935

East, Edward M. **Mankind At the Crossroads.** 1926

Evans, H[iram] W. **The Rising Storm:** An Analysis of the Growing Conflict Over the Political Dilemma of Roman Catholics in America. 1930

Fairchild, Henry Pratt. **The Melting-Pot Mistake.** 1926

Fulton, Justin D. **The Fight With Rome.** 1889

The Fund for the Republic, Inc. **Digest of the Public Record of Communism in the United States.** 1955

Ghent, W[illiam] J. **The Reds Bring Reaction.** 1923

Grant, Madison. **The Conquest of a Continent.** 1933

Hendrick, Burton J. **The Jews in America.** 1923

Huntington, Ellsworth. **The Character of Races.** 1925

James, Henry Ammon. **Communism in America.** 1879

King, James M. **Facing the Twentieth Century.** 1899

Kirwan (pseudonym of Nicholas Murray). **Letters to the Right Rev. John Hughes, Roman Catholic Bishop of New York.** 1855

Ku Klux Klan. **Papers Read at the Meeting of Grand Dragons Knights at Their First Annual Meeting.** [1923]

McCarthy, Joseph. **McCarthyism:** The Fight for America. 1952

McDougall, William. **Is America Safe for Democracy?** 1921

Monk, Maria. **Awful Disclosures.** 1836

[Morse, Samuel Finley Breese]. **Foreign Conspiracy Against the Liberties of the United States.** 1835

National Americanism Commission of the American Legion, Compiler. **ISMS:** A Review of Alien Isms, Revolutionary Communism and Their Active Sympathizers in the United States. 1937

Nevins, William. **Thoughts on Popery.** 1836

Pope, Or President? Startling Disclosures of Romanism as Revealed by Its Own Writers. 1859

[Priest, Josiah]. **Slavery.** 1843

Reed, Rebecca Theresa. **Six Months in a Convent** and **Supplement.** 1835

Roberts, Kenneth L. **Why Europe Leaves Home.** 1922

Ross, Edward Alsworth. **Standing Room Only?** 1927

Schaack, Michael J. **Anarchy and Anarchists.** 1889

Schultz, Alfred P. **Race or Mongrel.** 1908

Stripling, Robert E. **The Red Plot Against America.** 1949

Tenney, Jack B. **Red Fascism.** 1947

[Timayenis, Telemachus T.] **The Original Mr. Jacobs:** A Startling Exposé. 1888

Wiggam, Albert Edward. **The Fruit of the Family Tree.** 1924

Anti-Catholicism in America, 1841-1851: Three Sermons. 1977

Anti-Semitism in America, 1878-1939. 1977